S0-AKM-180

WHEN GOD CALLS

A FAITH-JOURNEY AUTOBIOGRAPHY

WHEN GOD CALLS

A FAITH-JOURNEY AUTOBIOGRAPHY

BY

FEDERICO I. AGNIR

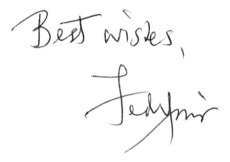

Best wishes,

Fed Agnir

Bookstand Publishing

www.bookstandpublishing.com

Published by
Bookstand Publishing
Morgan Hill, CA 95037
3952_5

Copyright © 2013 by Federico I. Agnir
All rights reserved. No part of this publication may be reproduced or
transmitted in any form or by any means, electronic or mechanical,
including photocopy, recording, or any information storage and
retrieval system, without permission in writing from the copyright
owner.

ISBN 978-1-61863-601-0

For orders, contact:

The Rev. Dr. Federico I. Agnir
6119 Weatherwood Circle
Wesley Chapel, FL 33545
(813) 991-1924
(813) 451-4267
agnir@juno.com

Also available at:
Amazon.com
BarnesandNoble.com
Ingram

Printed in the United States of America

ACKNOWLEDGEMENTS
AND
DEDICATIONS

To my wife, Ruby, love of my life,
my Kismet, fount of gifts and blessings
and partner in all endeavors

To my parents who gave me life, direction
and support through all my days

To my siblings for their guidance,
inspiration and invaluable assistance

To my children and grandchildren,
source of my pride and joy

To all my teachers, friends, classmates
and colleagues on both sides of the planet

And to God, the Ground of All Being,
who holds the Past, the Present and the Future

TABLE OF CONTENTS

Acknowledgements and Dedications v

Chapter I: Childhood in Claveria 1

Chapter II: High School Years 22

Chapter III: College at U.P. 34

Chapter IV: The Early Married Years 50

Chapter V: Student Life at Silliman 64

Chapter VI: Ministry at U.P. 78

Chapter VII: Teaching at Silliman 91

Chapter VIII: Syracuse University 104

Chapter IX: Greenfield Phase One 122

Chapter X: Greenfield Phase Two 139

Chapter XI: Greenfield Phase Three 156

Chapter XII: Back to My Roots 174

Photo Gallery 189

About the Author 194

CHAPTER I: CHILDHOOD IN CLAVERIA

I am sure that I was born at home on January 7, 1939, because in my hometown of Claveria in the province of Cagayan in the Philippines, there was neither hospital nor public maternity facility of any kind. There were no doctors that specialized in obstetrics at the time. By the time I was old enough to remember anything, there were only two doctors in our town and neither was an obstetrician.

The closest thing to professional obstetric help came in the person of the town visiting midwife who was a nurse. For many years, that person was Mrs. Fernanda Leaño. I recall when I was growing up that Nana Andang, as she was fondly called by everyone, could look almost anybody in the eye and confidently proclaim, "I brought you into this world." In the native tongue, which is Ilocano, the verb for the midwifing process is *paltot* and the midwife was called a *mam-maltot*. So she was Nana Andang, the beloved *mam-maltot*. The other person who doubled as midwife and visiting nurse was a woman whom I know only as Nana Dalong. So my hunch was that it was either Nana Andang or Nana Dalong who assisted my mother at my birth.

The lack of advanced public maternity facilities was a significant factor that determined my future. I was the fifth child and the one for whom my mother had the greatest difficulty both in conception and birth. I am told that I was a breech baby and that may have explained my mother's difficulty. Today, pre-natal procedures would have easily dealt with the problem but back then, there was not even such a thing as professional pre-natal care. My mother must have suffered at childbirth tremendously, much more than she ever did with the first four children, and she felt that both her life and that of her baby were in danger. So in her desperation, she called on God and promised that if the child would be born safely, that child would be dedicated to His service. This meant that the child would become either a minister or a deaconess. (In those days there was no such thing as a female minister.) So when I came out male, the decision was final. I was going to be a minister. Even before I knew what the term "career" meant, my future was already decided for me.

At this point, it is appropriate to talk about my parents because the decisions that they made about how and where to raise their family would ultimately affect the future of their offspring. One choice that they had to make early on was whether to stay in the capital city of Manila or go to the province. They had met and courted while they were both in Manila. He was a young lawyer and she was a nurse and

1

after they got married on March 30, 1928, they first tried to eke out a living in Manila. While they were there, they had two children – Esther, born in 1929, and Wenceslao, Jr., born in 1932. They then decided that my father, who was working for the Bureau of Lands, had a better chance of practicing and growing in his profession by moving back to their roots - to either my father's hometown of Claveria, Cagayan or my mother's of Banna, Ilocos Norte. They chose the former. For my mother, the move was a big sacrifice because it meant giving up her career as a nurse. Claveria had no hospital to take the place of the established ones where she had worked at in Manila, the last one being Manila Sanitarium in Makati.

For my father, it was a good move because Claveria had just a handful of lawyers to compete with. And there was always great demand in the outlying towns for municipal judges and government prosecuting lawyers known as fiscals. I later learned by piecing together stories from my father and people who knew him earlier in his life that my father had an ulterior motive for moving back to Claveria. It arose from a need to settle scores dating back to childhood.

By all accounts, Claveria is a young town compared to many of the other towns in Cagayan province. In fact, culturally and linguistically as well as geographically, Claveria is more naturally a part of the province of Ilocos Norte. The town is situated in the narrow northwestern strip that separates the province of Cagayan from Ilocos Norte in the west, the China Sea in the north and Mountain Province in the south. While Claveria is a distant 130 kilometers or 80 miles from the provincial capital of Tuguegarao, it is no more than 30 kilometers or 18 miles from the border between Cagayan and Ilocos Norte. Thus, most of the town's founders came from towns in Ilocos Norte near the border, such as Bangui, Vintar and Pasuquin. When I was growing up, Claveria was one of only three among the approximately 25 towns of Cagayan where Ilocano was the only language spoken by the inhabitants. Those of other towns spoke   Ibanag or Ilocano or both. Claveria's early settlers had been attracted by the land's rich natural resources and the abundance of uncleared and unclaimed land. There were two kinds of settlers. Those who sought fishing as their livelihood settled in what is now the town center, with many of them clustered in the northeastern section of town known as Minanga, where the Claveria river meets the sea. Then, there were the farmers who settled farther inland in some of the barrios that dotted the stretch between Claveria and the mountains of the south and west. One of these was the Claveria barrio of Union. It was there where my father's forebears settled, migrating from Sarrat, one of the towns in Ilocos Norte.

My father was born in Union on September 28, 1899 but his birth certificate says that he was born a year later. One plausible reason for the clerical mistake was that his birth occurred at the height of the Philippine-American War when everything was in turmoil. So his birth was probably recorded after American sovereignty was clearly established and everything had settled down. The discrepancy was never corrected and so all throughout life, my father officially was one year younger than he actually was. Since the practice of choosing names was based on the patron saint for that date on the Roman Catholic calendar, he was named Wenceslao after the "good king Wenceslas," who is celebrated in the popular Christmas carol. He was the third child of Salustiano Agnir and the former Eulalia Agmata and had three siblings, namely Anastasia, Eulogio, and Rufino.

Early on, young Wenceslao showed a very strong desire for schooling and so his parents sacrificed to satisfy the boy's yearning for education. Because there were no schools in the small barrio of Union, they let him leave the family so he could have his primary education in the central school in Claveria, which was a good 10 kilometers from Union. It must have been a lonely and difficult existence for a boy with meager resources. He had to scrape not only for a living but for materials to help him with his schooling. One of his neighbors during those days relates that he was so poor he could hardly afford to buy paper. So, sometimes, he would gather papers discarded by some of his schoolmates and patiently erase the markings so he could have something to use for his schoolwork. After finishing his primary education in Claveria, it was time to move on. In the company of his parents and neighbors, he traveled to Batac, Ilocos Norte where he studied at Batac Rural High School, eventually finishing seventh grade. At that time, that level of education qualified one to teach in the primary grades. So, armed with those credentials, he went back to teach in a school in Sanchez Mira, the next town east of Claveria.

He was in Sanchez Mira when he decided that he had to have more education. One thing that fueled his ambition was an incident involving a young woman with whom he fell in love and wanted to marry. The girl came from a local prominent family. When he approached her parents to ask for her hand in marriage, the father turned him down because he was "only a farmer's son." His pride hurt and his ambition fired up, he quit his schoolteacher job and went off to Manila. Years later, when he was already a well-educated person and on the verge of becoming a lawyer, he had his moment of psychological triumph. On one of his visits to his hometown, he was told that the old man who had ironically pushed him toward higher

3

academic and professional achievement by insulting him now wanted to see him. Respectfully, he went to Sanchez Mira whereupon the old man apologized for having mistreated him and offered his blessing if he was still interested in marrying his daughter. In response, my father said that he did not deserve to marry the old man's daughter because he was only a farmer's son. He then walked away and never looked back.

He finished high school at Far Eastern University and pre-law at National University. In the latter school, he honed his courtroom skills by joining the debating club. A debate team partner and lifelong friend of his was Edilberto Barot who later in life would become the Solicitor General of the Philippines. My father then enrolled and got his law degree at the Philippine Law School, which was then considered one of two premier educational institutions for future lawyers, the other being the College of Law of the University of the Philippines.

As to how he managed to make a living while going through school, he had to have been a working student, taking a number of jobs. It is said that he once worked for a family which probably belonged to the *ilustrado* class and where Spanish was the primary language spoken at home. There he picked up what was later to become one of the most valuable tools of his trade, fluency in the Spanish language. In his career as a young lawyer after his graduation, he enjoyed being bilingual, speaking both English and Spanish with equal facility. That skill came in handy because this was a time of transition from Spanish to English as the official language in the Philippines. Some of the older judges spoke only Spanish while the younger ones spoke English. My father would tell stories about how he would argue a case in Spanish one morning before an older judge and do the same in English in the afternoon before a younger judge.

As fate would have it, his mastery of the Spanish language and his somewhat egotistical penchant for strutting it in public was what got him to meet for the first time the woman who would become the love of his life. It happened one day in a bus that was bound from Manila to Laoag, Ilocos Norte. Among the bus passengers were my father, a young law student named Primo Lazaro and a young nurse named Cristina Ines. Mr. Lazaro knew both my father and Cristina through separate circumstances. My father happened to be striking a conversation in Spanish with another passenger, obviously in tones that everyone could hear. Both out of curiosity and mild annoyance, Cristina asked Primo who that braggart was who was showing off his skill in speaking Spanish. Primo not only identified the man but took him over and introduced him to the young lady. For my father, it was

4

love at first sight, though it was not the case for my mother. In fact, their first encounter almost ended in a spat that could have ended any relationship before it could even start. It was a cold day and the wind was blowing through the window and on the head of my mother who was napping. Very carefully, in an effort to protect her, my father spread a towel over her head. That soon woke her up and when she felt the towel covering her head, she grabbed the towel and yelled, "Who did this?" at the same time flinging it out. For my future parents, it was an odd way to start a romance.

My mother was the fourth among the five children of Santiago Ines and the former Rosalia Bala. In his youth, Santiago had migrated to Banna, Ilocos Norte from Sinait, Ilocos Sur, where the original Ineses came from. The Ines surname evolved from what used to be Ynes, a name beginning with the letter Y. Citizens of Sinait were assigned that letter when the Spanish regime started conducting the census in various towns in the Ilocos region. Today, surnames like Yadao, Ygnalaga, Yabes and Yuzon, to mention a few, are commonplace in Sinait.

Just like my father, my mother at a young age longed to have an education but she was not the only one in her family with such ambition. Her two brothers – Liborio and Faustino – both eventually became lawyers, practicing in the town center and raising their respective families there. My mother had two sisters – Catalina and Guillerma, neither of whom went beyond grade school. Of the five children of Santiago and Rosalia, only Catalina, whom we fondly called Auntie Alli, remained in the family's ancestral home in Ambagsang, Banna, where most of the family landholdings were located. Guilllerma, whom we called Auntie Immang, moved around a bit. When my parents moved to Claveria, Auntie Immang followed them soon after so she could help my mother with child-rearing and managing the family business, a small variety store located a few yards from our house. So for us siblings, much of our growing up was spent bonding and interacting with Auntie Immang, with mixed results. She herself was a strict disciplinarian especially when it came to keeping us children from getting our hands on the store merchandise. We were notorious for raiding the cookie jars when she was not looking.

After graduating from elementary school in her hometown, my mother was sent to the province's municipal capital of Laoag to board there while studying at Ilocos Norte High School. INHS, then as now, was the premier public secondary school that attracted the best students from all over Ilocos Norte and nearby provinces. She did not get to

5

finish her high school education because an opportunity came in the form of a chance to become a nurse.

In those days, one could go straight to nursing school right after graduating from high school and even before that. So she skipped her senior year and enrolled at Sallie Long Read Memorial School of Nursing. The school, located in Laoag, was established in 1903 by the United Christian Missionary Society, which is the missionary arm of the Disciples of Christ, one of several Protestant mainline denominations that came following the American occupation of the Philippines early in the 20th century. She later moved to Manila to continue and finish her studies at Mary Chiles Hospital, a facility that was also operated by the United Christian Missionary Society. After graduating, she joined the nursing staff of Mary Chiles.

For my Mom, being a part of institutions run by Protestants was a hard pill to swallow. Raised a Roman Catholic by a strict mother who observed a daily ritual of saying her prayers with her rosary, she avoided the services and devotions that were part of the daily routine. At night she would say her own prayers, doing so under the covers. However, she could not keep isolating herself and slowly she got exposed to the Protestant evangelical environment and eventually got converted. The rest is history.

How I got to be named Federico is an interesting story. Apparently, my parents had an arrangement whereby my mother would choose the girls' names while my father did the same for the boys. Each of them had a theme. It is customary among Filipinos to give two names to a child. My mother chose the Bible for a theme, meaning at least one of the names should be a character from the Bible. Thus, my two sisters, the oldest and the youngest of the six siblings, were named Esther Aurora and Amelia Ruth, respectively. As for my father, his chosen theme was that of historical figures such as kings, emperors, conquerors and prime ministers. The exception was the eldest boy whom he named Wenceslao, Jr. Then followed Carlo Caesar (after Charlemagne and Julius Caesar), and Orlando Napoleon (after the Italian World War I prime minister and the famous French conqueror). For me, he had chosen Frederick Alexander (after the famous Prussian king and the Macedonian conqueror, respectively)

My first grade teacher, Mrs. Amparo Bolante, had a unique way of teaching her pupils how to write. As soon as school started, she would go to the municipal building and search the birth records in order to get the exact name for each of her pupils. Then, she would make a thin slate made of cardboard about six inches long and one and a half inches wide for every one of her pupils. On each slate, she would write the child's first and last name. The children then learned to write by tracing the writing on their respective slates. When Mrs. Bolante located my birth certificate, she found out that I was listed as Federico Alejandro, not Frederick Alexander. How this discrepancy happened continues to be a mystery. Obviously, there was some kind of communication breakdown between whoever was assigned to go to the town registry and the clerk who made out the record. To compound the error, it took a long time for the mistake to be discovered by my family. I was already ten years old and in fourth grade when Rosella Batoon, a neighbor and classmate, visited our house. She said, "Federico is my classmate. He is very bright." My sister Esther, who was a month shy of ten years old when I was born and who assumed that my name was Frederick, exclaimed, "Who is Federico?"

That error which resulted in my being named Federico instead of Frederick must have rankled deeply in me because I resolved that when I had my own son, his name would be Frederick. So my son, who was born in 1967, is named Frederick. Incidentally, the clerical error in Claveria was to be somewhat replicated in another incident, this time involving my son. We were in Greenfield, Massachusetts, USA where our family had settled and lived from 1974 to 2004. My son must have been about ten when he had to go to the hospital for some treatment. When he registered at the desk, the clerk could not find his name in the computer. After searching the database using his birthday as a search parameter, it was discovered that he was mistakenly listed as Federico Agnir, Jr. In retrospect, I think it was selfish on my part to name him Frederick and that if I had to do it all over, I would give a name to my son that is as distant as possible from my own name.

One day when I was just a little boy, something happened at home that changed my life. On July 15, 1943, my sister Ruth was born. To understand the impact on me of my sister's arrival, it should be noted that I was already four and a half years old when she came. There is an Ilocano word - *buridek* - a descriptive title given to the youngest child when no more children are expected to arrive. Probably because I was the fifth child and my mother was in her mid-thirties when I was born, she did not expect to have any more children after me so everybody started calling me the "*buridek*." I got used to being referred to as such and felt very privileged - in fact, spoiled - by all the attention I got.

I remember the time when my father woke us all up early in the morning, summoning us to their bedroom so we could all see our new sister. We all were given a turn at holding the baby in our arms. It was a welcome event for the entire family and we all showed our delight, or so it seemed. But what I did not realize then was that I must have internalized my resentment at having my position as the *buridek* usurped, a feeling that took me many years to discover. All through my growing-up years, I had a recurrent dream. I would be holding a healthy baby and suddenly the baby would kick me in the stomach and that would trigger a phenomenon called *batibat* in Ilocano or by its more widely used Tagalog name of *bangungot*.

What happens in *bangungot* is that the victim suddenly is unable to breathe and in a lot of cases, it has been known to cause sudden death. Whatever causes it, most people who experience it would say that it is often triggered by a nightmare, as in my case. It is a life-threatening event and my *bangungot* happened so frequently – at least once a month and sometimes more often – that I had to learn how to deal with it. It took supreme mental and physical effort so that the moment I succeeded in waking myself up, I would be very exhausted and emotionally drained. That went on for years.

I must have been about 18 years old when I finally got liberated from my recurrent nightmare. I was already a college student and in one of my Psychology courses, I started reading the works of Sigmund Freud. What he wrote about dream analysis and the powerful influence of the id and super ego caught my interest. Suddenly, the entire picture became clear to me. I then realized that all those years, I had unconsciously suppressed and buried my feelings of resentment at the arrival of my sister. After that revelation, I completely ceased having my recurrent dream.

I look back and wonder if what happened when I was four and a half years old caused me to be sometimes mean to my sister when we were growing up. In any case, whether out of guilt or remorse and a desire to make up for all those lost years, my sister and I have become the best of friends, especially now as we are approaching the sunset of our lives. In fact, had it not been for my sister who kept urging me to write my memoirs, I probably would never have written this book.

Whenever someone asks me for my earliest recollections about my childhood, the first thought that comes to me is war. I was exactly a month short of my third birthday when Japan bombed Pearl Harbor on December 7, 1941. On that very first week that they showed up in Claveria, some Japanese soldiers came to our house at night to confiscate my father's most prized possession, a 1940 Ford sedan sitting in the garage. My parents almost lost their lives at that time because when they heard the commotion outside, they thought it might be burglars. My mother went out to investigate and suddenly found herself face to face with a Japanese soldier. She immediately retreated inside the house and related what happened to my father, who was already ready with his shotgun. Trembling in fear, they closeted themselves and waited, wondering what would happen next.

Eventually, things quieted down and hoping that the soldiers had left, my parents came out of hiding and found that the Ford sedan was gone. It broke my parents' hearts but there was no time to waste. They gathered us together and whatever belongings we could carry and hurried out. At first we did not know where to go. We eventually found ourselves about a kilometer west of our house in a sugar cane field belonging to one of the older settlers in town by the name of Catalino Aguinaldo whom we kids called Lolo Talling.

We would have stayed at Lolo Talling's cane field a long time exposed to the elements had it not been for the arrival of a proverbial Good Samaritan named Francisco Bumanglag. A farmer from Cabanuangan, a village several kilometers to the south, he had been looking for his carabao, which had gotten loose. After a whole day of searching, he found the carabao which had wandered to where we were hiding. Upon learning of our plight, he offered to take us to his home, convincing my parents that his place was safer than that of Lolo Talling's, which was adjacent to the main highway. My mother later explained best how blessed we were on that fateful day in 1941. She firmly believed that God led the carabao to us so that we could be rescued. Mr. Bumanglag, whom we kids called Tata Ikko, became our patron and his home our emergency shelter during the entire Japanese occupation. Our two families became very close, with both sets of parents becoming "kumpadres" when Dad and Ma became baptism sponsors for the Bumanglag daughter.

That was our first evacuation, one of many that were to come. Evacuations were the most vivid experiences I can remember of life during the Japanese occupation. In fact, the word "evacuation" was the first big English word that I learned at age three or four. At first it came to me in the corrupted Ilocano form, which was "bakwit" and later I learned what the correct word was. Presumably, Claveria was a strategically important piece of territory from a military standpoint because it sat in a cove facing the China Sea and made for a natural harbor. So both sides of the war coveted the place and there were a number of pitched battles between the Japanese and the guerillas who were active in the area. There were times when I would wake up late at night or in the wee hours of the morning and would realize that someone was carrying me. In the darkness, I would hear the hushed tones of people and the word "bakwit" kept coming up. It would have been one of those occasions when the word got around that the guerillas were coming. Everybody hurriedly packed up their belongings and headed south to the hills in order to avoid being caught in the crossfire.

I remember one morning that we were on evacuation and Tata Ikko was ahead of us clearing a path with his machete as we worked our way up the mountain to a safe haven. From the distance we could hear the sound of explosions and gunfire. Eventually, we arrived at a clearing where the adults set up camp by constructing a shelter made of bamboo and palm leaves. There we stayed for days waiting for calm to be restored in the town.

In the meantime, we lived off the land as best we could. We were lucky because the land was abundant in edible flora and fauna. Of course we had to make do with fare that was not part of standard cuisine. We learned to eat such things as wild mushrooms and frogs. I was told that a rare but special delicacy was a large snake, probably a python which the natives called "beklat." Although I don't remember eating any, adults swore that it tasted just like chicken or even better. Although life was not easy, we were never hungry because our elders were very resourceful. One resource that our family had was a cache consisting of canned foods. When the war broke out, my parents took out all the canned foods from the family variety store and buried them so that every now and then, we would have something to fall back on and add something different to our daily menu.

Even when things quieted down long enough for us to go back to our home, we were always at the mercy of the whims of the Japanese occupation forces. At one time, we even had to move out of our house and live in the variety store located a few yards from the house because Japanese officers had appropriated our house for their headquarters. Also, there were always Japanese scavengers looking for things they could lay their hands on. I distinctly remember one incident when some of them came to our house looking for food. One of them caught one of our ducks, which happened to be my pet duck. Right in front of me, he slaughtered the helpless creature with one swipe of his samurai sword, severing the duck's neck. That sight has haunted me all my life and to this day, I cannot eat duck meat.

The war years were not all a period of doom and gloom because there were some bright spots. For example, it was a time when the best of Filipino character emerged. Filipinos showed their incredible resiliency, learning to survive under the most difficult circumstances. Deprived of the necessities and conveniences of pre-war days, they either made do without them or invented substitutes.

One invention that I recall was to make up for the lack of adequate indoor lighting. Electric lighting had not yet come to Claveria homes. Before the war, one common form of indoor lighting came from a device called the "Coleman lantern," named after its manufacturer. The device worked by pumping a mixture of pressurized air and kerosene into a gauze bulb called a mantle. When the mantle was subjected to heat, it produced a light comparable in brightness to that of today's incandescent bulbs. It was a fairly expensive device and my family was lucky to have one or two of them. However, kerosene was in very short supply during the war so the Coleman was hardly ever used and only for special occasions.

That's when the town's elders came up with an invention. A certain tree had sap that they first learned was flammable from seeing it burst into flames when the tree was struck by lightning. Called *aningat* by the natives, the sap was in abundant supply in the forests nearby. They harvested the sap, dried it and ground it into powder. During the war, many homes, including ours, were often lighted through the use of a jerry-rigged lantern which had *aningat* for its fuel. One very clear childhood vision that keeps coming back is a typical evening when the family was gathered for our daily devotions. As we huddled together in a circle while my mother led the meeting with prayers, I can still picture the dim light from the lantern and can smell the sweet flavor from the *aningat*.

We children were just as inventive as the adults, if not more so. There were no department stores filled with toys like there are today so we had to create our own. My first toy gun was a spent 50-caliber machine gun shell mounted on a guava tree branch shaped like a pistol butt. My first musical instrument was a piece of hollowed-out bamboo with a hole which sounded one bass note when I blew on it. About a dozen of us neighborhood kids would use that instrument at Christmastime to form a "band" for caroling. We provided the background rhythm while we had a leader who played the melody with a flute made of a thin bamboo reed. We had only two tunes in our entire repertoire. The first one was the Ilocano love song called *Pamulinawen*. It was our marching song as we moved from one house to the next. The second was a lullaby entitled "Go to Sleep, My Dear Little One" which we played as soon as we got to our destination. No one ever questioned our choice of songs, which had nothing to do with Christmas, but apparently our neighbors enjoyed our performances. They loved to see us marching in our "uniform" which consisted of raincoats made from palm leaves and hats called *pittarok* made from craftily woven cane. In return for our efforts, we received from every

11

house enough rice candy called *patupat* or *sinuman* and sometimes a few coins to make it worth our while.

We invented our own games. One such game was the *barruga*. Played by a group of about half a dozen kids, it was a competitive game with firewood as an ante. The players each provided a piece of firewood about a foot and half long and the accumulated firewood were then formed into a pyramid. The players then stood about 30 feet away and took turns throwing another piece of firewood at the pile. Whoever succeeded in hitting and breaking it up won the whole pile. While some kids took the risk of surreptitiously draining their home firewood pile, the more enterprising kids prepared for the game by spending a day in the forest gathering firewood. For them and their families, it was a win-win situation in that they had their fun while building up their home firewood pile if they won. When the war was over and bowling lanes were introduced to Claveria, some of those who excelled in the new sport had their training in *barruga* to thank.

We had our own "gang wars" fought between us kids from the West (*laud*) side of town and those from the East (*daya*) side of town. They were relatively harmless with our most potent weapon consisting of a slingshot fashioned from a guava tree branch, rubber cut from discarded bicycle tires and leather from an old shoe. We each had a role to play. Manong Willie was always at the head of the troops, brandishing a bolo which he did not use as a weapon but only as a symbol of leadership. With his skill in the use of the slingshot, Manong Caesar was the sharpshooter. Manong Orly and I were the foot soldiers. My special role was that of ammunition carrier. My trouser pockets were always heavy with pebbles used for supplying the troops. As a result, my mother was always having a fit having to frequently repair my pockets that had holes torn by the weight of the pebbles.

Sometime early in 1944, a new enemy emerged in the form of bands of Philippine marauding renegade guerillas that moved into places temporarily vacated by the Japanese, terrorizing the area with impunity. Their expressed mission was to administer vigilante justice, directed at those whom they marked as collaborators. The most prominent and most notorious of these bands was one led by a certain Lt. Emilio Escobar who went by the *nom-de-guerre* of Sagad. That Ilocano word for "sweep" was an appropriate nickname because he and his band of about 300 would sweep into each town all over the Ilocos region and leave their mark on them. The first thing they would do was to arrest alleged collaborators and without the benefit of trial would execute them in public. The people they would mark for arrest and execution were the town's most prominent citizens, especially the two symbols of leadership, namely the mayor and the municipal judge. Even if they wanted to, the townspeople could not resist against this heavily-armed band. As he spread his brand of terror in the various towns of Ilocos Sur and Ilocos Norte, news traveled to us and fear gripped everyone thinking that it would not be long before he would cross the border between Ilocos Norte and Cagayan and we would be next.

It was at this point that Uncle Libor arrived. Uncle Libor was Liborio Ines, my mother's older brother who had settled in their native town of Banna, Ilocos Norte where he established a successful law practice. Eventually, he became the town's municipal judge, a position he held when the Japanese occupied. Like so many local officials all over the islands who held on to their posts in order to help maintain civil order, he continued to serve as judge. Thus, Sagad marked him as a collaborator and an instant target for arrest and execution. But before Sagad made it to Banna, Uncle Libor hurriedly left town and made his way to Claveria. He had to leave his family behind because there were neither private motor vehicles nor buses available at that time. Traveling by bull cart for three days along the 150-kilometer trip through the mountainous terrain, he finally reached the safety of our home.

In the meantime, while the townspeople steeled themselves for Sagad's anticipated arrival, the man of the hour came along in the person of Lt. Bonifacio de Guzman. He was an officer of the USAFIP, an acronym for United States Armed Forces in the Philippines. He joined the guerrilla forces after the Japanese occupied the Philippines. He himself was a family friend and my first time to see him was when we were in Cabanuangan during one of our evacuations. One day, he came to our place seeking medical help. His story was that he was walking along one of the narrow mountain passes and as he rounded a bend, he suddenly came face to face with a Japanese officer who attacked him with his samurai sword. Fortunately, Lt. de Guzman was able to draw his sidearm just in time to shoot and kill the Japanese but not before he was struck on the shoulder. When he arrived at our place in Cabanuangan, he was bleeding. Fortunately, my mother had kept as many medical supplies as she could and she tended to Lt. de Guzman's wounds.

It was Lt. de Guzman's leadership and bravery that saved Claveria from the scourge that was Sagad. The first thing he did was to organize a militia that would defend Claveria. He would have known that there was very little chance of military success against Sagad and his fully-armed band. Against Sagad's armory consisting of carbines,

13

Garands and grenades, all that de Guzman's men had for weaponry was a long knife called "bolo" and for which his men were nicknamed "the bolo men." But de Guzman devised a brilliant, although risky, strategy. With the aid of spies, he kept track of Sagad's progress. When news came to him that Sagad had reached the boundary between Ilocos Norte and Cagayan and had encamped there, he decided to go there and meet Sagad himself in order to deliver a message. He warned Sagad not to come to Claveria because the people were ready to resist and that Sagad would pay a heavy price for his effort. He was gambling that Sagad, before invading Claveria, would first try to ascertain whether or not de Guzman was just bluffing. Sagad took the bait and sent a scouting party. The party never reached Claveria because midway through, they were ambushed by a group of tribesmen called *Isnegs* who were recruited by Lt. de Guzman for the job. Convinced that de Guzman was telling the truth, Sagad retreated back to Ilocos Norte to continue his reign of terror.

Uncle Libor was a nice and gentle person who spent time with his nephews and nieces telling stories and teaching Ilocano songs. One such song I can remember was half joyful and half sad. It told about heroes who gave their lives for others and for their country and how lucky they were. It was only later when I was old enough and heard the story of his life that I understood the welter of feelings that he must have had to bear in those moments. On one hand, he must have been grateful and relieved that he had been saved from certain death at the hand of Sagad and his men. On the other hand, he was concerned about his family about whom he had not heard any word. What he did not know was that after he left, his family was able to evacuate to Ambagsang, a barrio near the mountains that separated the provinces of Ilocos Norte and Abra. They had relatives there who hid them from Sagad's men who even then were looking for ways to get Uncle Libor back to Banna. One day, a courier arrived in Claveria with a message from Sagad saying that he had captured my uncle's family and were holding them hostage. It was not true but Uncle Libor had no way of knowing. He had no other choice but to return to Banna and surrender to Sagad.

The days that followed at our home were grim. My parents were gripped with fear and concern for my uncle. My mother was virtually inconsolable, certain that any moment she would learn about her brother's fatal end. The moment of revelation came by way of an extra-sensory experience. As my parents related it, one night my father was awakened by a rustling sound coming from his office, which was a desk located in a corner of the living room. Given the uncertain atmosphere in those days, such sounds at night were always a cause for alarm. In pitch darkness, my father, armed to the teeth, slowly approached the source of the rustling sound, crouched and ready for anything. Unknown to him, another person in the house also heard the sound. It was Cirilo, our manservant, whom we called Manong Ilong. He was sleeping in another room and was awakened by the sound. Like my father, he proceeded to arm himself and slowly worked his way toward the source of the sound. The two men came upon each other and had they not recognized each other in time, could have killed each other. In the meantime, the sound coming from the desk got clearer. It was a distinct sound of typing followed by paper being snatched off the roller as though to start again with another paper. Apparently, someone was working the typewriter, except that when the two men looked closer, there was nobody there. My father returned to their bedroom to report what happened to my mother who by this time was also awake, waiting anxiously to find out what happened. When my father reported that there was nobody there, she went into hysterics, certain that her brother was dead and that his spirit had visited us that night. Sometime later, my parents learned from couriers that indeed my uncle had been arrested, imprisoned and executed by Sagad and his men.

It would not be the last such apparent visit by Uncle Libor's spirit. As reported by my siblings, one morning there came a distinct sound coming from the veranda on the east side of the house. It was the sound of a bed being dragged through the floor. That bed happened to be Uncle Libor's favorite spot for sleeping. Although a subsequent investigation showed no sign that the bed had been moved, my mother was convinced that her brother's spirit visited us that day.

The loss of Uncle Libor was one of two wartime tragedies that befell my mother's family. The other tragedy involved their youngest sibling, Faustino, whom we called Uncle Tinoy. Before the war, he was a young lawyer working for the government of Ilocos Norte headed by Roque Ablan, the provincial governor. When Japan invaded and occupied the Philippines, Ablan formed a guerilla unit and uncle Tinoy was part of it. The Ablan unit disappeared and was never heard from again. The story is told that when the Japanese army under the leadership of General Yamashita was advancing, Ablan retreated to the mountains and designated Uncle Tinoy to form the rear guard, instructing him to delay Yamashita's advance. Uncle Tinoy succeeded in his assigned task by burning a bridge which the Japanese forces would have needed to continue their pursuit. Upon learning about Uncle Tinoy's role, the Japanese put a price on his head. They found and apprehended him after he was betrayed by a fellow whom Uncle

15

Tinoy had prosecuted and sent to jail before the war for the crime of rape. Uncle Tinoy was executed in public by the Japanese at the Banna town plaza, along with 12 other prominent leaders of surrounding towns.

The loss of Uncle Tinoy was doubly tragic because he was on a fast track toward a bright political career. Before the war, Governor Ablan had been planning to run for reelection and was grooming Uncle Tinoy to be his running mate as a provincial Board Member. At that time, the latter was the second highest elective position in the province.

My uncles each left a grieving widow and young children. In the ensuing years, my parents reached out to my orphaned first cousins, some of whom spent time with us in Claveria while they were growing up. We bonded and treated one another like brothers and sisters and what began as a tragedy became a mutually enriching experience for our expanded family.

In late 1944, the liberation of the Philippines began. In fact, just as "evacuation" was the first big English word that I learned, "liberation" was the second. It meant that for the millions of Filipinos that suffered during the Japanese occupation, salvation was finally coming in the form of the arrival of liberating forces. In October, 1944, Gen. Douglas MacArthur fulfilled his "I Shall Return" promise that he had made three years before as he was leaving the Philippines following the fall of Bataan. He led a force that established a beachhead in Tacloban, on the island of Leyte, located in the east central part of the Philippines. The first thing he did upon wading ashore was to go on radio, addressing the Filipinos everywhere, saying, "People of the Philippines, I have returned." That message emboldened the guerillas everywhere who stepped up their campaign against the Japanese forces, thus paving the way for MacArthur's eventual victory.

One sunny morning, we heard the sound of several planes coming. It turned out to be three American fighter-bombers. They had spotted a Japanese ship that was anchored about a mile offshore. They then dived to a lower altitude and began their strafing and bombing run on the ship. For the people of our town, it was live theater and many, including my father, ran to the shore to witness the action. The rest of us at home huddled in the outdoor bathroom. From there, we could hear the explosion of bombs hitting the ship and sinking it. It was not long before my father came back excitedly telling us about the fate of the Japanese ship. He then took out an American flag from where he had hidden it for years and ran around the neighborhood with it, yelling, "Liberation! Liberation!" From that point on, it was only a matter of time before the American ground forces arrived.

16

All through my childhood and adolescent years, I obediently accepted and never questioned the decision that my mother made to dedicate me to the ministry. Those who are unfamiliar with Philippine culture need to understand that there are two cultural traits that keep Philippine society together, namely, respect for elders and fear of God. So for me, even just a moment's thought of considering a future career other than the ministry would immediately put me at odds with God and my parents. Furthermore, folk Philippine theology, which was a meld of old Filipino religions and Roman Catholicism, contended that devotion to God was a way of earning salvation not just for yourself but for the people you love. Conversely, disobedience to God could merit eternal damnation. To members of my family, I was the sacrificial lamb that supposedly guaranteed the safety of my family. That perception as the "family savior" reinforced my acceptance of my predestined future. It also helped that all through life I became the beneficiary of special protection and largesse from my parents and siblings.

Being Protestant in a town where eight or nine out of ten people were Roman Catholic made life difficult for me and my siblings. When I was in grade school, I could be the only Protestant in a classroom of 50 pupils. It was impossible for me not to feel constantly left out. We all went to a public elementary school and although the principle of separation of church and state was part of the Constitution of the new Republic of the Philippines inaugurated in 1946, it was hardly ever adhered to. For instance, the local Roman Catholic Church was allowed to conduct religious instruction at our school. Usually, a nun from the local convent would come and teach the class. Knowing that I was not Catholic, she would tell me that I was free to go out and play while the class was going on. I did not relish the idea of being outside all by myself so I stayed in class. I prayed the Hail Marys and sang "Mother of God" along with the rest of my classmates. Also, a number of my friends were acolytes of the local Catholic Church. After school, they would often go to the church which was just a hundred yards from the school. I often tagged along with them and mimicked everything they did. Once inside the church, I would tremble in fear wondering if God would send a lightning bolt to strike me dead. That's because my mother, a first generation fundamentalist Protestant, had pounded into our heads that associating with Catholics and entering their sanctuary was a sin. I never told my mother that when I was a boy, I attended Catholic Catechism and assisted my friends in the preparation of their church altar.

History records that one of the alleged reasons why the United States kept the Philippines after gaining control over the islands as a result of its victory in the Spanish- American war in 1898 was to bring the blessings of Western civilization and culture to the Filipinos. The offshoot of this policy was the establishment of the Philippine public school system. To guarantee that no child would be left behind, a public grade school was set up in virtually every town in the Philippines and, in some cases, even in villages that were too distant from population centers. One mark of a good grade school was having its own multi-room building, with a distinct architectural style called Gabaldon, in tribute to the former member of the Philippine Assembly named Isauro Gabaldon. In the early years of American occupation, Gabaldon authored the legislation that appropriated the money for the construction of the school buildings. They were U-shaped buildings with the base of the letter U at the front serving a lot of purposes, most commonly as a makeshift stage for school presentations and for the usual Monday morning flag-raising and Friday afternoon flag-lowering ceremonies. Claveria Elementary School was a quality school not only for having its own Gabaldon but by the fact that it had all six grades in its curriculum, good facilities and well-trained staff. For years after its establishment, the school produced many quality graduates who went on to more advanced schooling and became outstanding citizens in Claveria and elsewhere.

During the war, the Philippine Commonwealth under the leadership of Pres. Manuel L. Quezon functioned in exile. When MacArthur landed in Leyte in the autumn of 1944, Sergio Osmeña, who had assumed the Commonwealth presidency following the death of Quezon, was part of the liberating force that came ashore. Upon landing, Osmeña declared the reestablishment of the Philippine Commonwealth on Philippine soil although it was not until after the liberation of Manila the following February when concrete steps to set things up all over the archipelago took place. By the summer of 1945, the war was winding down and enough areas had been liberated to restore civil government and public services. Claveria Elementary School opened at that time and the work of enrolling those children who were held back for three years and distributing them proportionately into the various grades began. The chosen strategy was to accelerate some of the older kids, using a variety of criteria including intelligence tests and enrollment during the Japanese-occupation schools. All my older siblings were accelerated whereas at six years old, I was just at the right age to start at first grade.

Despite wide devastation caused by the war, the population was in great spirits and school opening was symbolic of a new beginning. It was also a time of anticipation because as provided for by

18

the law that established the Philippine Commonwealth in November, 1935, the United States was going to grant Philippine independence after ten years. The date for that independence was set for July 4, 1946, a celebration day replicating that of the United States. Philippine Independence Day coincided with the beginning of classes for the School Year 1946-47. By that time, I was seven years old and in second grade so I could understand the significance of the event and remember the details. We had a parade that went through the town and ended in front of the *presidencia* or town hall. For the last time, the *Star Spangled Banner* was sung as the American flag, which heretofore had been flying side by side with the Filipino flag, was lowered, leaving the latter flag by itself. The Philippines was finally independent.

My favorite subjects in grade school were Music and English. Although he himself was not a musician, my father loved music and one of his prized possessions was an old gramophone which he stocked with a variety of records. The part in his collection that I loved to listen to over and over was that of a banjo player who played works from great operas by such luminaries as Verdi, Mozart, Bizet and others. Although at that time I had no idea whose works I was listening to, it was for me a great early introduction to the classics.

We had two musical instruments at home. One was an old pump organ which our older sister Esther played in church until she left for high school. The other instrument was a piano bought by my mother when I was about nine years old. I am convinced that part of my mother's motivation for acquiring that instrument involved me. About that time, I started showing signs of growing interest in music and was particularly attracted to the violin after listening to some performances by a local violinist. I asked my mother if I could take violin lessons. She said, "No" and when I asked why not, she explained that her younger brother Faustino was a very good violinist and almost flunked law school because his friends frequently took him out serenading. Soon after that, she bought the piano.

The three of us younger siblings who were left behind - my older brother Orlando, my younger sister Ruth and I - started taking piano lessons under the tutelage of a certain Mr. Castro. He was a music teacher from Laoag who came to Claveria to take a job teaching at the Academy of St. Joseph, one of two secondary schools in town. To augment his income, Mr. Castro took in piano students who had their lessons at our home and used our piano for practicing. In return, he did not charge the three of us Agnir siblings for our lessons. By the time I was 11, I was arguably the most musically-knowledgeable among all my fellow sixth graders, a fact not unnoticed by my Music teacher who regarded me as both a help and a threat. There were times when in the middle of a music lesson, I would correct her if I caught a misplaced note, much to her chagrin.

As for the subject of English, it was what made me discover early on that I loved to write and speak. This interest was also fueled by my home environment. I was about ten years old when my Dad saw me toying with his typewriter. Instead of shooing me away, he decided to teach me how to type. I learned very quickly and by the time I was in fifth grade I was typing about 40 words a minute. With this new-found skill, something happened that literally opened the door to a lifetime of opportunity for me.

Just as in the case of the piano, there were very few places in Claveria that had a typewriter. One such typewriter was the one at the principal's office at Claveria Elementary School. Understandably, it was heavily used and people had to fall in line for it. One of those who were dependent on the typewriter and the services of the office clerk was my fifth grade home room teacher who needed them to prepare her tests. The process consisted of typing the test on a stencil, which would then be used for mass-producing copies on a mimeograph machine. Because she had to compete with others for typewriter and mimeograph time, she had to prepare the test days and sometimes weeks in advance and sign up to have the test prepared. Somehow, she learned that I could type and so one day she asked if I could cut stencils for her. That relieved her of the burden of having to await her turn at the principal's office. In turn, I had an advance copy of every test and although she could have exempted me from taking the tests, she decided to have me take the tests presumably to guard against anyone suspecting. Naturally, I aced all the tests. Pretty soon, some of my classmates started to suspect and one of them approached me and asked if I had advanced access to the test. I was faced with a difficult decision. Even if I denied it, I was too transparent to be able to get away with it so I knew they would not stop trying to get the truth out of me. I decided that it would be safest to let the secret out to just a handful and let them have advance copies but not before making them swear not to share it with anybody else. I also set things up such that they would deliberately miss enough questions to allay any suspicions. I was glad that the whole episode happened toward the end of the school year so that my ethical infraction involved just one test. On the other hand, I learned early on the true meaning of the saying "Knowledge is Power" and from that day on, I resolved that I would always try to be at the head of the line in learning how to use the newest production tools.

In April, 1951, I graduated from Claveria Elementary School as the salutatorian. Eppie Planta and Caroline Leaño were valedictorian and first honorable mention, respectively. Both girls were my best friends of the opposite sex. We did a lot of things together both in school and the community. Eppie is my god-sister for having been sponsored at her baptism by my father. For all our lives we considered each other as "favorite God-siblings." After elementary school, we parted ways when I went away for high school but we got together again years later as students at the University of the Philippines. Fortuitously, she and Ruby Ordinario, who was later to become my girl friend and eventually my wife, became college roommates and fast friends. We all continued to be close friends even after we started our own families. Eppie married her high school sweetheart and townmate, Edmund Daproza. We occasionally get together with them at their home in Maryland and elsewhere. As for Caroline, she eventually became a nurse like her mother, the town midwife of my boyhood. Caroline married, migrated to the States and settled with her husband Roy Alba and family on Staten Island off the harbor of New York City. The two have since retired and are now back in the Philippines.

Graduation Day in 1951 was a bittersweet experience, as I recall. The only person in my family who attended the ceremonies was my father. By that time, all my siblings, with the exception of my kid sister Ruth, were all away either in Laoag where they were studying at Ilocos Norte High School or in Manila at the University of the Philippines. My Mom was away on one of her frequent trips, having taken over management of the family's hardwood lumber business after my father had a mild stroke. For my Dad, my graduation was apparently not too happy an event because I could tell when he shook my hand perfunctorily when he came forward with me as I received my award. Aside from missing my Mom, he was evidently disappointed that I did not wind up higher in the honor roll. But as for me, there was neither time nor reason to brood. All I could think of was that the event marked the end of one big chapter in my life and the beginning of another. I was about to leave the town of my birth and boyhood for a new place, eager and ready for a new adventure.

CHAPTER II: HIGH SCHOOL YEARS

My oldest sibling, Esther, started the family tradition of going out of town for high school. In April, 1941, she graduated from Claveria Elementary School and was sent to Laoag in the adjoining province of Ilocos Norte to enroll at Ilocos Norte High School, the public secondary school that was highly regarded in the region. But her education was interrupted when a few months later, on December 7, 1941, Japan bombed Pearl Harbor to start America's, and by affinity, the Philippines' involvement in the war. A few weeks after Pearl Harbor, the Japanese started invading and occupying parts of the Philippines. Esther narrowly escaped being marooned in Laoag when the Japanese arrived, thanks to our uncles in Banna, Ilocos Norte who whisked her out to the safety of their town until a rescue party from Claveria could later go there and take her home.

Schools reopened all over the Philippines in late summer 1945 and my sister returned to Laoag to continue her education that had been interrupted by the war. For our parents, deciding to send her back to Laoag was a no-brainer even though by that time, Claveria had two local private high schools. Academy of St. Joseph was a parochial school run by the local Roman Catholic Church with the support of missionary educators of the Society of the Divine Word or SVD, which was one of several Catholic orders that had established themselves in the Philippines. My parents, or at least my mother, a first generation Protestant, was not about to let their children be placed under the influence of Catholic priests and nuns. On the other hand, Claveria Institute, although a secular school, had limited offerings by way of quality professional staff as well as curricular and extra-curricular activities.

By the time it was my turn to start high school, four siblings had already preceded me at Ilocos Norte High School. This unique situation had its advantages and disadvantages. On one hand, I could count on my older siblings to guide me with the benefit of their experience. On the other hand, I had to contend with whatever standards of achievement and behavior, good or bad, that each had set up. As what happens with families that go to the same school, standards set up by older siblings influence teachers' expectations for the younger ones.

Furthermore, I did not realize it at the time but there was one other major obstacle that I had to overcome. Our entering class in 1951 was going to be highly competitive, much more so than classes that preceded us. The reason was that this was going to be the largest class ever in the history of the school, consisting of children who entered first grade right after the war. Many of them were held back during the Japanese occupation and I remember that as a six-year-old first grader in the autumn of 1945 when schools first opened in Claveria, I had classmates who were three or four years older than I. My freshman class at INHS numbered more than 850 which, when divided into sections of about 50 each, totaled 17 sections. So unprepared was the school for this sudden influx of freshmen that finding adequate space was a problem. Some classes had to be held in the open, sometimes in the athletic grandstand about a kilometer away from the main campus and sometimes under the trees.

My first exposure to the level of the competition took place on the very first week of classes. I was told to show up to take a test. At the time, I had no idea how important this test was and how it would impact my future not just at the school but for the rest of my life. Apparently the school had a tradition of giving two free tuition scholarship awards to each of the four classes at the beginning of the year. For the entering sophomore, junior and senior classes, the criteria for choosing recipients were two, namely, that they had finished the previous year at the school and that they garnered one of the top two academic honors in their respective classes that year. However, for us entering freshmen, the criterion was the result of the test we were about to take, with the award going to the two highest scorers.

I never knew how they decided who were invited to take the test. I assumed that since there were not anywhere near 800 who were with me in the library where the test was administered, we were picked because we were at the very top in the honor roll of our respective elementary graduating classes. To the best of my knowledge, we all went into the testing room cold, which meant that there were neither advance notices nor review classes to prepare us for the test. I still remember every detail of the testing procedure because it was something I had never experienced before. The test was divided into sections and the teacher administering the test had a timer. We were told that when she would ring a bell and say "Pencils Up" we were to stop writing whether or not we finished that section of the test and be ready to move on to the next. The test was designed to measure our language and quantitative skills and it was immediately evident to me that speed was an important factor. That instant realization probably gave me a big advantage over others because several days after, I was informed that I scored highest on the test. Second place went to an out-of-towner like me named Constante Daoang from the nearby town of

San Nicolas. Soon after, we received our tuition scholarships, along with the others from the higher classes, during a convocation set up for that purpose.

The convocation itself must have been a highlight of the year not just for the school but for the town as well because it was attended by quite a few adults, many of whom were relatives of the scholarship recipients. My mother happened to be in town so she was around for the ceremonies too. A strange, somewhat comical, incident happened to me at the ceremony. I did not know that everyone was observing how the recipient would behave upon receiving the award. Apparently, some kind of custom had evolved through the years whereby upon receiving the award, the recipient would hand it to a parent or other relative seated at the gallery and usually followed with some gesture of affection or respect or both, such as a hug or a kiss. Nobody had told me about this custom. To make matters worse for me, the awarding sequence went from the lowest class to the highest so since I was the top freshman recipient, I was the first to be awarded and had no one to imitate. The award consisted of an envelope with seventy pesos in it, which in those days was a lot of money. As soon as I got the envelope, I behaved like a kid who had just been given a new toy. All I could think of was how I was going to spend all that money. Smiling and half-skipping, I scampered to my seat in the audience, far away from where my mother was seated in the gallery. When I heard the murmur from the crowd, I knew that I had done something wrong. That day and even long after, my mother and I became the butt of jokes over that incident.

More than any, topping the Freshman Scholarship Test started to open doors for me. I was an instant celebrity and, for better or worse, I became the object of attention and scrutiny from both my classmates and my teachers. For the latter group, there were two kinds. One group was very friendly to me while the other regarded me with suspicion. The attitude of the first group was natural. They looked at me as a rising star to be encouraged and developed. Some of them were my mother's friends and schoolmates from younger days and who acted as surrogate parents to us Agnir siblings. The second group's negative attitude toward me arose from the fact that I was another Agnir who had to be reckoned with. They each had an axe to grind with my siblings who preceded me at the school. Knowing all of these early on was a mixed blessing. From the outset, I knew who my friends and enemies were. It was knowledge that served me well as I navigated the four years of my secondary schooling.

My next hurdle was in the field of student politics. It was another new and fascinating experience for me. The presidency of my class was a much coveted and hotly contested position and so I was encouraged by my two older brothers – Caesar who was a senior and Orlando who was a junior - to run for the office of president of the freshman class. In the ensuing campaign, I was very busy because I had to visit all 17 freshman class sections. Given my celebrity status and the behind-the-scenes help of most of the home room teachers, I won quite handily. I look back and realize that I was extremely lucky to have overcome another obstacle, which was the regionalism of many of our fellow students, who favored the candidate that was a local person. We Agnirs were complete outsiders. At that time, you could count with the fingers of one hand the students whose home provinces were other than Ilocos Norte. I had to contend with this regionalism throughout my four years as a student politician.

Winning at those political contests was little more than a matter of visibility and prestige. There were hardly any responsibilities that came with the office. For most of us, with the possible exception of the senior class, the biggest event associated with our respective offices came at the end of the year when it was time to have our group picture taking for the school annual. For the 1951-52 annual, I was part of the group photo for the officers of the Freshman Council and of the Student Council in which I represented my class.

There was, however, one event associated with my position as Freshman Class president that I fondly remember. This was the celebration of United Nations Day. On October 24, 1951, the world was celebrating United Nations Day and for its part, Laoag had a parade which culminated in a program at the Laoag plaza. The main features of that program were two. One was a speech by the guest of honor, the young congressman of the second district of Ilocos Norte by the name of Ferdinand Marcos. The other was a short skit which was a mock session of the United Nations General Assembly.

The reason for the prominence given to the celebration was that the entire Philippine population was excited over the fact that a Filipino had recently occupied the prestigious position of chairman of the United Nations General Assembly in the person of Carlos P. Romulo. After the Second World War and a few years thereafter, Romulo was the most famous Filipino in the world. Some of his prominence arose from the fact that as a correspondent during the war, he chronicled the fall and later the liberation of the Philippines. He was pictured among those with General Douglas MacArthur wading ashore in Leyte Gulf in October, 1944. As a correspondent, he won many awards including the much-coveted Pulitzer Prize. From that position of prominence, he rose to become the best-known Filipino diplomat ever.

For some reason, the task of setting up that United Nations Day program in 1951 was assigned to Ilocos Norte High School. In turn, the school assigned the job of preparing the program to Miss Caridad Martin. Miss Martin was the advisor of the Freshman Council as well as the home room teacher of Section One of the freshman class. To this day, I am still bewildered that this highly important task did not go to the senior class but instead to a bunch of 12 and 13 year olds. Miss Martin wrote the skit and picked the players from Section One. There were probably a dozen of us who were part of that skit but of those who had speaking parts, I can remember only three. My part was that of then U.S. Secretary of State Dean Acheson. The Soviet ambassador, Andrei Gromyko, was played by Renato Ramos, and the part of Carlos P. Romulo by Agileo Guerrero. I also remember vividly that episode for another reason. When it was time for Congressman Marcos to speak, his first words were of praise for the job done by the players of the UN General Assembly skit. He singled me out and I later learned that the reason he mentioned my name was because he was reading the program in which the names of the officers of the Freshman Council were printed with my name as president on top. Marcos immediately became my hero. Subsequently, I followed his meteoric career and much later worked for his election to the presidency and supported him until we parted ways in the late 1960's when I got disaffected with him. As later recounted in this book, the development of my attitude toward Marcos and its consequences was one of the defining moments of my life.

On my sophomore year, I experienced a setback in my political career that taught me a valuable lesson. I lost in my bid for the presidency because of complacency. I had falsely assumed that my popularity would last forever and so I hardly campaigned at all. The person who beat me was Policarpio Miguel, a Laoagueño with a charming and engaging personality. I swore to myself that I would never be complacent again. So on my junior year, I rebounded and won in the presidential contest by working hard this time.

When I got to my senior year, I had a big decision to make. There were two high-profile positions that fourth year student politicians competed for. One was that of the Student Government presidency and the other was the Senior Council presidency. Each had its own merit. The Student Government presidency was more prestigious because it represented leadership over the entire student population. But whoever held the position was a mere figurehead because there were no regular activities save for the annual picture-taking. On the other hand, the Senior Council president was busy and very visible. There were at least two traditional activities for which the holder of the position played a prominent part, namely the senior prom and graduation ceremonies and for that reason I found it more attractive. So I chose to run for president of the Senior Council.

In the meantime, I had cultivated the friendship of Policarpio, the man who beat me in my sophomore year. Rather than risk getting into a contest with him again, I decided to forge an alliance with him. I convinced him to run for the Student Government presidency with the understanding that he and I would work together. We had a couple of formidable foes. Running against him was Froilan Estavillo, an out-of-towner from Solsona, Ilocos Norte who was tops in the honor roll and was the incoming editor-in-chief of the student paper. My opponent was Jose Ballesteros, a Laoagueño who was running in second place in the honor roll. Clearly, we were going to have a fight in our hands. In my case, I was also saddled with the usual disadvantages of the incumbent. Inevitably, there were enough of our classmates who were looking for a new face and for them I had been around too long.

Through the years, attrition had reduced our class size so that by our senior year, we numbered only 471. Ours was still the largest graduating class ever. As always, I made the rounds by campaigning at every section. On the day before the election, Policarpio came to me with a warning that I was losing, based on surveys that he had studiously made. He urged me to double up my efforts, to which I protested, saying that I had visited all nine sections already and was afraid that second visits would be counter-productive. I then came up with a unique idea. I chose to visit only one class, which happened to be an all-girl section. Fortunately, the section's home-room teacher, Mrs. Tumaneng, was one of my supporters. Instead of repeating my campaign speech, I took my guitar and serenaded the class. I won that class by a landslide, which enabled me to win the presidency by a squeaker. My friend and ally Policarpio was not so fortunate. Despite his charisma and political experience, he was no match in the eyes of the student body for Froilan's credentials as an honor student and student journalist.

As I write this part of my life story, I keep coming across stories about bullying in school and its harmful and sometimes disastrous consequences on individuals as well as society. In recent times, one of the deadliest outcomes of bullying took place at Columbine High School in Colorado in April, 1999, whereby two students went on a rampage, killing 23 students and teachers before committing suicide. The two claimed through their writings and their words that day that their actions stemmed from bullying that they suffered for years.

I had my own experience with bullying and fortunately I had both the luck and resourcefulness to deal with it. It happened at Ilocos Norte High School when I was a sophomore. One of my classmates had targeted me for bullying. His anger at me apparently resulted from envy over my achievements and the attention that I was getting from teachers and fellow students. During recess time or at the end of the school day, he would repeatedly challenge me to a fight. I would just walk away not wanting to create a scene. He interpreted my response as an act of cowardice and started taunting me in the presence of his friends. I knew that I could have accepted his challenge and easily vanquished him in a fist fight. The reason I was so confident was that I had developed fairly good boxing skills. Unknown to him, I belonged to a group of friends in my neighborhood who practiced boxing with gloves during the weekends and some weekday afternoons after school. My boxing skills were further sharpened with the aid of my older brother, Caesar. After graduation from Ilocos Norte High School in 1952, he went on to college at the University of the Philippines and on his freshman year, he elected boxing as his Physical Education course specialty. He came home at the break between semesters and taught me quite a few boxing tricks. With his coaching, I developed a powerful and deadly right cross.

One day after school, my friends and I were at our usual boxing afternoon exercises at the street near my house when my bully classmate happened to come by. He stopped to view the action. Since I was just standing by when he arrived, he assumed that I was just there as a bystander and not one of the fighters. The next thing I knew, he asked for a pair of gloves, put them on and came to me, challenging me to spar with him. Nonchalantly, I accepted.

I knew I had an excellent chance of decking him. It took me only a few seconds to find an opening for my right cross. I had already planned what I would do if and when that moment would come. The moment my right fist hit his face, I knew he was going to go down and as he fell, I let my body fall headlong forward and we both fell on the ground simultaneously as though both us only slipped. I quickly turned my body around so that both of us were facing up. For a few moments, we both lay on the ground and I tried to poke fun at ourselves by doing a mock knockout countdown, all the while laughing, as though to say that the whole thing was just a joke. That gave him just enough time to shake off the effects of my blow as we both scampered up. I could have done something different. I could have celebrated my victory, which for a moment I was tempted to do. But, thankfully, I was not in the mood to embarrass him. Instead, I chose to physically descend to his level, a gesture which he apparently appreciated.

The next day he approached me in school. Gone was the familiar expression of contempt which he used to show me. Referring to what happened the day before, he asked me if I had deliberately fallen down. Not wanting to patronize him, I lied and said I really slipped. From that time on, we became fast friends. Not only that; he would often come to my defense by discouraging other potential challengers, warning them that I was secretly taking boxing lessons and was good at it.

The adolescent years are a time for discovering and developing one's sexuality and I and my classmates were no exception. Most of us entered high school at 12 and 13 years old. At that age, we were in the transition stage in our attitude toward the opposite sex. We did not care much for them. That's the way it is supposedly for boys but probably not for girls because they allegedly mature earlier than boys. The school dealt with this reality by separating us by gender. Thus, on our freshman year, the brightest boys were in Section 1 while the brightest girls were in Section 2 and so on. Today, that decision to assign the girls to the lower of the top two sections would be criticized and labeled as male chauvinism. Besides, if girls mature earlier than boys, why should they not be assigned to the higher section? Go figure.

So girl-chasing was the farthest thing on my mind when I was 12 years old. All my leisure time was spent with the boys in my neighborhood with whom I enjoyed playing a variety of games and sports. It was at that time when I observed that a classmate of mine whom we shall call Fernando (not his real name) came frequently to play with us. I thought at the time that it was unusual for him to be around us so much since he lived quite a distance from our neighborhood. But it did not bother me until one day I learned why. I received a letter in the mail. Even before I could open it, I already felt something weird. The envelope reeked of perfume and upon opening it I found out that it was a love letter from Fernando. It was my rude introduction to homosexuality. I was completely unprepared not only by getting a letter from another boy but by the passion in the letter's language. Probably as a consequence of my shock and awkwardness, I reacted in a way that I later regretted. A few days after I got the letter, I gathered a few of my male classmates and let them read Fernando's letter. They decided to make a joke about it by memorizing parts of the letter and in Fernando's presence while we were in class, they started reciting passages of the letter while at the same time laughing, in an obvious act of ridicule. Fernando burst into tears and left the room. After that incident, he never spoke to me again. For the rest of my life, I have felt so guilty at the way I had treated Fernando. But the episode was, for me, an eye-opener and a useful one since it would not be the last time that I would deal with homosexuality both as a personal experience and as an issue.

It did not take long for me to get past the awkward stage of adolescence and by the following year, I began to feel attracted to the opposite sex and had crushes on my most attractive female schoolmates. It is quite common for people to have met the love of their life in high school but for me it was not the case. Many years later at class reunions, some of the girls would half seriously and half jokingly ask me why I never dated steadily any of them and I had a ready answer. I explained that I did not want to get committed to one girl because as a politician, I wanted to treat all the girls equally. That was only partly true because in reality there was a stronger reason why I did not attempt any serious relationships with any of my female classmates. It had to do with religion. In no uncertain terms, my mother had made it clear that getting serious with any but a Protestant girl was unacceptable. That unwritten rule applied to all of us Agnir siblings but it was more emphatically applied in my case because I was going to be a minister. Like a hawk, my mother kept a watchful eye over my relationships with girls and I later found out that she would even surreptitiously open any letter that came in the mail for me if it was from a girl. As for my classmates, the scuttlebutt by way of explaining my lack of serious relationships with them was that either I was gay or I had a girl friend somewhere else.

Actually, I had several girls who were special to me. With some of them I had a date but none developed into any romantic relationship. My first-ever date was Eufemia "Femy" Fermin, who was my military ball partner when I was a junior. My second date was Amely Lopez, who was my military ball partner when I was a senior. And my third and final date was Lilia Hermosura, who was my partner in the senior prom. Although attendance at those three social events was optional for most, I was required to be present because of my positions as highest-ranking PMT officer and as president of the Senior Council. PMT was an acronym for Pre-Military Training, the INHS equivalent of junior ROTC. In our junior and senior years, we took PMT as an adjunct of Physical Education and were taught and supervised by Mr. Gavino Bangloy, a World War II USAFFE veteran who doubled as the school's Corps Commandant. Part of his job was to assign ranks to us cadet officers. In both years, he gave me the highest ranks available for our corps. So in my junior year, I was the Cadet First Lieutenant and in my senior year, I was the Corps Commander with a rank of Cadet Major. Our battalion was mostly visible during school and town parades during which we marched with our wooden guns, and on Friday afternoons when we managed the flag-lowering ceremonies.

Two other girls were special to me because they were my singing partners when we represented the school in duet competitions, which were a side feature of the annual athletic meets among Ilocos Norte public high schools. On our freshman year, Natividad "Naty" Ramiro and I sang a duet entitled "Barcarolle," a selection from the opera Tales of Hoffman by Jacques Offenbach. On our senior year, Lydia Navarrete and I sang "Make-Believe" from the operetta Show Boat by Jerome Kern and Oscar Hammerstein.

Virtually everything I did during my high school years was designed to take the high ground. However, music was the one exception, which I did purely for fun rather than competition. Although, as I recounted earlier in this book, the piano was not my first choice for a musical instrument, by the time I was a teenager, I was good at *oido*, which is Spanish for playing by ear. I could play an entire piece without looking at a music sheet as long as I knew the melody. I also had a fairly good baritone voice and so that combination made me popular at parties and dances.

One day, I happened to recount to my buddies the story of how my mother decided against my taking up the violin so I would not wind up like my uncle who almost flunked in law school because his friends often took him out serenading. A few days after, I was relaxing at home when I heard the unmistakable beep of a car horn. I looked out the window and there were my buddies with a half truck and a piano in it. We spent the whole night all over town serenading our female schoolmates.

My musical career in high school had a bitter-sweet conclusion. As always, the operetta was a high point in the school's calendar and everyone, especially the members of the Glee Club looked forward to it, knowing that they would be in the cast. The school administration counted on it for the additional revenue and prestige it brought to the school. As usual, Miss Marcela Reyes, the Glee Club advisor, was preparing for it in advance. She had chosen an operetta with me in mind having a major role. In fact, she showed the play to me beforehand and asked my opinion about the role she had prepared for me. I told her it was OK. Then the damper to all her plans came. She asked the advisors of the clubs to which I belonged to give me free time for rehearsals. By that time, I was involved in so many leadership positions and was stretched quite thin. Aside from being president of the Senior Council, I was the PMT Corps commander, managing editor of the school paper, president of the Hi-Y Club and the Vocational Club, and a cast member of the Dramatic Club's play. I was also the school's entry to various provincial and regional oratorical contests. Nobody was willing to grant Miss Reyes's request.

I did not know until much later what was going on. But in retrospect, I would have willingly resigned some of my leadership positions because music and Miss Reyes were so special to me. However, it was not meant to be. In a fit of pique, Miss Reyes decided that for that year, and for the very first time since she started producing them, there wasn't going to be any operetta. She never discussed with me the main reason why but through subsequent conversations with some of the other teachers, I gathered what had happened.

For many years after, I felt guilty over my part in that unfortunate episode and in fact thought that Miss Reyes did not care for me anymore. Fifty years later, I found out the truth from no less than her niece, who was my schoolmate. She revealed to me that in the weeks before graduation, when it came time to decide on the honor roll, her aunt became my most ardent advocate and fought hard to convince the school that I should be the valedictorian chiefly on the basis of my strong extra-curricular record. Miss Reyes lost the fight and I wound up No. 3 or first honorable mention.

In a way, I looked at school as some kind of delaying action. I knew that eventually, I would have to go to the seminary or Bible School for training in the ministry and so I must have subconsciously looked at high school as my time to live it up. In fact, there was not a single one of my classmates to whom I had revealed the career set up by my mother for me.

Eventually, however, the proverbial cat got out of the bag and it took a special incident in class. One day, a few weeks before graduation, the school guidance counselor was invited to take over our home room class. The class session was going to be about our plans for the future and she asked each of us to go before the class and speak for a few minutes about what we were going to be. We were going to go in alphabetical order and although I would have been scheduled to be second because of my last name, I asked to be excused for a bathroom break, requesting to be the last speaker, which request was granted.

During the whole time that I listened to my classmates telling us how they were going to be lawyers, doctors, nurses, engineers and professors, I prayed that the bell would ring before it was going to be my time to speak. Alas, it was not meant to be. When it was my turn to speak, my first words were "I am going to be a minister" and tears started to roll down my face. I will never forget the expression on the faces of my classmates. It was a combination of shock and pity. All those years, they had known me as a politician, writer, orator, actor or musician. I had not even spoken a word about religion, formally or informally. In fact, the classmate whom we all assumed was going to be a minister was Remigio Acacio, an ardent member of the Jehovah's Witnesses who was always talking about his religion. In a few sentences I had let out what was heretofore the biggest secret of my life and there was no turning back.

From there on, it was all downhill for me. Graduation Day, April 1, 1955, came. I was just recovering from chickenpox which had kept me in the hospital for a week. Although I was well enough to be on my feet, I was strongly advised to stay away for fear of a relapse and also to protect my classmates from infection. The aftermath of my absence is that the program had to be changed in a hurry because half of it involved me. As class president, I was scheduled to give the valedictory speech and lead the class in the induction to the alumni association. As first honorable mention, I was going to provide the class prophecy. And I was to sing a solo entitled "Goodbye to Summer." The graduation exercises were held at the provincial athletic grounds where the grandstand was large enough to accommodate the audience. I was later told about how it went. Each time my number in the program would come up, the emcee would say "In place of Federico Agnir ...." and would give the name of my alternate. My vice president, Raymundo Arcangel, Jr. gave the valedictory address. Remigio Acacio sang my solo. My class prophecy was read by someone else. The week after the commencement exercises, I would run into a lot of complete strangers asking me about my recent illness and wishing me well. It was small consolation for missing my high school graduation ceremonies, which ranks as one of the most disappointing moments of my life.

CHAPTER III: COLLEGE AT U.P.

The summer of 1955 was a landmark period for me insofar as my career path was concerned. I had just graduated from high school and it was time to plan the next step. For the first time, my mother and I sat down for a lengthy heart-to-heart talk on the shape of my future. Actually, she was the one who instigated that critical meeting, which was bound to happen. For the first 16 years of my life, she and I never talked about plans for my post-secondary education.

We both assumed that after high school, I was going to study for the ministry but neither of us knew how to go about it in the best way. We each had our issues. For one thing, I was beginning to doubt the wisdom of investing my entire life in the ministry and had openly expressed my doubts to members of my family and my friends.

Also, I had been toying with the idea of becoming a medical doctor before going into the ministry. In part, my fantasy was fueled by reading about the life of Albert Schweitzer, the famed missionary who studied both for medicine and the ministry before going out to a remote village in Africa to be a doctor to the area's natives.

Somehow, word got to my mother that I had been expressing my doubts about the ministry and she decided to meet the problem head on. From the moment we got together, her very first words and her demeanor were unmistakable. In plain English, she asked me, "What do you really want to be?" Parenthetically, we learned early on that at home, as in virtually every Filipino home, when parents talk to their children in English as opposed to the vernacular, especially in a stern tone like my mother's, the business is serious and one better have straight answers. It was very clear that my mother was not about to allow her promise to God to go unfulfilled.

To cut a long story short, we hit upon a compromise. Instead of my going straight to Bible School or theological seminary as most future Filipino pastors were to do, we agreed that I would first go to the University of the Philippines (heretofore U.P.) so I could get a degree in Liberal Arts. One factor that helped convince her was that all my older siblings had gone to U.P. and I reasoned that it was only fair that I follow in their footsteps, as I did with all previous stages of my schooling.

I regard that historic meeting and agreement as having laid the seeds of what would become my life as a multi-vocational person. From that point on, I would grab every opportunity to broaden my knowledge, including enrolling in courses that were beyond the confines of the traditional theological course of study.

Actually, my mother had her own hidden agenda which in later years she would reveal to me. She herself had mixed feelings about sending her son straight into the ministry without looking at other options. Noting that many pastors she knew often wound up in poverty, she wanted me to explore alternate or supplementary occupations which could augment the pastor's standard income, which was usually very meager compared to that of other occupations. So in addition to focusing on a variety of elective courses, I wound up majoring at U.P. in two disciplines, namely History and Speech. As expected, I stayed longer than the normal four years it usually takes to finish a bachelor's degree.

That agreement between me and my mother for me to take the long route toward the ministry was, in a way, prescient. Unknown to either of us at the time, the shakers and movers in theological education in the Philippines were planning big changes in the formal preparation of future ministers. Their efforts would eventually lead to making a graduate degree the standard requirement for future ministers. As it was for those preparing for other professions such as law and medicine, it was deemed necessary for a person training for pastoral ministry to first acquire a bachelor's degree in the liberal arts before moving on to a graduate professional degree in theology. Thus, while I was in U.P., I bought enough time for the authorities to put into place their plans for an upgraded theological curriculum.

Established in 1908, the university's main campus was first located in Manila in the Ermita district along Padre Faura St. and in the Quiapo district along Hidalgo Street. Starting with three schools, namely the College of Medicine, College of Fine Arts and College of Liberal Arts, the university eventually outgrew its Manila locations. Thirty years after its founding, plans for a new campus were set up in Diliman, which was then a town in the province of Rizal. Construction of buildings on the new campus began in 1939. The first permanent buildings to be finished were those of the College of Liberal Arts and the College of Law.

When I arrived on campus as a freshman student in July, 1955, more new buildings had been constructed. The new buildings that attracted most of my attention were the Protestant and Catholic chapels. Located at the northern edge of the campus, they were set up to cater to the religious needs of the community. In previous years, people of all faiths shared one temporary building which they eventually outgrew, prompting construction of the two buildings.

35

The Catholic chapel was formally called the "Chapel of the Holy Sacrifice" while the other was at first called simply the "U.P. Protestant Chapel." In reference to the two buildings' unique architectural appearance, some people nicknamed them "the flying saucer" and "the covered wagon," respectively."In 1956 the congregation that worshipped in the latter organized themselves into a church. As a less than subtle response to the theological theme reflected by the neighboring chapel's name, the new church was called "The Church of the Risen Lord." That appellation or its acronym of CRL has since become the building's alternate name. Next to the chapel was a multi-purpose building that was subsequently named Gumersindo Garcia Hall, in honor of the late Dr. Gumersindo Garcia, Sr., a member of the university Board of Regents and a prominent lay officer of the National Council of Churches of the Philippines (heretofore NCCP). Dr. Garcia was a key instigator in obtaining the approval to have chapel buildings established on campus.

The Protestant Ministry complex became the second home for me and for many of the Protestant students on campus. Such second homes were a godsend for most U.P. students because a large number of them came from distant places with some being away from home for the first time in their lives. While most came from various provinces in the island of Luzon, others came from faraway places in the southern islands. It was a new inter-cultural experience for me. For the first time in my life, I was in the company of people who spoke something other than Ilocano as their primary language. All the major Filipino ethnic groups were represented.

U.P. was the leading post-secondary school in the Philippines, drawing the top 5% of the country's high school graduates. So well regarded was it as a quality institution that it was often referred to as the Harvard or Yale of the Philippines. Many families worked at great sacrifice to send their sons and daughters to U.P. Passing the entrance exams required for admission and eventually graduating from there were considered an honor in one's home environment. In order to stay enrolled at the university, a student had to maintain a minimum grade point average. For most, it required quite a bit of effort because of the nature of the competition. Many of their fellow students were high school honor graduates and oftentimes they would have teachers who graded by the bell curve. As a result, those who wound up at the lower end of the curve might receive a failing grade, often to their sheer shock for flunking a subject, usually for the very first time in their lives. Those who failed to make the minimum grade point average were "disqualified." That term on one's transcript was a student's most feared word. The colloquial equivalent was the phrase "kicked out," a stigma that would hound such students even long after they had left U.P. to continue their studies at other schools. For many, one's tenure at U.P. hung on the balance from semester to semester so much so that when students went home for school breaks, the first question that neighbors would ask them was whether they were "still at U.P."

Religious services at the Protestant Chapel were led by the American missionary who was recruited by either of the two primary member denominations of the NCCP, namely the Methodist Church and the United Church of Christ in the Philippines (UCCP). Each denomination took turns at recruiting the missionary who would serve as senior pastor. When I arrived, the pastor was the Rev. Richard Bush, a Methodist missionary who had the honor and pleasure of presiding over the inauguration of the new complex in 1954. He was succeeded in 1955 by the Rev. E.K. Higdon of the Disciples of Christ, one of the American denominations that sponsored the UCCP.

Student activities were held under the auspices of the U.P. Christian Youth Movement. Known by its acronym of UPCYM, it was first organized in the late 1940's by students at the old Padre Faura campus. After the transfer to Diliman, UPCYM became one of the most prominent and visible student organizations on campus, especially after it acquired its own quarters with the establishment of the Protestant ministry building complex. I worshipped regularly at the Church of the Risen Lord, singing in its choir. I also joined the UPCYM and through the years rose through the ranks, first becoming the editor of the organization's paper called UPCYMette and later getting elected as its president.

One of the reasons I joined the church choir was to keep an eye on an attractive young lady in the soprano section named Ruby Ordinario. At first glance, I already knew that she had a lot of the qualities that I admired in a woman. Eager to know as much about her as I could, I befriended her. Although she was from Davao City, which was located many miles to the south in the island of Mindanao, her roots were Ilocano just like mine. Her father, Roman Ordinario, was from Balaoan in the Ilocano province of La Union; her mother, Tereza Rubio, was from Batac, Ilocos Norte, the town famous for two of its citizens, namely Gregorio Aglipay and Ferdinand Marcos. Roman and Tereza had met in Davao to which they had each migrated as schoolteachers, married and had three children, with Ruby as the oldest.

Ruby was a child prodigy. At nine years old, she was the church organist for the large UCCP congregation in Davao City. In those days, the church's musical instrument was an old pump organ. A delightful story is told that because of her diminutive stature, Ruby's feet were not long enough to reach the pumps and so someone had to kneel on the floor while working the pumps manually as she played. Mentally, she was way ahead of her classmates. In elementary school she was accelerated to higher grades and eventually graduated from high school at the tender age of 13. At Silliman University High School where she went for her senior year, she was outstanding in the performing arts, excelling in declamation and acting. A voracious reader, she developed an interest in literature and wrote poetry at a very early age. At 16, she wrote a poem which was published internationally in a Harper Brothers anthology of Christian literature entitled "Christianity and the Fine Arts." At U.P., Ruby continued to set records for accomplishments. After she graduated in 1959, she was hired as an instructor at the university's Department of Speech and Drama. She was19 years old, making her one of the youngest ever to become a U.P. faculty member.

The more I learned about Ruby, the more I admired her and sought common interests that would draw us together. To me, she was the quintessential beauty and brains type and I was determined to win her over as my girl friend and eventually as my wife. There was just one problem. Early on, she was dating another man and I had to bide my time hoping that someday my opportunity would come. Slowly, between going to the same church, engaging in the same activities, loving the same shows and even being classmates in several courses, we grew closer to each other. Eventually, she and her boyfriend broke up. In December, 1958, she and I became engaged and three years later, we got married.

Going to other aspects of my life in U.P., I joined Beta Sigma Fraternity, one of four prominent campus fraternities. I joined a fraternity mainly for its snob value. It was commonly recognized that some of the most prominent campus figures were members of a fraternity or sorority. New frat members took delight in wearing their fraternity pin in public and, as in the case of their stateside counterparts, looked forward to the day when they could "pin" their girlfriend. As an indication of their elitism, frat men came up with a pejorative title for those who were not members of a Greek society, calling them "barbarians."

The mid-1950's was a critical period in the life of university fraternities and sororities. For a variety of reasons, their value and the role they played in college life were being seriously questioned and challenged. One of the issues being hotly debated was the nature of the initiation rites that an applicant had to go through. Hazing was a standard practice among virtually all fraternities on campus. There were rampant reports of injuries and one incident that became the focus of attention and publicity was the 1954 case of an applicant who died while he was being initiated. An investigation of the cause of his death revealed a connection to hazing. However, no amount of publicity or investigation was able to stop the practice and the issue was hushed up before it could make any further progress. One theory that was being whispered about was that there were too many alumni of the various fraternities who had since risen to national prominence. Some had become legislators and high court justices and in fact, an alumnus of the target fraternity was a highly placed legislator who would eventually become president of the Philippines.

An equally insidious issue had to do with the stranglehold that fraternities and sororities kept over student government and their questionable methods of maintaining control and dominance. At the time, student government at U.P. was set up such that the highest titular positions were elected by a few representatives. This was somewhat similar to the British parliamentary system whereby the prime minister is selected by members of the legislature instead of by popular vote. That set the stage for easy manipulation of the voting process through alliances and backroom horse trading.

At U.P. there were three top titular positions in student government, namely, the presidents of the University Student Council, the Senior Student Council and the Junior Student Council. A fourth position, which was not part of Student Government but equally prestigious, was the presidency of the Woman's Club. Competition for election to each of those titles was very intense. Aside from its prestige, the title also brought the power of political patronage for its holder. For instance, the University Student Council president appointed the editor-in-chief of the *Philippine Collegian*, which was the weekly school paper. The Senior Student Council president appointed the editor-in-chief of the *Philippinensian,* which was the graduation yearbook. He or she also had a strong hand in choosing those who provided ancillary services toward the *Philippinensian's* publication such as the printing and photography. Each of the three Council presidents had other sorts of appointments and largesse to distribute among supporters.

The man who spearheaded the fight to curb the influence of fraternities was a Jesuit priest named Fr. John Delaney. An Irishman born in Liverpool, England, who trained for and got ordained for the priesthood in the United States, he came to U.P. in the school year 1949-50 to become the full-time Catholic chaplain as well as spiritual adviser to the U.P. Student Catholic Action, or UPSCA for short. Fr.

Delaney was the Catholic chaplain during the transfer of the main university campus to Diliman. It was part of his enduring legacy to establish the Diliman chaplaincy and to supervise the design and construction of the Chapel of the Holy Sacrifice.

Fr. Delaney correctly analyzed the source of the dominance of the fraternities and sororities. For the typical member, a Greek society offered a closely-knit and fiercely loyal surrogate family as well as the pride of belonging to an elite exclusive group. Moreover, for the politically ambitious, membership was a ticket to achievement and campus-wide recognition. Such incentives were more than enough to attract applicants who were willing to undergo the rite of passage in the form of a rigorous, oftentimes brutal, initiation.

Fr. Delaney's battle strategy was two-pronged. One was to campaign for the abolition of fraternities and sororities. This he did by writing to university administrators, teachers, parents, students and the media, seeking their support. His other strategy was to mobilize the UPSCA to mount a challenge by fielding candidates for the various offices in Student Government and Woman's Club. To the fraternities and sororities and their various supporters, Fr. Delaney had thrown the gauntlet, igniting war between the two contending forces.

I first came to learn about the conflict between the fraternities and Fr. Delaney in 1954, the year before I arrived at U.P. One of my older brothers had brought home a copy of the *Philippine Collegian* which contained a full-page article entitled "Father Delaney Must Go." Written by Emmanuel Tipon, a law student and a member of Alpha Phi Beta, it clearly articulated the battle cry of the fraternities and sororities and showed how far the war had escalated. The article demanded that Fr. Delaney be expelled from the university on the ground that he was an alien meddling in university affairs in violation of the principles of academic freedom and separation of church and state.

The strain from building up the campus chaplaincy and fighting the war against the Greek societies must have taken a toll on Fr. Delaney's health and in December, 1955, he died in Baguio City while he was on spiritual retreat. In death, he was vindicated, though, because the following school year 1956-57, UPSCA won all the major council top seats as well as the presidency of the Woman's Club, thus ending many years of continuous fraternity and sorority hegemony.

The following school year, 1957-58, the war between UPSCA and the fraternities and their allies took a new form. This time, the issue was the choice of a new university president. Dr. Vidal Tan, who had served as university president, retired the previous school year, prompting a search for his replacement. Under the leadership of

Fernando Lagua, who had won a second consecutive term as president under the UPSCA banner, the University Student Council began complaining publicly that the Board of Regents, which was responsible for appointing the incoming president, was dragging its feet. It was believed in some quarters that UPSCA wanted to hurry the selection process because they had their own candidate, most likely the sitting interim president at that time who was known to be sympathetic to the local Catholic religious community.

Helping to stoke the fire was Homobono Adaza, the *Philippine Collegian* editor-in-chief who had been appointed by Lagua. Adaza wrote a series of editorials attacking the Board of Regents for their inaction. In December, 1957, Lagua and Adaza led a student strike that culminated in a motorcade of several buses filled with about a thousand students that went through the streets of Quezon City and Manila with a stopover at the presidential palace. There the strike leaders engaged in a dialogue with Fred Ruiz Castro, who was then executive secretary to the president of the Philippines. Embarrassed by the student strike and concerned over a possible escalation of hostilities, the University Council, consisting of administrators and faculty, declared an early Christmas holiday.

Unwittingly, UPSCA gained a couple of new adversaries in the Board of Regents and, indirectly, the office of the President of the Philippines, which had the final say on the choice of a new university president. It did not take long for UPSCA to feel the negative impact of its previous actions. A month after the strike, a number of student leaders petitioned that Lagua and Adaza be expelled for alleged immoral use of the *Philippine Collegian* to malign the Board of Regents and the university administration. Responding to the petition, the university Executive Committee suspended Lagua for nine months and divested him of his University Student Council presidency. In turn, Adaza was permanently dropped from university rolls.

The new U.P. president was Dr. Vicente Sinco, erstwhile Dean of the College of Law. One of his earliest objectives was to prevent student government from ever being dominated again by a single student organization. Accordingly, in June, 1958, he issued an Administrative Circular which limited any organization to just one representative in each of the student councils. Seeing the directive as an effort to curtail its dominance, UPSCA filed a case in court contesting the circular. The case dragged on for a couple of years before it reached the Supreme Court which dismissed the case on technical grounds, claiming that the petitioners should have exhausted administrative remedies within the university.

Thus, during the two school years 1958-59 and 1959-60, while the UPSCA petition dragged in court, student government was suspended. Except for a ten year hiatus early on, the University Student Council had enjoyed a long virtually uninterrupted history since it was created in 1913. It continued to function even during the Japanese occupation. And now, with the current suspension of student government, there were no more campus-wide student elections being held. That effectively pulled the carpet from under the feet of all aspiring future student leaders and their sponsoring organizations.

The two-year campus-wide election blackout affected me personally. School year 1959-60 was going to be my year. The summer before the opening of classes, some of my Beta Sigma brothers approached me for my permission to be nominated as the fraternity's representative to the Junior Student Council should student government is restored. In the years before the UPSCA ascendancy, the Junior Student Council had been a Beta Sigma bailiwick with a number of Beta Sigmans ascending to that council's presidency. Most of them were students at the College of Veterinary Medicine where there was always a large percentage of Beta Sigmans. I was told that the reason I was being groomed for candidacy was that they regarded me as the fraternity's "golden boy," which was their term for the one whom they considered the most popular Beta Sigman on campus at the time.

Indeed, I was quite visible on campus. I was in my senior year at the College of Liberal Arts and due to graduate that following November. I had just been elected president of the UPCYM. The previous semester, I represented Beta Sigma in the inter-fraternity oratorical contest and ran the first ever-inter-fraternity chess team tournament which attracted press coverage including weekly reports of the tournament's progress in the *Philippine Collegian's* sports page. I was a charter member and active participant of the U.P. Speech Association, a new organization whose flagship project was the annual Speech Festival, a week-long celebration that featured theater presentations and competitions in impromptu speaking, oratory, debate and other forensic events. I was also the head of the Jose Abad Santos chapter of the Order of DeMolay and although DeMolay was not a U.P. organization, more than 90% of the chapter's members were U.P. students.

At the start of classes, we waited eagerly for word from the administration for the go-ahead to hold student government elections. It never came as the UPSCA petition continued to be unresolved for another year. Attention then focused on the dormitory association elections. In past years, such elections were fairly nondescript side shows that attracted only lower-level student politicians. Now, with student government elections gone, they suddenly became the most prominent and potentially hotly contested elections on campus.

I was a resident of Kanlaon Residence Hall. Formerly called North Men's Dormitory by virtue of its location, Kanlaon was one of two men's dormitories on campus, the other being Mayon Residence Hall, formerly called South Men's Dormitory. Of the two, Kanlaon was the larger one. Its residents were also more economically and socially diverse. Kanlaon consisted of two components. One was a large two-story building where the better-heeled students stayed and the other consisted of the quonset huts that formed the original dormitory and where the less affluent students stayed. I had originally started at the quonset section, rooming with some of my DeMolay brothers. Later, I moved to the main building. Thus, I had the reputation of having resided in both sections, which gave me a demographic advantage over my potential opponents.

Beta Sigma put forward my candidacy for the presidency of the Kanlaon Residence Hall Association. My rivals were a couple of students from the College of Law both of whom were frat men. Joe de la Cruz was a Sigma Rhoan and Noel Laman was an Alpha Phi Betan. The situation became somewhat reminiscent of the competition between fraternities that featured student elections of the past.

The campaign that followed was one of a kind. It was totally one-sided and almost embarrassingly so. My fraternity brothers and friends at the dormitory got so enthusiastic that one by one, they came up with all kinds of ideas to advertise my candidacy. In contrast, my opponents offered little or no answer. I had very little hand in either planning or directing my friends' campaigning activity; most of it just happened spontaneously. Quirico Monje, a Beta Sigma brod, and co-alumnus of Ilocos Norte High School, started a media blitz. An Engineering student, he used ordinary everyday materials like a 45 RPM turntable, electrical wire and light bulbs to jerry-rig a neon flashing sign that read "AGNIR FOR PRESIDENT." Mounted on three window panes from the second floor and facing the street in front of the dormitory, the sight of the three words flashing in succession was quite something to behold at night by bus passengers and by pedestrians on their way to the nearby local shopping place called "Little Quiapo." Not to be outdone, Ellie Santiago, a Fine Arts student, a DeMolay brod and fellow UPCYMian put up a poster at the entrance of the dorm on the day of the election. On it was a cartoon depicting the finish of a foot race with me dressed like Superman, cape and all, hitting the tape ahead of my two opponents. The caption read: "Make Way for Super-Agnir."

The *coup de grace* was delivered by Jerry Dadap. Jerry was my best friend. We arrived at U.P. about the same time and got connected in so many ways. Both of us worshipped at CRL, sang in the choir together, joined the Order of DeMolay and organized a male quartet called The *DeMolay Dreamers* which performed extensively on and off campus. He was a student of the Conservatory of Music and was destined to become a household word nationally in music composition.

Jerry and I came up with a brilliant idea. We decided to ride the crest of the Agnir name's popularity in a tongue-in-cheek way. We did this by Jerry constructing a huge cloth banner which he hung above the dormitory's cafeteria in plain sight of diners. The banner read: "THIS IS A BETTER AGNIR." Almost everybody knew exactly what that meant and got a kick out of it. The Agnir surname was a virtual household name on campus largely because of the trail blazed by my two older brothers. My oldest brother Willie had been the president of the Senior Student Council in the school year 1955-1956 when I was a freshman. And my other brother Caesar was the sitting editor-in-chief of the *Philippine Collegian.* He had the unique distinction of being the *Philippine Collegian's* very first editor-in-chief who was not a political appointee. All previous editors were appointed by the University Student Council but because at the time there was no student government, the administration set up a test to select the editor-in-chief. He topped the test.

Manong Ces, as we younger family members called him, was also residing at the dorm at the time and some of his friends teased him about the banner. Not only did he take it good-naturedly but he had a great comeback, saying that while I might be the "better" Agnir, he was undisputedly the "best" Agnir. The "Better Agnir" banner was a sensation and people would later tell me that they thought that it sealed my victory more than did any of the other gimmicks. The memory of it stuck in people's minds for some time and for some, "Better" became my new nickname. At the inauguration program a few weeks later, that phrase got repeated often by program participants. So much so that the guest speaker and installing officer, Dean of Students Dr. Arturo Guerrero, got into the act himself with his opening statement, which went as follows: "This dormitory must be a big one to be able to accommodate two Agnirs."

So far, my narrative has dwelt heavily with extra-curricular activities. I may have chosen to do so because there were decidedly more interesting and unique highlights of the non-academic aspect of my life at U.P. However, my academic life certainly had its own share of interest and substance.

Those who were pursuing the Bachelor of Arts degree had a choice of either doing a straight general degree or one with a major subject. I chose the latter. As with everybody else, the first two years were spent in taking required general education courses in the arts and sciences. On the third year, we picked our major subject. As in most cases, my choice of major was influenced by two things, namely my experience with teachers in that field and the department's reputation.

One reason why I chose History was that my very first History professor was a very learned and interesting person. The course was titled "Introduction to World Civilization" and the teacher was Prof. Aurelio Estanislao. He did most of his graduate training in Europe, studying at Sorbonne, the famed French university. The man was a genius and Renaissance man. He spoke half a dozen languages and was trained and competent in a wide array of academic disciplines. One of his other areas of expertise was Music. Gifted with a strong baritone voice, he was a nationally recognized concert artist. In fact, he was also a member of the faculty of the Conservatory of Music teaching Voice. Estanislao eventually left the College of Liberal Arts to become full-time professor at the Conservatory. I idolized him in part because given my own wide variety of interests I could see myself pursuing a similar course.

One other History professor that attracted my attention was Prof. Teodoro Agoncillo. At that time, I was being exposed and drawn to the growing Philippine nationalist movement. One of the platforms of the movement was a demand for the rewriting of Philippine history. Until that time, history textbooks were written before the Philippines became independent from the United States so such books had a strong colonial bent.

Prof. Agoncillo was a leading figure in the move to rewrite Philippine history. He first gained national recognition for his book entitled *Revolt of the Masses*. The book focused on the life of Andres Bonifacio and the secret society Katipunan which he founded, and which launched the Philippine revolution of 1896. Aside from its unique flowing narrative style, the book appealed to me because of the emphasis on Bonifacio, whose stature had been eclipsed for a long time in Philippine historiography.

As a budding nationalist, I had wondered why Bonifacio was not getting the importance which I felt he deserved. One day, I stumbled on a plausible explanation in the form of an article in *The*

45

Philippines Free Press, the country's leading news magazine at that time. The article cited a statement made by H. Otley Beyer, a well-respected American anthropologist who spent most of his adult life in the Philippines. His accomplishments in teaching, research and writing earned for him the title of "Father of Philippine anthropology."

In his statement, Beyer allegedly revealed the hitherto little known background behind the choice of Jose Rizal as the Philippine national hero. According to Beyer, Rizal was chosen in 1901 by the Philippine Commission, the legislative body of the country at that time. Composed of Americans, that Commission chose Rizal over other Filipino patriots because of his pacifism. That decision completely left out Bonifacio and others who had led the Philippine revolution that began in 1896.

The notion of Rizal as an American-made Philippine national hero rankled deeply in me and helped to fuel my commitment to the nationalist movement. At the time, U.P. was a hotbed of nationalism and inevitably I got drawn into the company of students and faculty members who were leading the movement. We all began to see the American presence in the Philippines of more than 50 years in a different light. Instead of a benevolent and paternalistic sponsor whose mission it was to nurture the Filipinos toward self-determination, America to us was just a new breed of colonial master that was determined to keep the Filipinos subjugated politically, economically and culturally.

In 1958, I had a classmate named Jose Maria Sison. We called him Joe, which is a common Filipino nickname for Jose. Although neither of us knew it at that time, Joe was destined to become a leading figure in the nationalist movement and for which reason our paths would cross many times in the future. Ironically, we did not meet in a History class but rather in an English class, a course in advanced public speaking. It was a requirement in his degree program, which was Bachelor of Arts in English. I was just taking it as an elective. But I had a different agenda. We had another classmate in the person of Ruby Ordinario whom I was still courting. Like Joe, Ruby was an English major and I decided that taking the course was an opportunity to impress her. The three of us became close friends.

My other agenda was to use the course as a stepping stone to a second subject major, which was Speech. For much of my first four years of stay at U.P., there was no Speech department. The few courses under the rubric of Speech were offered by the English department and those who wished to make a career of teaching Speech had to become English majors with a concentration in Speech. In fact, that was the course of action that Ruby took. As for me, I did not care to be an English major, which focused a lot on Literature, a subject area that was not my cup of tea.

My opportunity came when, during the school year 1959-1960, U.P.'s Speech and Drama department was inaugurated. Immediately, I added Speech and Drama as my second major. For me, that meant staying an extra year after graduation. The year that I spent as a Speech and Drama student was one of the most enjoyable phases of my entire academic life at U.P. Much of that was from the quality of fellowship in the company of fellow Speech majors, something that had been lacking during my years as a History major. We were a closely knit bunch of eager beavers trying out new stuff. For example, there was the campus radio station DZUP, the management of which was turned over to the Speech Department. We all took our turn as DJs, sound engineers, and scriptwriters either as employees or students and interns while enrolled in Radio Production under the tutelage of Prof. Leticia Tipon, whom we fondly called Manang Letty.

We established the U.P. Speech Association, which was open to all advanced Speech students. Our big activity was the management of the Speech Festival, a week-long celebration of presentations and competitions in forensics, theater and public discourse that were opened to all university students. Through such activities, we played a role in discovering and nurturing new talent, some of whom would go on to prominence as leaders at the campus and, after graduation, of the larger community and even the country. For example, it was at the speech competitions that Enrique Voltaire Garcia II and Ben Muego first honed their public speaking skills. The two would eventually represent the university at international debate tournaments. Each later served as president of the university student council. I have no doubt that both owe some of their leadership skills to their forensic experiences that started with their participation in the activities of the U.P. Speech Association. Voltaire also went on to become a national leader, serving a term as a delegate to the Constitutional Convention of the early 1970s.

Toward the end of the school year 1960-61, Ruby and I started planning to settle down and get married. So I started looking for a job. For me, it was a rude awakening. In my entire 22 years of existence, I never had a paying job, having been completely dependent on my parents for support. I was completely out of my element.

Fortunately, I found out about a possible teaching position that could open up at a college in Manila. The college was the Lyceum of the Philippines, located in Manila's Intramuros district. I decided that my best chance was to seek the assistance of a person who held a key position in the school. The person was Dean Jose Lansang of Lyceum's School of Journalism. Dean Lansang knew me well because he was a U.P. campus resident who worshipped regularly at the Church of the Risen Lord. He had served in the church's governing board and was familiar with my work as an officer of the UPCYM and as a member of the church choir. He agreed to recommend me. Sometime after I had submitted my resume, Dean Lansang informed me that the Lyceum administration had accepted my application and that he felt confident about my chances.

On April 28, 1961, Ruby and I got married at the Church of the Risen Lord where we had met six years before, worshipped, sang in the choir and courted. Officiating were Rev. Bernard O. Brown and Rev. Eliezer Mapanao. My sister Esther was Ruby's matron of honor while Ruby's brother Sadiri was my best man. Our best friends, Jerry Dadap and Susan Montepio, were groomsman and bridesmaid, respectively. Rev. Brown's son Chris was thrilled when we asked him to be the ring bearer. We had three of the cutest flower girls. Two were Ruby's cousins from the Batac Rubio clan, namely Hazel Corpuz and Rosanna Pambid. The third flower girl was my niece Eleanor who is my sister Esther's daughter. Music was presented by vocal soloists Ed Nathan Drilon and Lydia Dirilo and organist Rey Paguio.

Choosing wedding sponsors was a balancing act. We wanted to have the people closest to us but our respective parents wanted to get into the act too. So we wound up with a larger than usual set of sponsors consisting of three groups. Our own choices were people who were closest to us during our years in Diliman. Rev. Chester Marquis was the interim minister at CRL before Rev. Brown's arrival. Mrs. Ruby Mangahas was close to us because of CRL and the Conservatory of Music. Besides, she and her husband Federico were our namesakes. Mrs. Flora Rivera was our choir director when we met. And of course, Dean Jose Lansang was very special to us for reasons mentioned above. At the suggestion of our parents, we named Mr. and Mrs. Pablo and Amparo Bolante, my childhood godparents and the same with Congressman and Mrs. Constancio and Ludivica Maglana, Ruby's childhood godparents. There was one very special person who was not around but whom we made as our "ninong." When Ruby and I became classmates for the very first time, Prof. Alejandro Casambre was our teacher and quasi matchmaker. During our wedding, he was abroad working on his Ph.D. at Ohio State University. So he became our wedding sponsor *in absentia*.

I remember distinctly how my last hour as a bachelor went. I was still at Kanlaon Residence Hall, living my last day as a dormitory resident. Classes had already ended and every one of my dorm mates had gone home. I felt so alone and I could not wait for the car to come and pick me up to bring me to church. I took a shower and went back to my room to get dressed. Before doing so, I paused for a moment, lay on the bed, looked up at the ceiling and saw my life pass before me. The future, with all its hopes and dreams as well as its challenges, beckoned. A new day was dawning.

I remember that upon reaching the church, one of my friends greeted me to assure me that Ruby had arrived although on the way they almost had an accident. Thank God she was safe. And when she walked down the aisle, she looked every bit as resplendent and beautiful wearing the gown that she had a friend sew instead of buying one from a pricey specialty store as one of her efforts to help keep expenses down.

Among the special things that characterized the ceremony, what stuck most to my mind was the quality of music. All three musicians were our friends and were outstanding in their respective specialties. We chose all the music with their consent. But there was a delightful surprise. Rey Paguio, pianist-organist extraordinaire, played as the prelude his own arrangement of our favorite piece of music and theme song, "Stranger in Paradise," which is based on the tune of Borodin's "Polovetsian Dances."

The reception was held at the Aristocrat Restaurant in Cubao, Quezon City. The food was good and the fellowship was great. Afterwards, we spent the night in a reasonably-priced hotel in downtown Manila. We figured a high-priced honeymoon was a luxury that we did not need at that time, so we were just happy that all our plans went without a hitch and we were ready for our life as a married couple.

CHAPTER IV: THE EARLY MARRIED YEARS

The months of May and June, 1961 were good for Ruby and me for a number of reasons. As a newly married couple, we needed the time to get settled. The weeks and months leading to the wedding were so hectic that we hardly had time to think about the hundreds of details of starting our life together. It helped that those two months were school vacation days so neither of us had any commitments at our respective places of work. Ruby was on her third year as instructor at the U.P. Speech Department. As for me, I was informed that my application for a teaching job at Lyceum was approved and was asked to report for new staff orientations in late June in preparation for the start of classes in July. I was very grateful to Dean Lansang for following up on my application and putting in a good word for me.

The reality of everything struck home. I was going to be working for a living and supporting a family. Until that time, I had never worked to earn money for school and living expenses, all the while depending on my parents for tuition and allowance. I realized then how lucky I had been compared to so many others. More than at any previous time, I appreciated the sacrifices that my parents made to get me and my five siblings through school.

Supporting all of us children through school was not easy. For our parents, the most difficult period happened during the mid to late 1950s when there were five of us who were away in school. Four of us were in college in Manila while the youngest was in high school. At the time of my marriage, my older brother Orlando was studying medicine at Far Eastern University and my younger sister was a college freshman at the University of the Philippines. Thus, I could understand the expression of relief written on the faces of my parents upon learning that I had a job.

Considering the circumstances they faced, my parents' efforts were nothing less than phenomenal. Having settled early in their married life in a small town where there were no opportunities to make enough money to finance the college education of their children just by practicing their respective professions, they both had to be very creative, resourceful and frugal. So they had decided to engage in a variety of business ventures, two of which were fairly large and successful enough to provide what they needed to put us through.

Their first big venture was the manufacture and sale of hardwood lumber. The forests in the mountains around Claveria and Langgangan (now Sta. Praxedes), the next town to the west, were lush with hardwood trees, the most common of which were narra, ipil and guijo. Thanks to friends who were in high places in the Philippine government, my father was awarded a government concession to harvest logs from those mountains. The logs were transported to our place for cutting into slabs at a makeshift factory located across the street from our house. The "factory" was run by a group of four to six workers who had to saw the logs manually because the wood was too hard for the instruments of a sawmill. The product was in high demand particularly for public construction projects and for a period of about ten years, my parents ran a successful business supplying customers all over Ilocos Norte and Ilocos Sur with hardwood lumber. There were no reforestation programs in the area at all so, inevitably, the Agnir hardwood lumber business had to be laid to rest and my parents looked for an alternate source of income.

At that point, my mother took charge. She saw a good opportunity in the gasoline business. At the time, there were no gasoline stations in Claveria but clearly, the demand was there. The major potential customers were the buses that plied the 220-kilometer route between Laoag, Ilocos Norte and Aparri, Cagayan. Claveria was at the mid-point of that route and was a perfect place for refueling and rest stop. To meet that demand, my parents built a service station at the Eastern end of town.

A few years later, a good opportunity to expand the business came up. There was a new company called Philippine Rabbit Bus Lines, heretofore PRBL. Founded in 1946 and based in Tarlac City, the company rapidly expanded and by the mid 1950's had become the dominant bus line along the route between Manila and Laoag and much of Central and Northern Luzon. Mama wondered if the bus line had any intention of entering the Laoag-Aparri route and whether there was anything holding the company back. Determined to know the answer, she went to Tarlac to meet with the company management. At those meetings, she did find out that they were thinking of extending their bus routes. My mother then proposed that if PRBL would enter the Laoag-Aparri route, she would have a service station set up in Claveria to cater to PRBL's refueling needs. To sweeten the pot, she offered to sell gasoline to PRBL at cost. It was a calculated move. She figured that if PRBL regularly patronizes the Agnir gas stations, other customers would follow suit, reasoning that the business could be trusted.

That was a stroke of business genius on Mama's part. Her proposal apparently struck a responsive chord with the company and soon after, PRBL entered the Laoag-Aparri route. Making good on her proposal, my parents then built a second service station at the Western end of town. The arrangement with PRBL worked well for years. The Agnir gasoline stations enjoyed virtual monopoly in the area. Thus, my parents found the financial stability to support their children's education.

In putting a high priority on their children's college education, my parents were following a key aspect of Filipino culture. The Philippines has one of the highest literacy rates in Asia and a big reason is that the typical Filipino family strives hard to help their children attain the highest possible level of education and would make sacrifices to achieve that end. A family's prestige in the community is often measured by how many of the children have obtained a college education.

As a result of my parents' efforts, all their six children attained a college education or even beyond. Our oldest sibling Esther became an educator. After several years as a public secondary school teacher in Manila, she and her husband Dr. Alex Viernes migrated to Tacloban and started a family. There she taught college, retiring as a professor at Leyte Normal University. Willie became a judge and rose through the ranks, retiring as an Associate Justice of the Court of Appeals. Caesar took up Law and wound up in educational administration spending most of his later years as president of Northern Christian College in Laoag City. Orlando became a doctor and upon moving to the United States established a successful practice as a cardiologist in Martinsburg, West Virginia. Ruth moved to the United States and became a nurse supervisor at the prestigious Columbia Presbyterian Hospital in New York City.

Once I got married and started working, my mother no longer brought up the subject of the ministry. I could tell that she had mixed feelings. Part of her was reluctantly resigned to the idea that I might have decided against pursuing the ministry. But part of her was also relieved that they had fulfilled their financial obligations with one child and could then pay attention to supporting the rest who were still in school. At the very least, the ministry was in the backburner as far as both of us were concerned. For the moment, I was entirely focused on my marriage and possibly starting a family.

Teaching at Lyceum was both exciting and challenging. Given my two majors of History and Speech and my wide and varied extra-curricular experience, I was in a good position to prove my value to the school. My workload consisted of courses in Philippine History and English. In addition, I was assigned to be the coach of the school's debate team and to help out with the school chorus. My achievement as a debate coach for the year consisted in preparing the team for a debate against the University of Naga in the province of Camarines del Norte. As for the chorus, I wrote for them a few choral arrangements which they sang at a choral festival held at U.P. Diliman.

From Day One, my mind started racing over the question of whether I wanted to be a college professor for the rest of my life and whether Lyceum was the right place. In any case, I figured that it would have to be a long haul that would include graduate studies either in the Philippines or abroad. And even then, there was still the monkey on my back, namely the potential guilt about abandoning my mother's promise for me to become a minister.

There were circumstances that disturbed me while teaching at Lyceum. One was the amount of time it took me away from home. Because about half of the student population at Lyceum consisted of working students who went to night school, my schedule was a mixture of day and night classes so I was on campus from morning till night. Added to that lengthy schedule was the long and tiring commute of two hours back and forth between Manila and Quezon City where Ruby and I lived. I was getting a taste of the kind of lifestyle that was so common among residents of Greater Manila and I had difficulty adjusting to it. I began entertaining thoughts of looking for a job elsewhere.

Ruby had her own reasons for wondering whether it was smart to stay in Manila. In November, a visit to her gynecologist revealed that she was pregnant. As soon as the thrill over the good news settled, we thought seriously about where Ruby would give birth. She wanted to do so at Brokenshire Memorial Hospital in Davao City where she herself was born. Besides, she strongly felt the need to be close to her parents for added emotional support at this critical phase of her life. So in April, 1962, as soon as classes were over at both institutions where we taught, we flew to Davao City and moved in with Ruby's parents.

We decided to investigate the possibility of moving to Davao permanently. Given my difficulties of living and working in Manila, I did not need much convincing. In 1962, there were eight colleges in Davao City, four of which were Catholic schools. Of the remaining four, two were located in the city's outskirts. That left two that were located in the center of town, namely Mindanao College (heretofore MC) and Rizal Memorial Colleges (heretofore RMC.) Both colleges were within walking distance from home.

Between the two, RMC was the logical choice for a lot of reasons. The family had long-standing connections with that school. Mama Tereza was one its founders and charter members when it was incorporated in 1948. Another enduring legacy of hers is that of having written the lyrics of the RMC song. A Bachelor of Science in Education graduate of U.P., she had taught in a number of public schools all over Davao province before the Second World War. When the family settled in the city after the war, she taught at the Davao City High School. After RMC's establishment, she moved to RMC to teach English, which she did until she left for Silliman University for graduate studies, receiving her Masters degree in English in 1954. Upon returning to Davao City to resume teaching, she became a full-time professor of English at MC but she maintained her connection with RMC by occasionally teaching a course or two when asked to do so.

The rest of the family also had close connections with RMC. Papa Roman, who along with Mama Tereza had taught in public schools before the war, made a career change by joining the staff of the provincial treasurer's office as a bookkeeper. After finishing his Bachelor of Science in Commerce degree at RMC, he advanced through the ranks and eventually became a Treasurer at some of the Davao towns. Late in life, before retiring from government service, he became the treasurer of Davao del Sur, one of three when Davao was divided into three separate provinces.

All of the Ordinario children studied at RMC. Ruby spent her first three years of high school at RMC before moving to Silliman University High School where she graduated n 1953. She then returned to Davao and took college courses at RMC before moving to Manila in 1955 to continue her education at U.P. Her younger brother Sadiri graduated at RMC High School and so did their baby sister Elizabeth.

The college president when we arrived was Atty. Leopoldo Abellera. He was a prominent lawyer who finished his law degree at U.P. and rose through the ranks of the Philippine judicial system, eventually retiring as an Associate Justice of the Court of Appeals. In evaluating my application for a job at the school, he was likely swayed both by the long-standing connection of the Ordinario family with RMC and the prospect of obtaining the addition of two young co-alumni of U.P. to the college staff. We and Atty. Abellera also had common church connections. His father had been a pastor in his native province of La Union. When Atty. Abellera migrated to Davao, he became an active member of the Davao City Congregational Church which later became the United Church of Christ of Davao City.

On Atty. Abellera's recommendation, I was hired as the college Registrar. With that full-time job plus the additional income coming from teaching an afternoon or evening college course or two, I got the financial incentive to consider permanently settling in Davao. The future looked bright for our professional advancement in Davao. I

54

turned in my resignation from Lyceum. RMC also hired Ruby to teach and she turned in her resignation from U.P.

It did not take long for me to adjust to my new environment, thanks in large part to the connections that the Ordinarios had developed in the community for which I was a grateful beneficiary. One institution that Ruby and I rapidly became a part of was the United Church of Davao. Located on the same street from our home just a stone's throw away, it instantly became our new church home. We both sang in the choir and became soloists for special presentations such as the yearly Christmas cantata. The church congregation was overjoyed over the return of the musician who started out as the church organist at the tender age of nine.

One person who was particularly delighted over Ruby's return was Atty. Constancio Maglana, a prominent businessman who was a member of the church. He was Ruby's baptismal godfather as well as one of our wedding sponsors. When we arrived, the church did not have an organ. The pump organ that Ruby had played as a youngster had long been retired. Instrumental music was being provided through a piano played by a young fresh college graduate of music named Vilma Mae Cataylo. Recognizing the church's need while at the same time overjoyed that his "hijada" was back in Davao to be both an organist and prospective mentor to young organists, Maglana decided to buy a brand new church organ. He asked Ruby for her professional opinion. At both Silliman and U.P, she had taken lessons in organ from Miriam Palmore and Flora Zarco Rivera, respectively, and in both campuses, the instrument she took her lessons at was a Hammond organ. So in response to Congressman's Maglana's question, she suggested that he buy a Hammond organ.

Maglana, who had made his fortune in the logging business, would occasionally go abroad. So on one of his trips to the United States, he bought a Hammond Spinet organ which he ordered shipped to Davao. The instrument arrived in time for his return from abroad. The occasion for the new organ's inauguration was memorable. In his presentation speech, Maglana mentioned the presence of his "hijada" as his primary incentive in buying a church organ

Papa and Mama met sometime in the late 1930's. Both were Ilocanos who, like so many first-generation migrants, went to Mindanao seeking a new life in what was dubbed as the Philippines' "Land of Promise." Papa came from Balaoan in the province of La Union, a town whose main claim to fame was being the hometown of Camilo Osias, a well-known politician, educator and author. The latter was best known for the "Osias Reader," a primer that grade school pupils all over the Philippines used during the Commonwealth period and shortly after the war. Mama came from Batac in the province of Ilocos Norte, a town which was best known for several heroes of the Philippine Revolution and Philippine-American War. Of these, the two most prominent were Artemio Ricarte, a general who served under Emilio Aguinaldo, and Fr. Gregorio Aglipay, the founder of the Philippine Independent Church. Another well-known Batac citizen was Mariano Marcos, a pre-war congressman whose son Ferdinand would eventually become the president of the Philippines. Mama and Papa had met and courted in one of the towns of Davao province where both had been assigned as public school teachers. On May 15, 1938, the two got married and started a family. They had their first child in February, 1939 but unfortunately, the child came out still-born after Mama went through a lengthy labor that lasted four days. They tried again and their effort was rewarded when Mama got pregnant and gave birth to Ruby on February 2, 1940. This time, on the advice of friends and relatives, Mama was taken to Brokenshire Memorial Hospital in the city where medical facilities were much better than those in the rural areas of Davao.

Japan bombed Pearl Harbor in December, 1941 and invaded Mindanao shortly thereafter. Papa and Mama evacuated to the Davao Penal Colony along with 60 families most of whom were headed by fellow government employees. The victorious Japanese forces took over the colony and administered it, putting everyone in the colony to work, oftentimes alongside the colony's prisoners. The schools were reopened and Papa was designated as the elementary school principal. On top of his teaching duties, Papa was conscripted by the Japanese authorities to work at the colony farm. It was an additional job that he performed well and enjoyed owing to everything he had learned growing up as a farmer's son in Balaoan. Moreover, his gardening and fishing skills guaranteed that there would always be enough food at the Ordinario table.

It was during their stint at Davao Penal Colony when their second child, Sadiri, was born on July 21, 1942. In April, 1944, the Ordinarios were reassigned by the Japanese authorities to Davao City to teach there. It was not the best time to move to the city. By then, the tide of the war had turned. The American liberating forces were working their way northward from Australia, successfully taking over one island after another. General Douglas MacArthur was getting ready to invade the Philippines. In the meantime, naval forces under the command of Admiral Nimitz had scored victories over the Japanese Imperial navy, taking control of the seas surrounding the Philippines. In preparation for the coming invasion, planes based on aircraft carriers began to bomb key targets to soften and isolate the opposition. Davao City always had a large Japanese population before the war and was now a major Japanese military stronghold. The city was one of those key targets.

Papa and Mama needed to decide whether to stay put or leave the city to escape the bombing or to evacuate to the rural areas. Neither prospect was attractive. The air raid shelters where the residents huddled during bombing raids were not the most comfortable places especially for Mama who was nursing a one and half year old infant. Moreover, they had no home of their own. They had been moving around so much and so frequently through the years and never had a chance to purchase or build their own residence. They were depending on the generosity of relatives who let them stay at their home. On the other hand, they were tired of the constant moving and were reluctant to pull up stakes again. It was Papa who made the key decision. In his entire life, whenever he was faced with a crisis, he would turn to his faith. He prayed to God and heard an inner voice telling him that God would take care of his family, whatever the circumstances. So they elected to stay put. It turned out to be a life-saving decision. Had they decided to evacuate to the rural areas, they would have been in the company of some of their friends who on their way out of town were intercepted and massacred by retreating Japanese soldiers.

After the war, Papa and Mama decided that it was time to sink their roots and the first step was to build a permanent home. One of the lots that were left vacant from the war and taken over by the city government was one located off Legazpi St. On Mama's strong urging, the two put in a bid for that lot and got the award in exchange for a nominal sum. The location of the Ordinario home was a Godsend. Legazpi Street is one of the main streets of the San Pedro district, which at that time was the oldest and most prosperous business center of Davao City. Thus, the new Ordinario home was close to everything.

Another key institution that Ruby and I instantly became intimate with was Brokenshire Memorial Hospital. It was originally built in 1908 as a small clinic at Magallanes Street under the auspices of the Board of Commissioners for Foreign Mission of the Congregational Churches in the United States of America. Originally, it was built as a response to the need for medical assistance for people who were afflicted by malaria, of which there was an epidemic at the time. The clinic grew and became Davao Mission Hospital. Eventually, it acquired its present name of Brokenshire Memorial Hospital in honor of Dr. Herbert Brokenshire who served as its director from 1926 to the outbreak of World War II. In 1954, the Brokenshire School of Nursing was established. Under the aegis of the Congregational Missions and then later the United Church of Christ in the Philippines when the Congregational churches joined other denominations to form a new Philippine denomination, Brokenshire continued to expand. In 1978 Brokenshire College was founded, with its campus located at Madapo Hill at the eastern edge of the city.

On July 24, 1962 our first child was born at Brokenshire Memorial Hospital. Ruby had inherited her mother's propensity for difficult childbirth. Fortunately, Caesarean section was already a common practice so when it was deemed to be urgently needed, the procedure was performed on Ruby by Dr. Virgilio Durban, Brokenshire's senior resident surgeon. Dr. Durban was arguably the best known and most skilled surgeon in Davao at the time. He was also a deeply religious man and in a way he epitomized the extensive influence that the Congregational missions had on the population of Davao City especially on the community around Brokenshire. Many of the doctors and nurses in the surrounding area were Protestant evangelicals and members of the United Church of Davao. And a lot of the lay leaders of the church at one time or another had a special relationship with Brokenshire.

Probably in part because he recognized me and Ruby as a typical young couple who could appreciate some help getting started and perhaps as a tribute to everything that Papa and Mama had contributed to the life of both the church and hospital, Dr. Durban generously waived his surgeon's fee. Other doctors and nurses adopted us as part of their family. Ruby was so touched that by all this generosity and she vowed to pay them in kind. One of the ways she did was by composing the Brokenshire School of Nursing song.

We named our firstborn Mirla Criste Jemima. Earlier, Ruby had been thinking of the name Mirabella, a name of Italian origin which means "lovely or wondrous." She settled for a shorter version of the name by taking the first and last syllables. Later, we were pleasantly surprised to learn that there were others who were named Mirla. The second name was created by combining the first syllable respectively of the names of my mother Cristina and Ruby's mother, Tereza. As for Jemima, it was actually the very first name Ruby and I had thought of. In fact, we had decided even before we got married that our first daughter would be named Jemima. We even wrote a song together by that name with me writing the music and Ruby providing the lyrics. We nicknamed our child Dawn because Ruby originally thought that Jemima is the Hebrew word for dawn. Actually it means "dove," as we learned much later. But the name Dawn stuck and that is what we in the family call her.

It seemed as though Ruby and I had the best of worlds. We had good jobs, had gained plenty of new friends and felt quite fulfilled with our activities in school and church. We just had our first child who got plenty of attention from everybody, especially from Papa and Mama who were thrilled at having their first grandchild.

However, it did not take long before I began to feel restless. It was as though there was an emptiness inside of me that longed to be filled. Apparently, I had not succeeded in putting away all thoughts of going into the ministry. Although there was a tacit agreement between me and my mother that I was now free to do what I wanted, my feelings of emptiness were more profound than just a mere guilt over disappointing her. I felt like I was being hounded.

I used the term "hounded" because my thoughts were strongly influenced by the poem entitled "The Hound of Heaven." Written by Francis Thompson, a 19th century English poet, the poem uses the metaphor of the hound chasing the hare to symbolize God in pursuit of the fleeing human soul. The poem first came to my attention four years before when I was in college. It was introduced by two of my classmates during our class in Oral Interpretation whereby they did a lecture recital on the poem. Later, the two performed it as an event in the Speech Festival for that year. The poem's first stanza sets its theme as follows:

> I fled Him, down the nights and down the days;
> I fled Him, down the arches of the years;
> I fled Him, down the labyrinthine ways
> Of my own mind; and in the mist of tears
> I hid from Him, and under running laughter.
> Up vistaed hopes I sped;
> And shot, precipitated,
> Adown Titanic glooms of chasmed fears,
> From those strong Feet that followed, followed after.
> But with unhurrying chase,
> And unperturbèd pace,
> Deliberate speed, majestic instancy,
> They beat--and a Voice beat
> More instant than the Feet--
> "All things betray thee, who betrayest Me."

I needed help and I was very fortunate that I found it from a new friend to whom I could turn for spiritual and psychological guidance. This was the Rev. Edmundo Pantejo, the pastor at Davao City United Church. At the time of our arrival in April, 1962, Pastor Pantejo was just starting his second year as minister of that church. He and his wife Ophe and their child of six months, Barbara Jean, had arrived in September the year before. Ed and Ophe had been sweethearts while they were college students at Silliman University. They parted ways before they graduated. After Ophe graduated from the prestigious Silliman College of Nursing, she migrated to the United States where she worked as a registered nurse. In the meantime, Ed, who had graduated from Silliman's College of Theology in 1957 served for a year as pastor of the Surigao UCC Church in Northern Mindanao before going abroad for further studies. The two met in Boston, courted again, got married and started a family. After Ed finished his Bachelor of Divinity and Master of Sacred Theology degrees at Andover Newton Theological Seminary, UCCP Bishop Proculo Rodriguez urged him to come home to the Philippines so he can be the pastor of the Davao City United Church.

Pastor Ed and I immediately hit it off. He and I began extensive conversations about life in general and more specifically, our respective plans for the future. He would become my lifelong friend and mentor. As it turned out, both of us had similar concerns. Although we both had reasons to be happy by living and working in Davao, we shared a common feeling of restlessness.

On the other hand, Ophe made quite an impression on Ruby. Upon arriving in Davao, Ophe continued to pursue her career by joining the faculty of the Brokenshire Memorial Hospital School of Nursing. What impressed Ruby most about Ophe was that the latter represented an image of a minister's wife that was completely different from what she knew. Unlike most ministers' wives, Ophe was independent-minded, professionally visible and not perceived as a mere extension of her husband's ministry.

For Ruby, this was a turning point. It was for me too because I knew that Ruby had long held a negative perception of the life of a minister's wife. One of her favorite stories on that subject happened when she was a high school student at Silliman. Ruby was then living at Channon Hall dormitory where her mother was the matron. At that time, Channon Hall was where the female students of the College of Theology lived and so quite a few of the male Theology students would come to court their classmates. Some of them were clearly attracted to Ruby and made no effort to hide their feelings and intentions. But she would stop them dead in their tracks, telling them that she was certain that they were only interested in getting a ready-made church musician for free. By that time, Ruby already had a reputation in local circles as an accomplished organist and singer, on top of her other talents.

The moment that Ruby and I got engaged, I revealed to Ruby the promise that my mother made to God for me to become a minister. I often wondered whether in fairness to her, I should have revealed to her my secret earlier when I was still courting her. At any rate, she accepted my fate, albeit grudgingly. As it turned out, despite her protestations, she revealed to me a faith that in more ways than one was deeper than mine. It was based on her conviction that God is in control of our lives and whatever road we wind up taking, God would always be leading the way. Later in our married life, her faith would often be an invaluable source of strength for me during times when my own faith would waver.

When I finally found the courage and composure to lay it all on the line, I told Ed my life story – my mother's promise, my mixed feelings over what she did, my efforts to avoid and delay the inevitable, and my feelings of profound guilt over my years of vacillation. His response was like a breath of fresh air to me. He told me that there was nothing unusual about what I was going through. He said that based on his observations as a former theological student, minister and pastoral counselor, he knew that a large number of Theology students go into the ministry for the wrong reasons. Some find out early enough and change careers in time while others find out when they are already ministers. But what floored me was his confession that he was one of those who realized when he was already a full-fledged ordained minister that he had gone into the ministry for the wrong reasons. He told me that what saved his career and his sanity was his success in finding the right reasons for staying in the ministry. He never told me what were his alleged wrong reasons for entering the ministry but I did not feel I had to know. I just felt better knowing that I was in good company.

It was time for me to finally cross the bridge and go to the seminary to train to be a minister. The question was where and when. The answer to the first part of the question was a no-brainer. I had made that decision five years before. In October, 1958, I decided that should I go on to study for the ministry, Silliman University would be my top choice. That month, I visited the campus for the first time. I was then a junior at the University of the Philippines and was part of an UPCYM delegation at a national conference of the Student Christian Movement being held at Silliman. Upon arriving there, l found that all that I heard about the university and its ambiance was confirmed and more. I was smitten.

The only issue I had at that time was that Silliman's College of Theology did not have a graduate program, offering only the Bachelor of Theology degree, which was an undergraduate degree. However, I was also informed that plans were afoot to upgrade the college to a graduate level. Four years later, the planned upgrade did take place. In 1962, the college inaugurated the Bachelor of Divinity degree, which required a four-year undergraduate degree as a prerequisite. At the same time, the college was renamed the Divinity School and moved to its own campus with Dr. Paul Lauby as its first dean. The latter was formerly pastor of Silliman University Church, which position he held when I first visited Silliman.

I was eager to find out more about the new Divinity School. Ideally, a personal visit to Silliman was in order but at that time I was too busy with my job at RMC plus taking the trip to Dumaguete would have required extra money which I did not have. Again, Ed turned out to be a lucky recourse. In the summer of 1963, he went to Silliman University at the invitation of the Divinity School to teach a class in Pastoral Psychology and inaugurate the school's Clinical Pastoral Education Center. It was no secret that given his excellent credentials and his academic specialty which was in great demand, the school was trying to attract him to join the faculty. For Ed, it was a very tempting prospect. Before he left, I asked Ed to learn as much as he could about the state of the Divinity School and its prospects for the future.

After his summer stint, Ed came home to Davao with high marks for the Divinity School. He also reported to me that he had conversations with Dean Lauby during which he mentioned to him my interest in enrolling in the B.D. program. Dr. Lauby reportedly showed extraordinary interest in me. Ed's report gave me more incentive to study at Silliman. It was just a matter of deciding when. One thing gave me pause. Ruby was pregnant with our second child and was due to give birth in July, 1964. Thus, moving the family to Silliman for that year was out of the question so I set my sights on enrolling at Silliman no earlier than the next school year, 1965-66.

And then the most unlikely event happened that made me reconsider my plans in a hurry. In March, 1964, a big fire wiped out the entire San Pedro business district. Two of those that were consumed were Rizal Memorial Colleges and Brokenshire Memorial Hospital. Although my office records had been saved in time, I knew it would take quite a while before things could go back to normal at RMC. Moreover, I could not help thinking that the timing of the fire was a portent of sorts. Once again, thoughts of The Hound of Heaven swirled in my mind. I felt that for my peace of mind, I had to give in. I decided to start my theological education right away and leave for Silliman right after our second child was born.

Makeshift temporary buildings were set up at Brokenshire in a hurry and on July 23, 1964, Ruby gave birth to a baby girl. Since Ruby was going to undergo Caesarian section again, we could have scheduled the date of birth. We discussed the possibility of scheduling it on July 24, in which case both our children would have the same birth date but we decided against it. Ironically, though, in the years after, we wound up celebrating their birthdays simultaneously anyway.

We named our second daughter Rowena Nirda Leilani. Ruby came up with the second and third names, the latter being a common Hawaiian name. Rowena is a common English name but it was also influenced by the first syllables of the child's maternal and paternal grandparents, respectively. Ro was taken from Roman and Wen from Wenceslao.

A week after Ruby came home, we had Rowena baptized. Standing as sponsors were Ed Pantejo and Vilma Mae Cataylo. With mixed feelings, I left a few days afterwards for Silliman, leaving my family behind until it was the right time to bring them to Dumaguete.

CHAPTER V: STUDENT LIFE AT SILLIMAN

I arrived in Silliman on the last week of July, 1964. From Davao City, I flew into the airport at Mactan island in Cebu City and from there boarded a Philippine Air Lines shuttle flight to Dumaguete. It would still be a few more years before the jet age would catch up with that city. In 1964, the Cebu to Dumaguete airplane was a two-engine propeller-driven DC-3. The plane, also known by its military name of C-47, was the workhorse transport during the Second World War, and long afterwards was a mainstay of many a national airline in Third World countries including the Philippines.

The Dumaguete airport is adjacent to the Silliman University campus so while seated on the left side of the plane, I looked out the window as we started our descent over the bay. That way, I was able to catch my first glimpse of the campus from the air. It was a breathtaking sight and from that moment I began to understand the fascination behind the oft-repeated phrase "Silliman beside the sea." That phrase is the last line of the refrain of the Silliman song, a song that would often be a main program feature of every gathering of Sillimanians on campus and elsewhere. As I was to learn later, "Silliman beside the sea" is more than just a line in a song. It stands for a culture.

From the airport I was taken to Woodward Hall where I was going to reside for a semester. It was a déjà vu experience. Three years after graduating from U.P., getting married and starting a family, I was a student once again living in a college dormitory. I had left my family behind in Davao City with the intention of bringing them over after one semester. That period of a few months gave Ruby time to recover from the birth of our second child and for me to make the preparations for the family's transfer to Silliman.

Knowing that my dorm experience was going to last for only a few months, I resolved to enjoy and learn from it as much as I could. And I did. I had a specific role that only I could play among my dorm mates. I was arguably the oldest dormitory resident and the only married person so they looked to me as advisor, resource person and model. That role helped me to stay in the straight and narrow. Some of my dorm mates became lifelong friends.

One particular friend was Federico Ranches, my roommate and *tucayo*, the Spanish word for namesake. He and I became lifelong buddies. I was his matchmaker with Carmen Mendoza, a fellow Divinity School student whom he later married. We also became *kumpadres* and when we migrated to the United States, we both settled in Massachusetts and visited one another's families often.

Another dorm mate who became my lifelong friend was Gideon Alegado. He started out as a Divinity Student but later changed his course to Education in response to the urging of his family so he could help out with Gingoog Christian College, the school founded by his father. We later reunited many years later when we both migrated to the United States. By that time we were retired from our respective professions and were both active with SUACONA, the umbrella organization for Sillimanian alumni and friends residing in North America. Shortly after his retirement, he was summoned to Gingoog to become the college's president. At about the same time, he was elected to head SUACONA as its president.

My decision to wait a semester before bringing my family over was also good for another reason. The Divinity School was building a housing project specifically for married students and their families. It was due to be finished at the end of that calendar year. So my timing was just right. In December, I went back to Davao to spend the Christmas holiday with my family. On the first week of January, we left for Dumaguete by boat. After about a month living in temporary quarters, we moved into the brand-new Divinity School Housing Compound. It was going to be our home for the next two and a half years.

Our house was a two-floor building, with walls made of woven bamboo slats called *sawali,* and a thatched roof. The lower floor contained the bathroom and toilet and the upper floor was the living quarters consisting of a living room, a kitchen and two bedrooms. The quarters were rather cramped but we managed. We were just grateful for the generosity of the Divinity School who gave us subsidized accommodations. This helped to keep our housing budget low, with the biggest expense item going toward utilities.

Before I made the decision to enroll in the seminary, I discussed the matter at length with my parents because how to finance my education was a primary concern. I made it clear that I had to be a full-time student in order to focus on my studies. Fortunately, my parents consented to give me a monthly allowance equivalent to what a single graduate student would have for board and lodging, tuition and books. Moreover, I got a gift from them of a Honda motorcycle to help with my transportation needs.

To meet the rest of the family's financial needs, Ruby decided to take a full-time job. Fortunately, an instructor position opened up for her in Silliman's English department. Doubtless, her four years as a college teacher, two of which were spent at the University of the Philippines, was a positive factor. Moreover, Ruby's experience as an instructor at U.P.'s Speech and Drama department evidently appealed to Dr. Frank Flores, the head of the English department at the time. He focused on strengthening the department's Speech and Theater area to balance the department's erstwhile concentration in English Literature. His efforts included recruiting teachers whose specialties were in Theater. One of them was Amiel Leonardia who had just arrived from abroad after obtaining his Masters degree in Theater. Dr. Flores also had a Speech Laboratory built in the premises, which was administered by the English department. He developed a Bachelor of English degree program with a concentration in Speech and Theater. Also under Dr. Flores's direction and encouragement, an annual event called *Dia Eufonia* was inaugurated. Similar to U.P.'s Speech Festival that Ruby and I had been part of, it featured a week-long series of speech competitions and a major theater production. Dr. Flores's moves put the English Department, or at least its Speech and Theater division, at the front and center of the campus extra-curricular calendar.

Readers of this part of the narrative who are Westerners may wonder how Ruby could have managed to have a full-time job and at the same time take care of her family with two little children, one of whom was a six-month-old baby. The answer is that in the Philippines, inexpensive domestic help is part of the Filipino way of life. We always had at least two live-in help who shared the babysitting and household chores, thus freeing enough time to enable us to pursue our various professional and academic activities. In addition, Ruby was able to take undergraduate courses in Music and graduate courses in English, the latter eventually earning for her a Master of Arts degree in English Literature.

Before I went to Silliman, some friends warned me about what were being taught at the College of Theology or Divinity School. Some even went so far as to say that the school often destroys the faith of its own students. I got a less condemning and more intellectual view of what to expect from conversations with Ed Pantejo before I left Davao. He told me that a lot of incoming Divinity students are unprepared for the challenge of theological education to their faith. As a result, a good percentage of them wind up dropping out after their first year. But he also thought that the first year is a necessary part of a winnowing process, saying that those who survive the first year and go on to finish the degree program are the ones who really belong in the ministry, anyway.

Despite my own religious background, none of those warnings bothered me at all. I was raised in a Christian fundamentalist religious environment where it was assumed that everything written in the Bible is literally the word of God. My mother frequently led the family in devotions, and grace was spoken or sung before every meal. In Sunday school, we were encouraged to read the Bible frequently and were brought up to admire the few who could memorize the Bible from cover to cover. But unlike some of my fundamentalist friends, I did not have a deep religious commitment. After all, I was studying for the ministry mainly to fulfill my mother's promise for me to become a minister. In fact, I treated many of what I learned about Christianity as a child and young adult with a jaundiced mind. Moreover, the secular education and the emphasis on academic freedom to which I was exposed at U.P. enabled me to approach everything with an open mind.

The issue that appears to divide fundamentalists from their opposite counterparts is the place of doubt. I recall an incident when I was growing up in which doubt was an important criterion in the evaluation of a young minister in my church. It seemed that the pastor had been heard expressing to some parishioners his doubts about what he was taught in the seminary. As soon as word got to the church elders, they called the pastor to a meeting and demanded an explanation. The pastor admitted his doubts, a position the elders found unacceptable for a minister of the gospel. They then successfully prevailed on the church to dismiss the pastor. I felt so bad for the pastor who, for being honest about his thoughts, paid dearly for it. Incidents like this made me develop a negative attitude toward fundamentalists and a more accepting view of the place of doubt.

If there is one person who influenced my thinking on the subject of doubt, it was Dr. Ricardo Pascual. When I was a student at U.P in the mid 1950's, Pascual was the head of the Philosophy department. While studying in England, he came under the influence of Bertrand Russell, the British philosopher and mathematician who is best known for his part in the development of analytical philosophy and its handmaiden, Logical Positivism. Russell and Alfred North Whitehead wrote the book *Principia Matematica*, a work which led to the introduction of symbolic logic as an analytical tool in the service of language. As a result of Pascual's background and influence, course offerings in Philosophy at U.P. were slanted toward analytical philosophy to the virtual exclusion of, or at most lip service to, other traditional subject areas such as Metaphysics and Ontology. The introductory Philosophy course, which was required of most Liberal Arts students, was devoted exclusively to Symbolic Logic.

Pascual was widely regarded as the most prominent atheist at U.P., although he himself denied being such, preferring instead to be labeled an agnostic. His position was no mere exercise in semantics. He was echoing his mentor Bertrand Russell who himself had said that he is technically an agnostic although practically an atheist. Russell's position was based on the central thesis of Logical Positivism that only empirically verifiable statements can be regarded as true. Therefore, statements such as "There is a God" are, to him, meaningless because God's existence is not verifiable through the empirical method. Pascual himself went on to say that he could not be an atheist because atheism would presuppose a negative claim such as "There is no God" and according to Logical Positivism, one cannot prove a negative statement. To his credit, Pascual never sought a public forum to espouse his lack of belief in God but was always ready to express himself unequivocally when confronted by students and colleagues on the subject. I regarded him with respect and was fascinated by his views on the existence of God. Even though I was an active churchgoer and officer of the U.P. ChristianYouth Movement, the seeming conflict between philosophy and religion did not bother me because I tended to compartmentalize the two as separate and existing in different worlds.

As I started my Silliman education, I realized that I belonged to what I considered the most privileged, if not pampered, student group at the university at the time. Thanks to the efforts of the former Dean of the College Theology, Dr. James Mckinley and the Divinity School Dean Dr. Paul Lauby, we had for ourselves a brand new campus. It consisted of three buildings that adjoined each other, namely the Chapel of the Evangel where we had devotions regularly three times a week, Proculo Rodriguez Hall which housed classrooms and administrative offices, and the school library. Added to that privilege was the housing arrangement for Divinity students. Previously, I mentioned the subsidized Married Student Housing compound where several families including ourselves stayed. Considered part of the special housing arrangement were Woodward Hall and Channon Hall. Both located just a stone's throw from the Divinity School campus, they were the first housing choice for single male and female students, respectively, of the Divinity School and they had preferential status in both dormitories.

Furthermore, we had a faculty with an extraordinarily high percentage holding the highest postgraduate degrees. Not a single one of our 13 teachers had anything less than a master's degree and eight of them had an earned doctorate. All of them obtained their advanced degrees abroad. With the exception of one, they all studied at one of the universities in either Northeastern United States or California. Six of the faculty members were missionaries under the auspices of their respective missionary boards while the other seven were Filipinos.

From the outset, I was very curious about what it was in the Divinity School curriculum that reportedly challenged the faith of incoming students to the point that quite a few dropped out after their first year. What I found out had the opposite effect on me. It became a fillip to my inquisitive mind and gave me a reason for pursuing my theological education other than the mere desire to please my mother. It was a blessing of sorts that I had gone to a secular school for my undergraduate degree. That way, I had no prior exposure to any kind of religious education other than my Sunday school classes while I was growing up. So virtually everything I was being taught was new. I plunged into my studies like a kid who just found a new toy and became a serious student like I had never been before

I found out that the biggest stumbling block for many new students was the Divinity School's approach to the study of the Bible. At the time, Biblical Studies were heavily influenced by Form Criticism, a method of analyzing Biblical texts to determine how and when they were written and by whom. To prospective ministers who were taught that every word of the Bible is literally true and that each book was written by the same person to whom it was ascribed, the mere idea of questioning the authenticity and authorship of the Bible was tantamount to heresy.

Scholars of the Form Criticism method concluded that the so-called Synoptic Gospels, which consisted of the first three books of the New Testament, and which tell the story of Jesus and his ministry, were written not by single authors but by groups of authors. Evidently, those groups, who may have been disciples of the gospels' named authors, combined bits and pieces of narratives based on a variety of literary forms, both written and oral.

Some of the material consisted of supernatural events, which were acceptable to the time and culture in which they were written but not to the modern scientific mind. Most notable of such events were the miracles attributed to Jesus. Therefore, much of the Bible, especially the Gospels, could not be relied upon as history. This conclusion led to a couple of scholarly pursuits. One was an intensive search for the historical Jesus. The other was a search for the core of Jesus' teaching, otherwise known as the *kerygma.* Both searches involved deconstructing the gospels by eliminating unacceptable material for perceived lack of historical authenticity.

This deconstructing process is called *demythologizing,* a term used extensively in his writings by the German theologian Rudolf Bultmann. Recognized as one of the most influential theologians of the 20th century and a proponent of Form Criticism, Bultmann claimed that the Jesus of history and the Jesus of faith are two distinct entities. Such a statement was the cornerstone of liberal theology which touched off a profound discussion that characterized much of 20th century thinking.

The central question that both proponents and critics of liberal theology had to grapple with was the relevance to modern Christians of Jesus and his teachings. If all that is known with absolute certainly about Jesus is that he was born, lived and died, what is the relevance of the Gospel? Since liberal theology challenges all supra- and super- natural events, including such orthodox claims in both the Bible and church doctrine as the Virgin Birth and the Resurrection, what is left of the Christian message?

My search for answers to the above questions introduced me to the thoughts of some of the greatest thinkers of the time. Perhaps the most prominent of these was the Swiss theologian Karl Barth. His theology was popularly dubbed "neo-orthodoxy" for seemingly providing a bridge between the two extremes of fundamentalism and liberal theology. His thoughts centered on his definition of revelation, making a distinction between God's absolute act of revealing Himself through Jesus Christ, and humanity's interpretation, imperfect as it may be, of that revelation. Other luminaries that excited me were Martin Buber for his treatise on the "I and Thou," Soren Kierkegaard for his concept of the "leap of faith," Paul Tillich for introducing an alternate term for God as "The Ground of All Being," and Reinhold Niebuhr who used the paradoxical phrase "impossible possibility" to express the authority and urgency of Jesus' ethical teachings. On the subject of doubt, none stirred my brain as did Bishop John Robinson's "Honest to God."

When presented with such an impressive array of theological demigods, if I may call them such, one is bound to have a favorite and such was the case with me. My favorite, whose name I have withheld for last, is Dietrich Bonhoeffer, the German theologian, pastor and martyr. Bonhoeffer was a brilliant and precocious man who chose discipleship over scholarship as a way of life. Graduating *summa cum laude* in college and obtaining his doctoral degree in theology at the tender age of 21, his early writings and speeches attracted attention among theologians all over and merited invitations to teach at various seminaries. He could have spent the rest of his life as a respected writer and professor abroad but chose instead to stay in his native country of

Germany where he felt that he was needed. Nazism had risen to power in the 1930's and Bonhoeffer decided to publicly oppose Hitler. He conspired with others in founding the Confessing Church, which became a forum against the policies of the state church that had been co-opted and controlled by the Nazi regime. Convinced of the need for Hitler's removal from power, he joined the resistance against Nazism, going as far as being involved in the plot along with some officers of the German Military Intelligence Office to assassinate Hitler. The plot failed and those who were involved including Bonhoeffer were rounded up and jailed. Bonhoeffer was hanged in April, 1945, just a few days before the concentration camp where he was jailed was liberated by the Allied forces.

What amounts to Bonhoeffer's theological manifesto is found in his best-selling book The Cost of Discipleship. In the book, he rails against the historical watering down within the church of Jesus' call to discipleship resulting in what he calls "cheap grace." According to him, manifestations of this cheap grace include such things as forgiveness without repentance, communion without confession, and baptism without discipline. Criticizing the institutionalization of religious discipline to a reserved few such as in monasticism which, he claimed, leads to a double standard of religiosity, he urged that all faithful Christians should heed the call of Jesus to take up his cross and follow him. To him, it meant that discipleship is to be practiced not just in the cloister but, more importantly, in the world by responding to the call for justice and righteousness.

What is perhaps Bonhoeffer's most eloquent and frequently quoted statement is one that came from The Cost of Discipleship, "When Christ calls a man, he bids him come and die." More than any, that statement encapsulates Bonhoeffer's courage, determination and commitment to be a disciple of Christ through word and action, even if it means paying the supreme sacrifice for one's faithfulness. Equally touching were his last words which he wrote in prison just before his death, "This is the end – for me, the beginning of life."

One reason I was attracted to Bonhoeffer's way of thinking was that it validated my decision to keep both feet squarely on the church and the world. I reasoned that theological education and spiritual reflection have their place but would not matter much if all that learning is not applied in the trenches. It was not easy to resist the temptation to stay put within the comfort of the academe. In fact, some of my professors in Silliman paid me a high compliment by suggesting that I should consider a career in theological education.

The mid-1960s saw the start of a period of international political turmoil that lasted a decade. The two main centers of political activity were the United States and China. The American scenario was fueled by protests against involvement in the Vietnam War. In 1964, President Lyndon Johnson, who had taken over the U.S. presidency following the 1963 assassination of President Kennedy, decided to escalate the conflict by introducing combat troops. Before that, American involvement in the conflict consisted of military advisers to the South Vietnamese regime. As America's commitment to the war expanded, the anti-war movement grew and protests occurred almost daily all over the country. Most of them happened at university campuses with students leading them. Meanwhile, satellite television brought the specter of mass demonstrations while they were happening right into living rooms all over the world. Protest became a dominant subculture of the 1960s, affecting all areas of life including music, theater and other arts.

In China, Mao Zedong launched what he called "The Great Proletarian Cultural Revolution." Its announced purpose was to purge society of so-called capitalist revisionists. Following Mao's direction, young people went on a rampage, publicly denouncing prominent citizens and humiliating them in public. The list of victims included bureaucrats, college professors and even established Communist party members. Many were punished by forcing them to work in the rural areas so that they could "learn from the masses." Mao's Red Book, which expounded on the principles of the Cultural Revolution, became the Bible of the movement, which both sympathizers and detractors labeled as Maoism.

Although both of the above protest movements had differing agendas, they produced a common result. Political consciousness was awakened among the masses and with mass media's pervasive influence, the phenomenon spilled over to other countries, including the Philippines.

1965 was a watershed year in the history of the Philippines. At the November elections of that year, Ferdinand Marcos was elected President. The loser and incumbent president, Diosdado Macapagal, became the latest in a succession of one-term presidents. With the exception of Manuel Roxas and Ramon Magsaysay who both died while in office, every president during the 20-year existence of the independent Philippine republic had been voted out of office amid charges of electoral fraud, rampant corruption and crony capitalism.

To many people, Ferdinand Marcos represented hope for change. Much of that hope arose from Marcos' legendary personality.

To a citizenry that admired intelligence and charisma, Marcos was the perfect choice to lead the country into the future and represent his people to the rest of the world. His personal and political resume was lengthy and impressive. An outstanding orator, writer and student politician in college, he graduated *cum laude* from the prestigious College of Law of the University of the Philippines. He topped the Philippine Bar examinations despite the fact that he reviewed for the tests while in jail for a murder charge. Although he was convicted by the lower courts of the charge, he won the verdict's dismissal by arguing it before the Supreme Court. He was a war hero, having led a guerilla outfit during the Japanese occupation of the Philippines. Soon after the establishment of post-war government, he entered the political arena, and steadily rose through the ranks, first as congressman and then as senator. When he launched his presidential candidacy in 1965, he held the country's highest legislative office as Senate president and had been in government service continuously for 15 years. To add to his popular appeal, he married Imelda Romualdez, a former beauty queen and scion of a prominent family in the Southern Philippines. Inevitably, comparisons with the equally legendary John Kennedy of the United States came up.

Aside from all the above, I had my personal agenda. It had been 14 years since I first met Congressman Marcos while I was a freshman in high school. I had closely followed my boyhood hero's meteoric career and supported his candidacy for various legislative positions as soon as I was eligible to vote. I joined Marcos's organization, campaigned hard among my colleagues at Silliman University and basked in his victory in the 1965 presidential elections.

However, once Marcos took over the presidency, it dawned on many that he was not going to be much different from the other presidents that preceded him. Early public opposition to the Marcos administration came mainly from his failure to chart an independent policy from the United States and the consequences of that failure. To be sure, he inherited the problem from previous administrations but contrary to the hopes and fears of the populace, he did little, if any, to do anything different. Instead, he made it clear that he was going to continue the country's long-standing political, economic and cultural dependence on America. One of his first acts along that line was to successfully convince the legislature to send a military contingent to the Vietnam War. Ironically, when Pres. Macapagal tried a similar move earlier, Marcos defeated the proposal by leading the Congressional opposition. Marcos' complete reversal on that issue became a sore point. The country could ill afford such foreign adventures given the serious problems at home that needed more attention, such as soaring inflation, increasing gaps between the rich and the poor, and human rights abuses, to mention a few.

I joined the ranks of the opposition. It seemed that I was destined to take a leading role where I was. Up until that time, Silliman was a haven of peace and quiet. From the time it was established by Protestant missionaries at the beginning of the 20th century, the school had gained and maintained a reputation as a place where one could get a high quality college education in a beautiful and serene semi-rural setting, free from the stresses and conflicts that were part of a metropolitan environment. In fact, it was no secret that some prominent families in Manila sent their children to Silliman to get them away from the day-to-day distractions of life in the city. At Silliman, a significant part of co-curricular and extra-curricular activities revolved around the development of Christian fellowship. Student activism of the kind that was going on in Greater Manila and other metropolitan centers was non-existent at Silliman.

It was clear to me that the Silliman academic community needed to be awakened to the problems that plagued the country. I thought that the best way to do that was to bring into the campus some outside resources. I decided to invite Jose Maria Sison, my friend and U.P. classmate, to visit Silliman. Sison had acquired a reputation as a leading activist who led demonstrations in the Manila area against Philippine involvement in the Vietnam War and the inequities of the country's political and economic system. He started lecturing on his views about the forthcoming revolutionary struggle, labeling his movement "The Struggle for National Democracy." That phrase became the title of his first book which got published in 1967.

My application to invite Joma, as he was fondly called by friends and followers, was met with stiff opposition from the Office of Student Affairs, which had jurisdiction over such applications. As expected, the reason for the opposition was that Sison was too radical to be acceptable to the Silliman community. My project would have died had it not been for the intervention of Dr. Paul Lauby who, as Vice President for Academic Affairs, reasoned that Silliman would be publicly criticized if it refused to provide Sison a forum.

Joma's lecture was well attended and served as the catalyst to awaken the campus from its political and social slumber. From that moment, Silliman would never be the same again. Activist groups sprouted on campus and Silliman became a microcosm in the widespread battle for the minds of the citizenry, with the battle fought along ideological lines. On one side were those who defended the status quo and whom their opponents pejoratively called reactionaries. On the other side were a number of progressive groups of various stripes depending on their ideological bent. Of these, three stood out, namely *Kabataang Makabayan*, (Patriotic Youth), *Malayang Pagkakaisa ng Kabataang Pilipino* (Free Union of Philippine Youth), and Young Christian Socialists of the Philippines. The three groups were together in the conviction that things were terribly wrong with the country's political, social and economic system but differed in their views on how to remedy the problem. Some advocated a complete change in government structure and ideology while others preferred staying with the present structure while vigorously pressing for reforms.

Eventually, the struggle moved outside the walls of the academe to the countryside. The shift was logical, inevitable and long-coming. The island of Negros was the scene of some of the most horrendous examples of economic and social inequality. The situation was rooted in Spanish colonial times with the establishment of the hacienda system whereby huge tracts of land were put into sugar production. During the American era, sugar became the primary Philippine export, thanks in large part to the American policy of protecting sugar producers both at home and in the colonies by setting an artificially high price of sugar well above world prices. After the Philippines became independent, the protection policy continued to be extended to the country by giving it a share of the so-called sugar quota. This made the production of sugar in the Philippines a very attractive business. Sugar producers became some of the wealthiest and most influential people in the Philippines. In turn, the attention focused on sugar and other agricultural commodities, such as coconut and abaca, created an economy heavily skewed toward agricultural production. The ready availability of a market for such agricultural exports discouraged diversification and industrialization, thus keeping the Philippines mired in a backward economic system.

More than half of the sugar produced in the Philippines came from Negros Island where the Silliman campus was located. Almost half of the island's population lived in extreme poverty because of the exploitative nature of the hacienda system. The master of the plantation, called the *hacendero*, lorded over the property and its inhabitants and treated workers as virtual slaves. The work of preparing the fields, planting sugar cane, weeding and harvesting was backbreaking and often involved spending many hours under the hot tropical sun. Moreover, with no labor unions to protect them, the workers were paid subsistence wages well below the country's minimum wage. A large part of the labor force consisted of migrant workers called *sacadas*. Because the wages were so low, children as young as seven years old were often pressed into work in the fields to help support the family.

I took a leading role in advising and nurturing the broad coalition of student activists as their ranks grew on campus. Many of them were in their late teens to early twenties and very few had experienced any form of protest activity before they came to Silliman. My task was to impress upon them that they were engaging in a very serious and possibly risky endeavor. They had to know what they were getting into and had to be strongly committed. Already, the apologists for the Establishment were digging their heels and were determined to take all measures needed to preserve the status quo. Thus, the struggle was not for the faint in heart and shallow in thinking. Moreover, as students in a Christian institution of learning, it was incumbent upon them to realize and affirm that what set them apart from the average activist was that their involvement was a logical outgrowth of their faith and sense of mission.

My background as a History major in college, as an instructor of Philippine History and my years of involvement in the nationalist movement both as a student and teacher gave me the wherewithal to discharge my role. Besides, my position as a graduate student in the Divinity School provided me the perspective in Christian social justice to convince them that I was one to be taken seriously. I was able to use several media outlets. These included the Weekly Sillimanian, the campus student paper in which I was an editorial staff member and regular columnist; the campus radio station DYSR where I would go on the air as a guest commentator; and the Visayas Chronicle, the town's newspaper where I contributed feature articles. I also got maximum mileage from the "teach-in," which was an occasional lecture-discussion among campus activists. What we did in preparing the students for the struggle turned out to be a foreshadowing of what was to come. The conflict between protesters and the Establishment progressively got sharper and more contentious so that when, several years later, the government started to target them for censure and persecution, they were not caught off guard.

Some of my most enjoyable extra-curricular activities were in the field of Speech and Theater. In a way, I got involved in that field for much the same reasons I did when I was at U.P. I was engaging in a field that Ruby and I loved to do together while at the same time supporting the Speech and Theater Arts department where she was a faculty member. Moreover, I wanted to stay active, improve my skills and add to my credentials in that field, anticipating a future need.

I looked forward to the annual speech festival called *Dia Eufonia* which the department ran. I was in demand as a coach for the various forensic competitions such as oratory, impromptu speaking and debate. I was also responsible for instigating a debate between the Divinity School and the College of Law and starting an annual tradition. The very first debate between the two schools was held in 1965. I was the captain of the Divinity team. Reflecting the hottest international issue at the time, we debated whether or not Communist China should be admitted into the United Nations. Taking the negative side, our team won the debate with me chosen as best debater.

I acted in several plays produced by the Department of Speech and Theater Arts. They were directed by either Dr. Frank Flores or Prof. Amiel Leonardia. Some were performed at the Woodward Hall and some at the university theater. One that had a theological theme was performed at the Chapel of the Evangel for the benefit of Divinity students. The most prominent of our plays was Arthur Miller's "Death of a Salesman" in which I played the part of Uncle Ben. Silliman President Dr. Cicero Calderon was so impressed by and enthused over our performance that he decided it was worth exporting. So under his sponsorship, we took the entire play – cast, crew, set and props – to Manila and performed it at what was then the city's premier showplace, the Philamlife Auditorium. Our two evening performances were very well-attended and received very good reviews in the Manila papers.

In April, 1967, I finished all my course work at the Divinity School. I had been there three years, a period that seemed to go so fast I hardly noticed. The reason was that I had never enjoyed studying as much as I did in Silliman. In class, all I wanted to do was learn as much as I could from my professors and never had to bother about whether I was going to get a good grade from them.

To complete the degree program and graduate, I needed one year of internship in the field as a student pastor. An opportunity to fulfill that requirement came in the form of an offer to be the assistant chaplain at the University of the Philippines Protestant Chapel and assistant pastor of the Church of the Risen Lord. I welcomed that offer for several reasons. For one thing, it gave me a chance to practice my new profession in a setting I was quite familiar with. I had previously spent five years there as an undergraduate student, worshipped at the church, met my future wife and were married in that same church. For another, I was eager to recharge my intellectual batteries. As it turned out, I wound up spending two years at U.P., first as a ministerial student intern and later as a full-time pastor.

CHAPTER VI: MINISTRY AT U.P.

In April, 1967, we started to make our move to our new home. Our third move since we got married, this was going to be more involved than previous ones. For one thing, our family was growing. Ruby was pregnant with our third child, who was due to arrive the following month. So the first step was to go to Davao so that Ruby could give birth at Brokenshire Memorial Hospital where our first two children were born. When she and the children flew to Davao, I gathered the few worldly goods that we wanted to bring with us and took them to Manila aboard one of the inter-island boats that plied the route from Dumaguete to Manila. Upon arriving in Manila, I deposited the cargo at the home of Auntie Immang in Quezon City. This was going to be our temporary home while we looked for more permanent housing. In early May, I flew to Davao to be present at Ruby's delivery.

Three years had gone by since the big fire that consumed the San Pedro business district that included Brokenshire Memorial Hospital. During our absence, the hospital board decided not to rebuild the burned complex that consisted of the hospital and the Brokenshire School of Nursing. Instead, thanks to a generous subsidy from a missionary body in Germany, a new and modern facility was going to be constructed at a property in Madapo Hill, located at the western end of town. In the meantime, temporary buildings were set up at the old Brokenshire site.

Dr. Durban was still Brokenshire's chief surgeon. The man was truly a gift God sent to us. As in the case with our first two children, he generously offered to perform the delivery by Caesarean section without charging for his services. Before everything, Ruby and I discussed how big a family we wanted to have. Our concern was that this was going to be her third birth by Caesarean section and I had no desire to put her through the pain and difficulty of a fourth operation. On the other hand, we dearly wanted to have a son. At that time, there was no way to accurately determine the baby's gender ahead of time as the technology for doing that was still far into the future.

We decided that this was going to be our last child no matter what. And while there were a number of birth control options that we had at our disposal, we wanted to be absolutely sure. The way to insure that was for Ruby to have a so-called tubal ligation, a relatively minor operation which could be conveniently performed in conjunction with the Caesarean section.

Accordingly, I got together with Dr. Durban to discuss the matter of performing the tubal ligation. His first reaction was to ask whether I was absolutely certain. He wanted to make sure we would not regret our decision should the child turn out to be another girl. I assured him that Ruby and I discussed the matter at length and prayed about it before making our decision.

On the morning of May 20, 1967, Ruby was wheeled into the delivery room, which consisted of a temporary building about the size of a bedroom. In addition to Dr. Durban, the group performing the operation included two other doctors and a couple of nurses. All of them were our friends, some of whom we had known since 1962 when we first moved to Davao. One of them had been Ruby's classmate in grammar school days. They were also members of the United Church of Davao where we had worshipped and were still members.

I had made the unusual request to be present in the delivery room and it was granted. Accordingly, they suited me up, complete with surgical dress and mask. The operation did not take very long but the suspense over the outcome was both tense and exciting. Everybody in the room shared my anxiety and as the moment of truth drew near, there was noisy chatter among the attending party. For a moment, it reminded me of the noise from the gallery at a *pintakasi*, that popular Filipino cockfighting sport, when everybody cheers for their favorite rooster to win. I could not see the baby when it finally came out but I immediately knew what it was because everybody suddenly burst into a loud cheer. Thank God, we had ourselves the baby boy that we had fervently wished for.

Mama Tereza and Papa Roman had been outside, anxiously waiting. The delivery room being a temporary building, it had thin walls and was not sound-proof so Mama clearly heard the cheering coming from inside. When she did, she stuck her head through the door of the operating room and with a smile she said, for everyone in the room to hear, "I think I have a grandson."

We named our baby boy Frederick Rowen Leander. The name Frederick was my long-held ambition to make up for the Claveria clerk's mistake in registering me as Federico instead of Frederick. As for the name Rowen, it was a combination of the first syllable of my father-in-law's name, Roman, and that of my father's name, Wenceslao. The boy's third name was a combination of a part of Ruby's second name, Leah, and that of my own would-have-been second name, Alexander.

On the last week of June, we arrived in Manila for me to start my internship year at the U.P. Protestant Chapel/Church of the Risen

Lord. With me and Ruby were two daughters, a one-month old baby boy and two helpers who would share the household chores and babysitting. No previous arrangements had been made for housing on campus. At that point, my senior minister, Rev. James Palm, and his wife came up with a practical solution. They offered to share the parsonage by vacating the basement and letting us stay there. That gave us four small rooms to share, which was relatively cramped but adequate.

The best part of the deal was that I could live in the church premises and was available at all hours of the day. There was a second reason why I loved the idea. I thought it would be a great intercultural experience for us to live next door to the Palms. This was especially the case for our two young daughters whom we hoped would be able to keep their English language skills intact by interacting with the Palm children. At Silliman, we had no worries in that area because English was a very strong second language there. However, we were not so sure about the language environment in Manila. It all turned out to be an unexpected double blessing. The Palm children, or at least the two oldest ones – Ellen and Cobbie – were perfectly bilingual, speaking English and Filipino with equal ease.

Our next objective was to look for a job for Ruby. Fortunately, there was an opening at the Department of Speech and Drama at U.P. We were also lucky that our *ninong*, Dr. Alejandro Casambre, was the head of the department. We were happy to meet him again since we had not seen him since our student days. It was in his Speech class that Ruby and I first became classmates and sweethearts and so for that reason Dr. Casambre had a special place in our hearts. So when we got married in April, 1961, we wanted him to be our sponsor. At that time, he was in the United States finishing his Ph.D. at Ohio State University. So we wrote to him and he agreed to be our *ninong in absentia*.

The instructor position had been advertised earlier and there were other applicants who had lined up to apply for the job. But our timing was just right. Had we arrived a week or so later than we did, the position would have been filled by somebody else. So between our close relationship to Dr. Casambre and her having taught there several years before, Ruby was considered the best qualified for the job and was hired on the spot.

Eleven years had gone by since the creation of the Church of the Risen Lord in 1956. It had been a big step in the development and growth of the U.P. Protestant ministry. Up until that time, the Protestant complex functioned primarily as a chapel where students and

80

staff gathered for worship on Sunday morning and held midweek services on Wednesdays. There was no formal church organizational structure.

All of that changed in 1956. The architect of the move to an organized church was Dr. E. K. Higdon who had taken over as Protestant chaplain following the conclusion of his predecessor Rev. Richard C. Bush's term. In a way, the emergence of an organized church was inevitable. The Diliman campus had a growing resident community of university students, faculty and staff. They found it convenient to worship at the U.P. Protestant Chapel which, to many of them, was just a short walk from where they lived. As the congregation grew in numbers and became increasingly diverse, many of them expressed a desire to expand the ministry's program in order to cater to the needs of the congregation's families. In response to their requests, Rev. Higdon set in motion what led to the creation of the Church of the Risen Lord.

The move was not without its share of controversy. I was then a sophomore at the College of Liberal Arts and part of the UPCYM leadership, holding the position of editor of the organization's newsletter, the UPCYMette. Through conversations with other UPCYM leaders, especially the organization's pioneers, and with pastors and active laymen connected with the National Council of Churches of the Philippines (NCCP), I got a fairly accurate understanding of the issues surrounding the organization of a Protestant church at U.P.

It was felt by most of the UPCYM leadership that the demands of maintaining an organized church risked jeopardizing the student ministry, which, after all, was the main reason for setting up and building the Protestant complex on campus. I felt it my duty to articulate that concern, which I did by writing an editorial on the subject. That did not earn for me Dr. Higdon's friendship. The Sunday after the UPYCMette issue containing my editorial came out, he spent his entire sermon refuting my editorial, sentence by sentence.

As for the NCCP, a big concern of theirs was over the church's lack of denominational connection and support. The Protestant ministry at the Diliman campus was a project of the NCCP, which was a federation of several mainline Protestant denominations. Through their efforts, the lease of a piece of property on campus was obtained from the university and money was raised for the construction of a complex consisting of a chapel, a parsonage and a Fellowship Hall. Pastoral leadership was to be supplied through an arrangement between the two main NCC denominations – UCCP and Methodist Church -

whereby the two would take turns securing the services of a missionary from the United States to be the Protestant chaplain at U.P. Diliman. Not being itself a denomination, the NCCP had neither the desire nor the wherewithal to take CRL under its wing as a local church. And joining one of the member denominations instead was out of the question.

Rev. James Palm arrived at the Diliman campus in 1962. Sent under the auspices of the U.S. Presbyterian Missionary Board, he was the sixth chaplain to serve at the U.P. Protestant ministry following Rev. Bliss Billings, Rev. Richard Bush, Rev. E.K. Higdon, Rev. Chester Marquis and Rev. Bernard Brown. Unlike his predecessors, though, Rev. Palm was not a new transplant. Diliman was actually his second Philippine assignment. Previously, he spent years as pastor of the Church Among the Palms at the U.P. campus in Los Baños, Laguna. Thus, he was already a step ahead insofar as previous experience in campus ministry and familiarity with Philippine life and culture. He and his wife Louise had arrived in Los Baños in 1956 where they served for four years. While they were there, they started a family and had the first two of their four children.

Compared to the Church of the Risen Lord, the Church Among the Palms had a long history as well as a firm denominational relationship. The congregation was first started by the Presbyterian missions in 1914 when the school was not yet a part of the University of the Philippines and was then called the College of Agriculture and School of Forestry. Three years later, a chapel was built on a 1.7 hectare lot adjacent to the college campus that the Presbyterian Missionary Board had acquired.

In 1948, the United Church of Christ in the Philippines came into being as a federation of churches that had been established by missionaries belonging to a number of mainline denominations. The Church Among the Palms became part of the new denomination along with other Presbyterian churches in the Philippines. During his tenure, Rev. Palm encouraged the congregation to become independent and acquire the services of a Filipino pastor. The congregation responded positively and in 1960, Rev. Palm finished his tenure, having succeeded in accomplishing his objective with the church calling its first Filipino pastor in the person of the Rev. Ciriaco Lagunsad, Jr.

Rev. Palm's previous experience as pastor of a church caring for residents of a college campus served him well at Diliman as he proved equally comfortable and adept at relating to the adults in the church and the students in the UPCYM. Under his stewardship, the church program and structure of the Church of the Risen Lord grew. At the same time, the student ministry took on new features.

When I arrived on campus in 1967, one focus of activity was the expansion of the church's educational program, which had outgrown the facilities. A Nursery School had been opened that catered mostly to the children of faculty and staff of the university. The church decided that a new building needed to be constructed in the premises. Accordingly, architectural plans were laid out and a fundraising drive started to finance the new building. However, the plans had to be scaled down when the university did not approve the proposal for a new building on the ground that it was not covered by the provisions of the lease agreement between NCCP and the university. Instead, a one-floor wing extension to the Fellowship Hall was built for the purpose. Overseeing the church's educational program was Gloria Tormo, who served both as Christian Education Director and Church Secretary while Dada Wale was in charge of the Nursery School.

Meanwhile, the Church of the Risen Lord congregation had grown in membership and scope of outreach. Aside from the resident faculty and staff that provided the church's lay leadership from its beginnings, the church drew strength from U.P. alumni and their families who lived in the surrounding areas of Metro Manila. Some had been active members of the UPCYM and members of the Church of the Risen Lord when they were students and, after graduating, left the campus. Many of those who settled in the Greater Manila area continued to be active CRL members. Others joined because of family affinity. Such was the case with some spouses and parents of U.P. alumni. A couple of examples of the latter were Sonny Belmonte, a former journalist turned politician who had married Betty Go, a U.P. alumna and scion of a prominent Filipino Chinese family; and Dr. David de Leon, a physician who retired from the armed forces to be a professor at FEU School of Medicine. His daughter Carminda was a U.P. alumna and shared with Ruby the position of CRL organist in the 1950s. Both men, at one time or another, served as chairmen of the CRL Church Council.

With his previous extensive campus ministry experience, his academic breadth and his folksy style, Rev. Palm, whom students called Uncle Jim, had much to offer to students who flocked to join the UPCYM and participate in its activities. He attracted young campus intellectuals by leading study retreats on books whose subjects ventured beyond the boundaries of theological orthodoxy such as those by John Robinson, Harvey Cox, Paul Tillich, Dietrich Bonhoeffer and Rudolf Bultmann. He and U.P. Professors Rex Drilon and Agustin Pulido and prominent journalist Federico Mangahas inaugurated the Diliman Forum, a monthly event at the Fellowship Hall in which a well-known person in his field, frequently a U.P. professor, would speak and lead a discussion on a current social, political or religious issue. He also encouraged student creativity in the fine arts. A theater group called the UPCYM Playhouse produced plays that were performed at the sanctuary. The UPCYM choir, conducted by his wife Louise, developed a repertoire that combined sacred and secular music and was invited to perform by various community and church groups. The choir's most ambitious project while I was there was a 1967 national tour sponsored by the Philippine Association of National Minorities (PANAMIN), an organization established and led by Manolo Elizalde. Later, the choir cut and marketed a 33-rpm record album that contained their repertoire.

I was engaged by the Church of the Risen Lord to assist Jim with church and UPCYM activities. It was clear that the rapid growth of both institutions were getting to be more than one person could handle. I also suspected that my employment was Jim's way of getting the congregation used to a Filipino pastor. Just as he did at the Church Among the Palms, Jim was encouraging CRL to become independent of foreign missions. In fact, I was not the first Filipino ministerial assistant at the church. I was preceded by Jose "Joe" Malayang. A Silliman Bachelor of Theology graduate and ordained UCCP pastor, he came to U.P. to earn a Masters degree in Sociology and served as Jim's assistant for one year. He and another assistant, Nic Primavera, were chapel scholars the school year before I arrived. Joe and Nic attended to church and UPCYM tasks respectively.

I was just an intern fresh out of school but Jim took little time in getting me fully involved in church leadership. Within a few weeks after I arrived, he asked me to preach. Except for one sermon that I had done at the Davao UCCP Church while on vacation from my theological studies, all my previous preaching was in Homiletics class at the Divinity School. This was my first time to preach to a group of university faculty, staff and students, so I had every reason to be nervous. I still recall every detail of that service, especially before and after I preached. I was inside the preparation room at the back of the sanctuary when Jim came in and informed me that Dr. Gregory, the general secretary of the United Board of Christian World Missions was in the sanctuary. Based in New York, he was apparently visiting the Philippines. My heart began to pound. Jim then stepped inside the sanctuary for a moment and came back to tell me that he saw Silliman University president Dr. Cicero Calderon and his brother, Joe, sitting there. The latter was a prominent Philippine politician. By the time I got to the pulpit, I saw sitting in the congregation Augusto Caesar Espiritu and Johnny Flavier, two prominent national figures who were UPCYM pioneers. I felt like almost dying that morning. But I also thought that after that incident, I could confidently preach to any congregation, which I subsequently did.

In August, 1967, just two months after my arrival, Jim put me fully in charge. He had been asked by the World Student Christian Federation to co-direct a leadership training program, designed for Student Christian Movement leaders in Asia. The first portion was held at Tozanzo, a YMCA Conference Center in Japan, which meant that he was going to be away from UP till the middle of October. While a part of me felt overwhelmed at such a big responsibility, I also felt honored at Jim's confidence in my ability. I immediately set myself to the task. My first step was to obtain the proper credentials to enable me to fully discharge the duties of a pastor. Fortunately, the Greater Manila conference of the United Church of Christ in the Philippines awarded me the title of licentiate pastor, which authorized me to administer the sacraments.

In retrospect, I consider that year I spent as an intern at the Church of the Risen Lord a highly invaluable experience that I would not have traded for anything in the world. The three months that Jim was away went very quickly as I became more and more confident and efficient in my work. Before he left, Jim lined up a number of guest preachers to ease the burden on me. That way, I did not have to spend time in sermon preparation and could devote my energies to the preparation of the liturgy and other pastoral tasks such as visitation, administration and work with the young people.

I would be the first to say that things did not go perfectly during my brief tenure as pastor in residence. While there were a lot of wonderful moments, the ones that easily come to mind, oddly enough, are those of the mixed blessing variety. For instance, what I remember most clearly from those three months is the case of the liturgical dance. One day, a lady approached me and introduced herself as a teacher of dance. She was a New Zealander who had come to the Philippines to teach dance. She was venturing into the area of contemporary liturgical dancing and wanted to test out what she had taught to a group of local students. She wondered if she could incorporate one dance number into one of our worship services. I knew just enough about liturgical dancing from having seen it done at Silliman when some fellow students in the Divinity School were experimenting with it as part of their worship courses. I was impressed with its possibilities for enhancing worship. But the Silliman students were a bunch of amateurs and I thought that here was a chance to see liturgical dancing done by professionals. So I grabbed the opportunity and set it up for the following Sunday morning service.

The event did indeed turn out to be a mixed blessing. The dance was very artistically done and the performers' movements were all precise. But neither the congregation nor I were prepared for what we saw. Based on my previous experience, I had been expecting the dancers to be clad in white robes and their movements slow and stately. Instead the dancers were scantily clad in bright colors and their movements were anything but slow and stately. Thus, instead of enhancing the service, it became a distraction for most.

To their credit, the congregation tolerated the spectacle and sat quietly throughout. After the service, they filed out without a word, hardly even making eye contact. Fortunately, only two people showed outwardly negative response. One walked out during the service and the other later chastised me, using sarcastic language. But the subject never came up in any subsequent conversations or meetings so I escaped a potential crisis. Apparently, the rest of the congregation had forgiven me for letting things get out of hand. However, that experience taught me a valuable lesson. It reminded me of the old but reliable simple rule in decision-making, which is "Look before you leap."

One reason I enjoyed my time at the place was that I hardly needed to get adjusted. I was back home. The place was where Ruby and I met, sang together in the choir, dated and married. Half the faces were familiar. Among the church's senior adult leaders that were still there were The Riveras, the Ensiedels, the Lansangs and the Mangahases, to mention a few. Some of my fellow UPCYMians of the 1950's were now young adults and had become leaders of the church. There were former campus couples who were friends from earlier times like Ruben Ganaden and Mildred Sevilleno, Pio "Peps" Caccam and Gloria Quitco and were newly married. From all of those holdovers, I got a lot of support and encouragement.

And then there were the young DeMolay boys. In earlier years, my Jose Abad Santos Chapter brods and I had started the DeMolay presence at UPCYM because so many of us were students at U.P. Diliman. It was more convenient to gather on campus and hold some of our activities there rather than travel the 25 kilometers to the Masonic lodge at San Marcelino St. in Manila. After our batch graduated, a new generation of DeMolays continued the tradition that we started. Among the young DeMolays who were there were Sol Abellera, Ernest Gonzaga, Sam Macagba, Manny Agulto, Albe

Dumlao, Ron Paraan, Danny Galang, Rene Atienza, Ernest Gonzaga and Amor Oribello. Another DeMolay who was an active UPCYMian was Ed Decenteceo, who was a member of Leon Kilat chapter in Dumaguete. To them and other UPCYMians, I was like a big brother whom they called "Manong Ed."

I don't want to give the impression that I was totally dependent on the DeMolay boys for leadership support because there were quite a few non-DeMolays whom I had the pleasure of getting to know well and enjoyed working with. Of them, the one that stood out the most was Carlos "Pahteets" Castro. In many ways, Pahteets was not the typical UPCYMian. He was a scion of a nationally prominent political family. His father, Fred Ruiz Castro, had served in the Executive branch of the Philippine government and at one time was the Chief of Staff under President Ramon Magsaysay. The elder Castro later joined the judicial branch of government and eventually wound up as Chief Justice of the Philippine Supreme Court.

Ironically, Pahteets belonged to a devout Roman Catholic family. Apparently Pahteets had previously gotten very friendly with some UPCYMians who introduced him to the fellowship at the Protestant complex and he liked what he experienced. So instead of gravitating toward UPSCA across the street, he got heavily involved in UPCYM activities and became one of the organization's leaders. When I arrived on the scene in June, 1967, UPCYM was about to induct its new officers for the year led by Pahteets Castro as president.

UPCYM was very fortunate to have Pahteets as president because he was just the right person at a critical time. As with any typical organization, UPCYM had its own share of challenging group dynamics. What was needed at the time was a leader who was enough of an outsider so as not be identified with any of the UPCYM sub-groups but who had the personality and persuasiveness to be able to harness their energy. Pahteets did not fit the stereotype of an UPCYM officer, neither a regular CRL worshipper, nor a member of the UPCYM choir, nor having personal or family Masonic connections, nor being a spiritual activist. But just because of the entire above plus his strong leadership skills, I found it refreshing and helpful, as the organization's adviser, to work with Pahteets for the time that he was president.

Nobody could say that the Protestant ministry was a one day a week phenomenon. The main reason is that just about every day, the students were around. Aside from being there for worship on Sunday mornings and Wednesday evenings, they could be practicing at the choir, carousing with the Palm and Agnir kids, having officer meetings and strategy sessions or just simply hanging out. The Fellowship Hall, which in the intervening years had been named Gumersindo Garcia Hall, GG Hall for short, was the students' gathering place. They called it their "tambayan," a colloquial Tagalog word whose root verb is "tambay," a corruption of the English word "standby." I looked forward to the afternoon hours when they were all there. They kept me busy. Many of those occasions were what I would call "spontaneous pastoral moments" dealing with a wide assortment of concerns that came in the life of every student. Every now and then, I would get a phone call at night and at one time, one of them woke me up and got me out of bed at 2:00 in the morning. I did not mind those rare events and in fact appreciated their trust which I had earned within such a short time.

In her own fashion, Ruby did something to infuse new life into the daily fellowship. She loves to cook, probably the least widely known of her many skills. One afternoon, she prepared one of her favorite snacks, a native delicacy called *guinatan*, which consisted of taro and yams in coconut milk. One day, she just happened to make more than the usual amount for the family and so she decided to offer the rest to a few of the students who happened to be around. The *guinatan* became an instant sensation as the students asked Ruby if she could offer it again and this time they wanted to pay. That got the UPCYM mini-snack corner started. Every afternoon, Ruby, with the assistance of our household help, prepared snacks for students and it gave students added reason to frequent GG Hall. She added to the daily menu, introducing such dishes as spaghetti and meatballs and occasionally some rice cakes. Not intended as a money-making business, it just broke even but its biggest value was in providing additional variety and enjoyment for the students.

Worship was a key responsibility for me both as an adviser and as pastor. I was pleased to find out that the Wednesday evening service that was a regular UPCYM activity from the very beginning continued through the years without any interruption. The students led and designed the service with me as consultant working with a committee headed by a chairman who was designated by the UPCYM Executive Council. On my first year there, the chairman was Daphne Madrid, whom I loved working with in part because I had known her from my student days when she was still a young girl. Her mother, the former Esther Samonte, was church choir director for a couple of years and Ruby and I sang in her choir. Although nervous when she started out, Daphne was a quick and eager learner and before long she was doing a very good job. The service was fairly simple and brief, consisting of prayers and meditations led by students, using a variety of presentation styles. The service was a good midweek spiritual respite for the 25 to 50 students who attended, most of them campus residents.

Toward the end of my internship year, I started a Sunday evening worship service as an experiment. I wanted to reach out to anybody who could not make it to the morning service because of work and other responsibilities. I had no idea who would come but I considered it worth a try. Not wanting to duplicate any of the regular worship services, I wanted the service to have a different format. I decided to pattern it after the Sunday evening vesper service at Silliman University. The main feature of that service was sacred music provided by a guest performer or group. In place of a liturgy and sermon, there were readings from Scripture and inspirational literature.

I had no difficulty finding performers who graciously donated their time and expertise. It helped that I was a former student there and was familiar or friendly with local musical talent. Some of them were established musicians. My former History professor, Aurelio Estanislao, who, by then, had moved to the Conservatory of Music to be a full-time professor of Voice, was one of my first invitees. Others whom I engaged were personal friends from college days who had graduated from the Conservatory of Music and had started their own musical careers. Numbered among them were Ray Paguio, Jerry Dadap and Elmo Makil. One man whom I was fortunate to have as a resource was Constantino Bernardez. He was a professor at Silliman University who with his rich baritone voice was always in demand as soloist for church services and public events. A former manager of the DYSR, the Silliman campus radio station, he was engaged by its counterpart Protestant Evangelical radio station in Manila to spend a few years as its manager.

At first, just a handful attended but slowly, the congregation grew so that by the time I left a year after I started the service, it averaged about 25 to 30 worshippers. In 1980, I visited the campus and went to CRL on Sunday evening. I wondered what I would find. To my delight, I found out that the Sunday service that I started a dozen years before had grown into a full-blown worship service. The church was full with hardly an empty seat.

In 1967, the CRL and NCCP, responding to Rev. Palm's urging, started the search for CRL's first Filipino senior pastor and Protestant chaplain. Their efforts led to the recruitment of Rev. Bonifacio "Boni" Mequi, Jr. A U.P. alumnus and former UPCYM president, Boni had migrated to the United States and studied at Garrett Theological Seminary in Evanston, Illinois where he obtained his

Master of Theology degree. At the time of his recruitment, he was serving as an associate pastor at a Methodist church in Iowa. He and his wife Suzy accepted the offer to come to U.P. to take charge of the ministry.

In the meantime, with my internship year over, I was due to graduate at Silliman University. So in April, 1968, I traveled back to Dumaguete to receive my Bachelor of Divinity degree with *magna cum laude* honors. I did not have to worry about having to move to a new post because CRL asked me to stay on as associate minister at least for another year. My presence was needed in the transition to its first Filipino senior minister. Concluding his tenure at U.P., Rev. Palm had accepted a new assignment abroad so I had to be in charge until Rev. Mequi arrived.

I was thrilled to be working with Boni. He and I were old friends, schoolmates, and CRL choir members in the mid 50's. He was UPCYM president in the school year 1956-57 while I was editor of the UPCYMette. It was during his presidency that the UPCYM had an enjoyable and memorable retreat between semesters that was held in Lucena, Quezon.

By staying an extra year, I provided the transition that helped Boni get acclimated to his new surroundings. We shared equally virtually every aspect of the work. We were co-advisors of the UPCYM and alternated at the pulpit. We also continued the past practice of sharing the parsonage.

The year went by quickly. My work at the Church of the Risen Lord was done and I set myself to the task of looking for my next assignment. I had offers from a couple of churches. One was a church in the Roxas district in Quezon City in what used to be called Project 1. The other was the UCCP Church in San Fernando, La Union. In the meantime, Silliman University was looking for an instructor in the Religious Studies Department. At the same time, the Department of English wanted to have Ruby back at her old position. We decided that going back to Silliman was the best choice for us and the family. In May, 1969, we said goodbye to our friends at CRL and UPCYM and went off to Silliman.

CHAPTER VII: TEACHING AT SILLIMAN

Finding a place to stay was quite a challenge this time around. No longer having the housing privileges that we had when I was a student at the Divinity School as well as a graduate ministerial intern at U.P. Diliman, we were now on our own. We searched for a place to rent for several months and made three residential moves before we found one that was close enough to the campus, offered enough space for our growing family, and was within our price range.

The house was located in the nearby district called Piapi, along the main street that connected the Silliman campus with the university's beach property called Silliman Farm. Our landlord was Mr. Enrique Tenorio, a retired public school principal. Our house sat in the same compound where his house sat just a few yards from us. We were told that our house was once occupied by his daughter Lilia before it got vacated and offered for rental. Lilia was a professor at Silliman's Language department teaching Filipino. We became friendly with her because she would later come and visit her old home to indulge her nostalgia.

The house had a charm of its own. It was a typical old Filipino type of dwelling with a thatched roof, walls made of woven bamboo called *sawali*, and a floor made of bamboo slats. It reminded us of the house we had at the Married Student Housing when I was a Divinity student. We lived in the second floor of the house because the lower level was a dirt floor where presumably in times past, animals were either kept as pets or raised for future consumption. We knew that our modest quarters would not qualify us for acceptance by Dumaguete's established gentry. On the other hand, we felt some solidarity with many of those who lived nearby, who were students and simple folks. Given my activist background, I regarded them as my kind of people.

It did not take long for us to get acclimated to our new situation. We were back in familiar territory with just a few adjustments. Ruby returned to her old job at the College of Liberal Arts as a faculty member of a new academic department named Speech and Theater Arts. The latter was created when Dr. Edilberto Tiempo returned to the Philippines to resume his former post as head of the English Department after several years abroad for studies. In the meantime, Dr. Frank Flores, who had been English Department head in the interim, moved to Manila where he took a job teaching at a Language School in Quezon City. Heading the new Speech and Theater Arts department was Prof. Amiel Leonardia, whose subject specialty was Theater. He had arrived a few years before, having obtained his Master of Fine Arts degree in Theater at the East-West Center of the University of Hawaii. Subsequently, he began collaborating with Dr. Flores in producing some high-quality plays that were presented on campus and elsewhere.

Ruby's main course assignment was Speech 101, which dealt mainly with fundamentals of Public Speaking. The English Department also assigned her courses in English Composition. As for me, I was an assistant professor with the Department of Religious Studies. My main course assignment was Introduction to the Bible, which was required of all Silliman undergraduate students. I also taught a course in Christian Ethics, which upperclassmen took as an elective. Rounding out my teaching load was a course in Argumentation and Debate for Speech majors.

Teaching college-level courses in Bible literacy was an interesting and fulfilling experience. As with any subject that I ever handled, I learned more about the Bible in two years as a teacher than I did in four years as a Theology student. However, it did not take long for me to realize that teaching Bible was not the kind of career I wanted for the rest of my life. For one thing, I missed being a pastor, especially as one serving in an academic setting like I did at U.P. For another, if I was going to be a college professor at all, I wanted to teach in an area in which I felt most competent. That area was Communication and its various specialties.

I felt like I was being led as, one by one, things seemed to fall into place. One day, the dean of the Divinity School approached me, telling me that they needed someone to teach Homiletics. He asked whether I would be willing to take it on. Homiletics is the branch of theological education that deals with sermon preparation and delivery. I gladly accepted the offer, reasoning that not only would it be a new and exciting experience, but it would also be a good addition to my resume, plus Speech was my second undergraduate major. In addition, I had spent two years in the ministry at the Church of the Risen Lord during which I had my own share of preaching before an elite congregation composed largely of university professors and students.

I began to think of a new career goal, which was to be a full-time professor of Speech at the College of Liberal Arts and an adjunct professor of Homiletics at the Divinity School. To reach that goal, I figured I needed more education and the best place to obtain it was abroad. Accordingly, I started researching schools in the United States that offered established advance degrees in Speech.

My research led me to three schools where I wanted to seek admission, namely Northwestern University, Ohio State University and Syracuse University in that order of preference. For me, the first two were no-brainers. Ever since our student days at the University of the Philippines, Northwestern University was the dream school for me and my classmates. We had heard so many good things about the school from two people who graduated there, chiefly Mrs. Consuelo Fonacier and Miss Leticia Tison, our professors in Oral Interpretation and Radio Production, respectively. Furthermore, during my senior year, Dr. Wallace Bacon, a visiting professor from Northwestern came to teach at U.P. I did not get a chance to take a course under him but Ruby did. She had nothing but superlative comments about her experience. As for Ohio State, I chose it mainly because it was our wedding godfather Dr. Alejandro Casambre's alma mater and I figured I could get a good recommendation from him. I had no special reason for choosing Syracuse University except that on paper it had a School of Speech with a solid faculty and a good and varied slate of Speech offerings at the graduate level that would lead to a Master of Arts degree in Speech Communication. Although I did not know anyone who had studied there and who could share experience with me, I made Syracuse my third choice. I started the process of seeking admission to each of the three schools by ordering their application forms.

In the meantime, I busied myself in a variety of Speech-related activities in part as a way to pad my credentials. The annual *Dia Eufonia*, which was a whole week of Speech and Theater activities that was inaugurated several years before, had become firmly established as a premier campus event that attracted a lot of talented students. I offered my services as a coach to some of them, specifically in two areas I specialized in: Impromptu Speaking and Debate. In the former, I developed some speakers who went on to participate in forensic competitions on and off campus.

It was as debate coach that I had some of my most memorable moments. Ever since that first debate in 1965 when I led the Divinity School team against our College of Law counterpart and won best debater honors, I had continued my involvement in Silliman forensics even after I left the campus. For example, in the school year 1967-1968, while I was serving as assistant chaplain at U.P., the National Union of Students staged a nation-wide debate tournament and invited member schools to field their own teams. Silliman fielded a two-man team consisting of Fred Dael and Elfren Quial, better known to his friends as Dodoy. Fred and I were long-time associates and got involved in a number of forensic and theater activities together when I was a student at the Divinity School. One of his achievements was to win the Impromptu Speaking event at one *Dia Eufonia* with my help as his coach. The NUS tournament, which went for a whole school year, consisted of a series of elimination rounds to determine which teams were going to represent their various regions. The regional winners then debated one another until the field was down to two teams for the final debate to determine the national winning team. Fred and Dodoy won their elimination contests to earn the right to compete for the national championship debate, which was to be held in Manila. So Fred and Dodoy came to Manila to prepare for the debate. They asked me to coach them and we spent a few weeks together doing the work necessary to prepare.

The final debate pitted them against the other finalist, a team from the University of San Agustin. It was held at the auditorium of the Philippine Women's University before a packed audience. Unfortunately, we lost the debate. I wish I could say that we did in spite of our best efforts but I cannot. Something happened that, to this day, I regret and feel guilty about.

As their debate coach, it was my duty to give my team my undivided attention, especially on the day of the debate. I did not. I allowed myself to be distracted at a critical moment. During the weeks that Fred and Dodoy spent a lot of time with me at the U.P. Protestant Chapel campus preparing for the debate, they got acquainted with some of the students who frequented the place, including a few girls who were quite obviously attracted to the pair, both of whom were young, good-looking and unspoken for.

One of those girls was one whose name will never see the light of day, at least not from me. On the day of the debate, she came to me with a special request. She asked to come with me to watch the debate. With the benefit of hindsight, I can say now that I wish I had refused her request. But not wanting to disappoint her, I consented. So we drove to Philippine Women's University and sat together in the audience to watch the debate. All the while, I was thinking that I probably should have been backstage with my debaters giving moral support and last minute pointers. However, I figured that I had prepared the two sufficiently and they no longer needed me.

A standard debate consists of two parts. The first part is called the constructive phase, where each debater gives a prepared speech. He is then cross-examined for a few minutes by the next speaker, who is a member of the other team. After all speeches are done, there comes the second part called the rebuttal phase when each debater delivers a brief extemporaneous refutation of some of the points presented by the other team. The rebuttal stage is oftentimes the most critical phase of the whole debate and could mean the difference between victory and defeat, especially if both teams are evenly matched. The rebuttal phase tests each debater's skills in listening and quick analytical thinking.

All the debaters showed that they deserved to be the finalists of the tournament. They all delivered their constructive speeches well and were effective in the cross-examinations. Suspense hung in the air and one could sense the excitement from the audience who knew that everything now depended on the outcome of the rebuttal phase.

At that point, the unexpected happened. The stage curtains suddenly closed. I was shocked. In all my years as student debater and coach, I had never seen that happen. The rebuttal phase had always followed right after the constructive phase without any interruption while the debaters remained in their place at the stage in full view of the audience. It immediately became clear to me that the reason why the curtains closed was so that the debaters could retire backstage to prepare their rebuttal speeches. Presumably, waiting in the wings were their respective coaches and handlers. Since neither I nor my debaters were warned that this was going to be part of the debate procedure, I was not there backstage to help them out. Thus my debaters were put at a disadvantage. It was obvious to me that the other team had made up their minds on how to win the debate at all costs.

I was glad to be back at Silliman where I could practice debate coaching in much friendlier territory without running into any unpleasant surprises like I did in Manila. During the ensuing two years that I taught at Silliman, I coached three debates, each of which had its own share of interesting highlights.

In the first, I coached a School of Divinity Team which faced a College of Liberal Arts team. That debate was an elimination contest to determine which team would represent Silliman in a forthcoming invitational debate between Silliman and the University of San Carlos, a school located in Cebu City. The debate resulted in a split decision of sorts with the Liberal Arts team winning the debate but with Best Debater honors going to one of my Divinity debaters.

Silliman's next task was to decide on the composition of the team that would face that of the University of San Carlos. It seemed logical that the Best Debater of the previous round should be a part of the Silliman team. However, the Liberal Arts team consisting of Bobby Café, Roldan Dalman and Ernest Gonzaga, wished to stay together and so they asked me to talk to the Divinity debater. Fortunately, the latter gave his blessings. It did not take much to convince him because he felt relieved that he did not have to do any more debating, which had taken much time away from his studies. The Liberal Arts team was thrilled that they could stay together. They also asked me to be their coach for the debate against the University of San Carlos.

Silliman hosted USC for the debate, which was held at the campus theater. The debate topic was whether or not to change the term of the Philippine president from four years to six years without reelection. It was one of several hot issues at a time when the country was preparing for a constitutional convention. Silliman took the affirmative side. We agreed that that this was going to be a friendly debate where instead of declaring a team winner, only one prize was going to be decided, which was that of Best Speaker. That honor went to Roldan Dalman.

As with all the teams I had coached, one of the delightful outcomes of working with Ernest, Roldan and Bobby was to see them blossom as they developed their talents and acquired self-confidence that enabled them to go on to bigger and better things individually and collectively. For instance, they teamed up in the ensuing student government elections with Ernest and Roldan running for president and vice- president respectively while Bobby was in the party's senatorial lineup.

The third and final debate that I coached at Silliman was so different from any other that I had done before. Several developments converged to make it happen. One was my longtime fascination with the issue of who should be the Philippine national hero. My views on that issue started way back when, as a student in History at U.P., I learned that Jose Rizal was chosen by a Philippine legislative body composed mostly of Americans, which reportedly used as a primary criterion for their choice the fact that Rizal was a man of peace. While teaching at Lyceum of the Philippines in Manila following my graduation from U.P., I wrote an article for the student paper questioning the legitimacy of Rizal as the national hero. The article elicited a lively discussion on the subject among students and fellow teachers.

I wondered whether the issue would be an appropriate topic for a debate at Silliman. An opportunity came in June, 1971. The school year was about to start and preparations were being made for the annual *Dia Eufonia* that was to take place in the first semester. The event's organizers asked the Divinity School and the College of Law if they would continue the practice of doing a debate as a feature for the week's activities. Both parties agreed. I persuaded the two parties to do a debate on the following proposition: "Resolved that Andres Bonifacio should be the Philippine National Hero" with the Divinity team taking the affirmative position.

We agreed that the debate would be conducted in the Cebuano language. It was a novelty which we hoped would attract people in the areas surrounding the campus, especially members of the lower class who had little more than rudimentary competence in the English language. By this time, activism had spilled out beyond the confines of the university. Nationalism was a dominant theme of the frequent discussions taking place between student activists and their counterparts in the larger community. We figured that the latter would be interested in the topic, especially if they knew that the debate would be conducted in their native tongue.

The Divinity team consisted of Francisco Ugsad and Joel Tabada. I enjoyed working with the two as we prepared for the debate. One of the benefits to me was being forced to immerse myself in Cebuano, enabling me to pick up a third Filipino language, after Ilocano and Tagalog. To my regret, though, I was not going to be present for the actual debate because by that time I was getting ready to leave for the United States for graduate studies. Ruby, who stayed behind and moderated the debate, reported to me that it was very well-attended and as we had hoped, quite a few residents of the area surrounding the campus attended. She sent me a tape recording of the debate which I enjoyed listening to. Best Debater honors went to Francisco Ugsad, who delighted the audience with his witty one-liners during the cross-examination.

Twenty five years later, I visited the Silliman campus during the celebration of the annual Founders Day and had a chance to learn about the impact of that debate experience on the two. I met Francisco Ugsad who was attending the annual Pastors Convocation sponsored by the Divinity School. He had gone into politics in his town and he told me that his experience in debating helped him in his political career. As for Joel Tabada, I was delighted to know that he himself became a debate coach. He had developed a career in prison ministry and one of his projects was to form debating teams among the inmates. His teams got to be so good that they were often invited to debate others outside the prison.

One other extra-curricular activity that I enjoyed was theater. In virtually all campus activities, especially the performing arts, nationalism became a pervasive theme and theater was no exception. Following that trend, Amiel Leonardia decided that the next major theater production that he would direct should be in the Filipino language. For that, he chose a play entitled "Donya Clara," a Filipino adaptation of "The Visit," a play written by the Swiss dramatist Friedrich Durrenmatt. The play revolves around an old lady named Claire who had become rich over the years and returns to the town of her youth with a dreadful bargain. In exchange for enough money to revitalize the struggling town, she wants the townspeople to kill one of their own - a man named Alfred III who had jilted her and for which reason she was forced to leave town. At first, the townspeople, shocked by the woman's proposal, indignantly refuse and vigorously express their disapproval. But as the play progresses and Claire waits in the wings, the townspeople's attitude slowly changes and greed takes over.

At the time, the play's most famous adaptation was a 1964 20th Century Fox movie by the same title starring Ingrid Bergman and Anthony Quinn. Unlike the movie which ends with Claire changing her mind at the last minute and letting Alfred III live so he can spend the rest of his days among the townspeople that had forsaken him, the Filipino version closely follows the Durrenmatt script which ends with Alfred's execution. The title role of Donya Clara was played by Nora Ausejo while I played the role of Antonio, her former lover. The rest of the large cast who played the part of townspeople was a mix of faculty and students. For us all, it was a surreal experience as virtually none of us had previously acted in a play where the language was Filipino. Although half of the cast had spent their entire lives in the Visayas area where either Cebuano or Ilonggo was the language spoken at home, they all quickly adapted. Performed several times at the Woodward Hall to capacity audiences, the play was a hit and got excellent reviews in the local press.

Broadcast journalism was the one activity that I did in those two years which most clearly defined me in the minds of people in the community. I was signed up by DYSR, Silliman's radio station, to do a weekly radio column. Early on Monday morning each week, I was on the air providing radio commentary on a variety of subjects, mostly on national politics. At the time, DYSR was the most prominent radio station in the province of Negros Oriental so I had a very large audience. The country was going through a political crisis. Dissatisfaction with the political and social establishment was rampant and demonstrations occurred frequently in nearly every major population center in the country, especially in college campuses. Silliman had its own share of student demonstrations. There was even talk of an impending Philippine revolution. Everywhere the situation became very polarized and the battle for the minds of the citizenry pitted progressives against reactionaries. Inevitably, I became the mass media voice of the progressive sector in the area.

It did not take long for my broadcasts to catch the attention of the Philippine government. It was common knowledge that prominent leaders of the opposition were marked for inclusion in what was referred to as "the blacklist." Those on the list would be targeted for arrest and imprisonment should the political crisis deteriorate to the point that the president would place the country under martial law. So I was not surprised when I learned from friends who had access to military intelligence that my name had landed on the "blacklist."

The threat of martial law was very real and most of us in the opposition were sure that its proclamation was just a matter of time. I seriously began to plan my means of escape should such a terrible event take place. One option was to go to the hills and join the guerilla forces. The other, far safer, option was to leave the country and stay away for a while till the political situation improved. My hopes for the second option hinged on my admission to any of the three schools I was applying to and the availability of a means of support while I was there.

Fortunately, all three of the schools where I applied for admission accepted me and invited me to start my studies in the school year 1971-1972. However, the question of the means of support was up in the air. I had applied to all three schools for financial aid, which usually comes in the form of a fellowship or assistantship. All of them acknowledged my application for financial assistance and told me that I would be duly informed once a decision was made. I inquired when to expect such a decision so I could make my plans, and was told that the decision would be made on or about April, 1971. I waited with bated breath for months and when April, 1971 came and went without a word, I concluded that I had not qualified for financial aid and resigned myself to staying in place at my job at Silliman.

Meanwhile, a tragedy was about to take place that was going to change my life. It all started when one night in April, I had a terrible dream. In that dream I saw my father getting shot to death. I woke up in a start, which awakened Ruby who assumed that I was having another one of my *bangungot* episodes. I told her about my dream and she advised me to pray, which I did.

I decided to warn my father and so the next morning I wrote him a letter. I wanted to be subtle and did not tell him about my dream. Instead I asked him to watch his back, saying that I read somewhere that in his area of the country, there were people who would kill for a piece of land. I concluded my letter by asking him to "love your neighbor." To this day, I cannot explain what made me write those words. They all just seemed to come to mind spontaneously as I wrote.

The passion in my father's response was something I did not expect. He wrote me a very long letter of several pages in his handwriting, the most detailed one I had ever received from him. He protested, claiming that he had not done anything to deserve my warning. He gave a long recitation of all the things that he had done in the past as a young lawyer for the poor and downtrodden. He then demanded an explanation behind my warning, expressing the hope that rather than a portent of something terrible that was to happen to him, it was just a general word of caution from a "man of God" (to use his words) who was concerned about social justice and love for his fellowmen.

I did not have a chance to write to him again because events happened too fast afterwards. On the morning of May 19, I received a shocking telegram from my mother. I still remember every word of that telegram which contained only five words. It said: COME HOME DADDY SHOT DEAD. I had to read that telegram several times to convince myself that I was not just having a bad dream. My feeling of disbelief was mixed with extreme guilt. I wondered if I could have prevented the tragedy by telling my father about my dream, thereby putting him on guard.

What happened was that on the night of May 18, my father had just finished business for the day and had closed the Shell service station that our family owned. He and Carmen, the station manager, were walking toward our house, which was just a block away from the station, when suddenly a gunshot rang out from behind them. My father fell forward, mortally wounded. As Carmen turned around to see where the shot came from, she found herself face to face with a man holding a gun and pointing it at her. All the man had to do was pull the trigger and Carmen would have been instantly a second casualty because in her fright and shock, she just stood there frozen still. But for some strange reason, the man did not shoot and instead turned around, ran and disappeared into the night.

Subsequent interviews of Carmen and circumstantial evidence appeared to suggest that the triggerman may have belonged to or been engaged by a family that had just lost a court case involving a dispute over a piece of land. Such disputes were commonplace in the area because of spotty recording and documentation of land ownership. It was believed that my father may have been targeted as a scapegoat by the aggrieved family for no apparent reason except that some members of the party that won the court case were his distant relatives. Thus, they may have assumed that my father, who was a lawyer and at that time the sitting municipal judge of the next town, was involved in the case. In truth, he was not involved at all.

The case was never solved. The authorities were never able to identify anyone responsible for the crime and no arrests were made. The event sent shock waves all over. Heretofore a calm and peaceful place, the rural town of Claveria had never lost any of its prominent citizens in this manner and what happened triggered a lot of soul-searching among its inhabitants. Memorial services were held at the church and at the town hall, in which officials of the town participated. Our family became the beneficiaries of a generous outpouring of support by the townspeople. Afterwards, my father's remains were transported to Manila for a week-long vigil held at a funeral home in Quezon City. Town mates in the area and members of our family and clan came from all over to pay their respects, including my two siblings Orly and Ruth who traveled from the United States for the funeral. After the final memorial service, my father was interred at a memorial park located in nearby Marikina, Rizal.

Throughout the observances, I kept a low profile owing to the fact that I was going through a period of spiritual turmoil. I found it difficult to accept my father's death, especially its circumstances. I began to question my faith. In seminary, we constantly talked about the problem of evil and how to deal with it, but now that I was face to face with evil, my theological training failed to help me. I was angry with God for letting it happen, more so because all my life, I thought that by dedicating myself into God's service, I was shielding my family from danger.

I kept my dream about seeing my father being shot to death and our ensuing exchange of letters a secret from everyone. Finally, when things quieted down and I was ready to go back to Silliman, I took my mother aside and told her the whole story. She made me promise to give her the lengthy letter that my father wrote in response to my warning. I had intended mailing that letter to my mother as the very first thing I would have done as soon as I got home. But something happened that made me forget to do so.

I got home to find a pile of mail that had accumulated in the two weeks that I was away for my father's funeral. As I sorted the mail, one letter caught my eye. It was an envelope with a return address of Syracuse University. Excitedly, I opened the letter and found out that it came from the university's School of Speech informing me that I had been awarded a graduate teaching assistantship that would enable me to finance my education. The news was a complete surprise. It was already June by the time I got the letter and I had given up hope of ever getting an award. So I wondered if the mail had just been delayed in transit. I looked at the date when the letter was written and was met with another shock. It was dated May 18, 1971, which was the day my father was killed. I found it hard to believe that it was a mere coincidence.

The days and weeks that followed were hectic as there were a lot of arrangements to be made. I wrote to Syracuse to accept the award and started work on my travel papers. There were passports and visas to be processed, travel itineraries to be set, fare money to be raised and a lot of other tasks that kept me hopping from one place to another. I had completely forgotten about my promise to my mother to mail my father's letter to her. It took an extra-sensory experience to remind me. I was at home asleep when I heard a distinct noise coming from the wardrobe dresser that was just a few feet away from the bed. It was the sound of the door being forcibly opened. I looked and saw nothing that would cause the noise. I then remembered that it was in the dresser that I had kept the letter that I had promised to mail out. I sat up, turned to the dresser and said, "OK, Dad, I will mail the letter out tomorrow" and the noise stopped. The next day, I mailed the letter to my mother with a note apologizing for the delay.

I grabbed every opportunity to learn from others who had been to the States for studies, especially from fellow graduates of the Divinity School. A valuable piece of advice came from some of my professors. They encouraged me to get myself ordained into the ministry before leaving for the States. With full ministerial credentials, I was told, I could more easily affiliate with denominational judicatories upon arriving in the States. Following their advice, I petitioned the Southern Mindanao Conference of the United Church of Christ through the Davao UCCP Church which had sponsored me into the ministry in 1964 and which continued to be my home church. My petition was approved and on June 21, 1971, I was ordained as a UCCP minister through the Service of Laying of Hands by clergy members of the Conference. My family, together with Papa and Mama Ordinario, were there to support me and be a part of the ordination service. The Conference gave me a gift of a Bible; Papa and Mama donated my clerical garb; and Ruby installed on me the stole that was symbolic of my new professional title. I finally acquired the right and privilege to be called The Rev. Federico Agnir.

On August 15, 1971, I said goodbye to my family and friends and boarded the plane that was to take me to Manila. I was scheduled to fly out of Manila to San Francisco on August 21. Upon arriving in Manila, I went to visit Liz Pajaro, one of the UPCYM members that I was close to when I was serving as assistant chaplain and assistant pastor at U.P. She had already graduated and was working for a travel agency. During that visit, she introduced me to an offer that she was sure I could not refuse. She said that they were trying to fill seats in a large airplane and if I would change my plans and take that airplane instead, they would set me up for one-day stopovers in Hongkong and Tokyo with all my hotel expenses paid for. The condition was that instead of my original plan of leaving Manila on August 21, I would leave on August 23. They also offered to contact whoever was supposed to pick me up in San Francisco, who, in this case, was my cousin Alfredo Pascua. She gave me a day to think the offer over.

The offer was indeed very tempting, especially the part about stopping over in Hongkong and Tokyo. However, something told me that I had to get out of the country as quickly as possible and even a day's delay was unacceptable. The next day, I told Liz my decision. She was, of course, disappointed.

It was my first time to take such a lengthy trip and it felt like it took forever. I finally reached San Francisco where my cousin Manong Fred and his wife Manang Conching met me and took me to their home. I was so tired from the trip that I promptly went to sleep. The next morning, I picked up the morning paper and upon reading the headline news, I realized why I had to leave the Philippines right away. I had left Manila on the day when a big rally was being held in the main square of Manila called Plaza Miranda. Before a crowd of about 4,000, the opposition Liberal Party was showcasing its slate of national and local candidates for the forthcoming elections that were to be held in November. While the rally was going on, two grenades were thrown on the stage. Nine people were killed including a child, and many of those on the stage were injured, some of whom were maimed for life. Among those who were injured were prominent candidates of the opposition party.

President Marcos blamed communists and leftist radicals for the Plaza Miranda attack. He then suspended the *writ of habeas corpus* and ordered the military to round up activists and intellectuals all over the country. Ruby would later tell me that in the days that followed, my friends in Dumaguete, who were worried about me, wanted to know whether I was able to leave the country in time. She told them that I was due to fly out the afternoon of the Plaza Miranda bombing and so was confident that I was safe. I was glad that I did not tell her about Liz Pajaro's offer and how close I came to being left behind.

CHAPTER VIII: SYRACUSE UNIVERSITY

For anyone moving to the United States and staying there for any length of time, adjusting to one's new circumstances can be a daunting challenge. Most people choose their destination carefully so as to minimize adjustment problems. For Filipnos, perhaps the two most important criteria are weather and social support. For this reason, many Filipinos migrating to the United States wind up in Hawaii and Southern California where the climate is relatively mild compared to other places and where there is a large Filipino population. In fact, the chances are usually good that one will find some friends and relatives who are already there.

By going to Syracuse, I could not have chosen a more difficult place to adjust to. Located in upstate New York where the so-called Northeast JetStream dumps more than a hundred inches of snow a year, Syracuse has one of the bitterest winters in the country. At Syracuse, the first snowfall occurs in October and has been known to keep going into early May. According to the Weather Bureau, the average annual snowfall there is about 125 inches. Actually, on my first year there, the snowfall was a record total of 164 inches. As for social support, the nearest relative I had were my sister Ruth, a nurse working in New York City which was five hours drive away. My brother Orlando, a doctor practicing in Martinsburg, West Virginia was even farther away. Alone and with my own family ten thousand miles away, I knew I was going to have to deal with and fight loneliness and homesickness while I was in the States.

I had hoped that I would be able to quickly develop a circle of friends among those who were already there, reasoning that the chances were good that there would be a few Filipino graduate students there. Indeed, I was right. But what came as a delightful surprise was that nearly all of them were people I already knew from my days at Silliman and U.P.

Foremost of the Sillimanians were Claro and Riorita Ceniza, a couple who were working for their Ph.D. and Masters degrees, respectively. Claro and I had been classmates at the Divinity School in the mid-60's. We parted ways when I left for two years at U.P. In the meantime, Claro decided that instead of finishing his ministerial studies, he was going to become a Philosophy professor. By the time I moved back from U.P. to Silliman in 1969, Claro and family had already left for Syracuse where he was a doctoral student under a fellowship grant. Another Silliman couple was Tony and Nilda

Magdamo whom I previously knew mainly by name. He was an engineer going for an advance degree. Eventually he would return to Silliman to be the Dean of the College of Engineering. Rounding up the group of Filipino graduate students from Silliman was Mary Ellen Rutherford, who arrived the same time I did.

Among the U.P. alumni, the most special to me was Sammy Tan, a doctoral student at the Maxwell School of Citizenship and Public Affairs. He and his wife Luming and their three children were the very first ones to welcome me when I arrived on campus. They had heard about me from the university's International Student Center, which apparently had a policy of informing the compatriots on campus of any new international student who was coming. Their apartment was in the same building as mine and I spent many evenings with their family and was often invited for dinner, including my very first meal on campus.

Arriving at Syracuse to start their studies about the same time I did were three young Filipinos whom I had known quite well from my days as a ministry intern and pastor at U.P. Two of them were Cipriano, Jr. and Ianthe (nee Castro) de Leon. Both scions of prominent Protestant families in Manila, the two were college sweethearts at U.P. and were married at the Church of the Risen Lord while I was there. Cip was in Syracuse for his M.B.A. degree while Ianthe was going to be my classmate in the Master of Arts program at the School of Speech. The third of the young Filipinos from U.P. was Moreno Requiza, who was one of the UPCYM leaders while I was in Diliman. He and I had an even closer relationship by family affiliation. He is a godbrother of my wife Ruby, having been sponsored at baptism by Papa Ordinario way back in the 1940's when he was an itinerant schoolteacher living in the Requiza hometown of Digos, Davao.

Arriving the next school year were Fernando "Nanding" and Linda Lagua, both of whom were my contemporaries as fellow students at U.P. in the mid 1950's. They were both prominent campus leaders, with Nanding serving as Student Government president, at that time the most coveted and prestigious student political position in the university. After U.P., he moved on to La Salle College where he earned his M.B.A. degree. He came to Syracuse to get a second Masters degree in the field of Computers. Linda also obtained her Masters degree in the Philippines and while in Syracuse took post graduate courses at Maxwell.

I stayed at the Vincent Apartments, a housing complex near the main campus that was intended for graduate students. When I was still in the Philippines working on my papers, which included making housing arrangements, I was given a choice between having a room to myself and sharing a room with a fellow student. I chose the latter, an easy decision because I already knew who my roommate was going to be, a friend named Jayaprakash Ramanujam, Jay for short.

Jay was a native of Sri Lanka who went to Silliman for his undergraduate degree. His father was a Sri Lankan diplomat who had met and became friends with Dr. Cicero Calderon when they were their respective countries' representatives to various gatherings of the international labor community in the 1950's. In 1967, the elder Ramanujam sent his son Jay to study at Silliman because his friend Cicero was already the university president. Jay spent four years at Silliman, graduating with a Bachelor of Arts degree in Political Science. He and I had become good friends. We had both applied for admission and got accepted at several U.S. universities including Syracuse. But we never dreamed that we would wind up together in the States until I heard the wonderful news about my financial aid award. Luckily, he was still on campus when I returned from my father's funeral in June, 1971. He and I got together and agreed that we would be roommates in Syracuse.

Jay and I had something in common. We both came from a culture where the cooking was done mostly by the women at home. In his entire life, he had never prepared a meal by himself. At least I knew how to cook rice and boil an egg. Moreover, Ruby gave me a book entitled <u>Cooking for Beginners</u>. I still remember the dedication she wrote at the back of the front cover. It said: "Just because I am not with you does not mean that you are going to starve." She also told me that an easy way to vary the taste of my dishes was to use different sauces. I followed all of Ruby's suggestions. Jay was so impressed by my cooking that he often bragged to his friends that he had a roommate who was a great cook. He and I split household tasks. He did the grocery shopping while I did the cooking, an arrangement I really appreciated especially in the dead of winter when I did not have to slog through the snow to get to the grocery store which was a couple of blocks away from our apartment.

I was eager to survey the place where I was going to study and work so as soon as I got settled, I went to the main campus. The Syracuse School of Speech was located on the second floor of the Hall of Languages, one of the campus' oldest buildings. It sat prominently on top of what was intimately referred to as "the hill." My first stop was the office of Dr. Beulah Rohrlich, the head of the Speech Department. She was the one who had written to me informing me of my graduate assistantship award and who presumably was going to be both my work and academic advisor.

After the initial greetings and getting acquainted, I asked her how I got to be chosen for my award and why the announcement came later than usual. She explained that the award was originally offered to someone else who declined it in favor of an offer from another school. I got it because I was the second in line. I then asked her the big question that had been nagging me since I received her letter. I told her I was curious to know when she wrote and mailed her letter to me. Momentarily, she paused, obviously puzzled and wondering why I was asking. She recalled that she had written the letter at home and then on the way to work stopped at the post office to mail it. I asked her what time she got to the post office. She said, "Eight o'clock in the morning." In a slightly quivering voice, I said, "That was eight o'clock at night in the Philippines." I felt that I had to get out of there so I excused myself and left.

The next day I visited Dr. Rohrlich again. I apologized for my behavior the day before and explained why I left in a hurry. I told her about my father's assassination and that it happened on May 18, 1971, which was the date on her letter. I said that I had been intrigued by the coincidence in dates but when she told me that she mailed the letter at the exact time that my father was killed, I was completely overwhelmed. I explained that among my people, it is believed that such coincidences are signs of divine intervention. She thanked me for sharing my story with her and offered her condolences. I felt relieved at being able to unburden myself to someone who would become my teacher, advisor and friend.

For my graduate assistantship, I was assigned to teach two sections of an undergraduate Speech course called Small Group Communication. Most of the students in my classes were students majoring in Speech or Mass Communication. My daily routine consisted of teaching in the morning and taking graduate Speech courses in the afternoon and evening. I enjoyed my job as a teacher because I learned as much from it as I did from my course work, if not more so. This was my first time to teach a class composed of American students, virtually all of whom were Caucasians. I also found out that Syracuse had a very high proportion of Jewish students so, through my interaction with them, I learned a lot about Jewish culture. On my second semester, I was offered to teach a course in Public Speaking at the University College, Syracuse University's extension department located in downtown Syracuse. Aside from providing me extra income, it exposed me to a different inter-cultural experience. The class consisted of ethnic minority students who lived and worked in the inner city.

As time went on, I began to have mixed feelings about the future. I enjoyed both my teaching and my studies and was due to graduate with my Masters degree in Speech Communication at the end of the school year. Silliman University, from where I had taken a leave of absence, was waiting for me to return and teach at the College of Liberal Arts and the Divinity School. However, something made me think twice about going home right away. Ruby had been writing to me with some ominous news. She reported that members of the state police called Philippine Constabulary had been visiting our neighborhood inquiring from people there about my whereabouts and asking when I was coming back. In the meantime, the political situation in the country continued to deteriorate and Ruby was apprehensive about their safety. She was afraid that should a political emergency arise, my family might be held hostage to force me to come home and be apprehended. She urged me to look into the possibility of getting them to join me.

Realizing the urgency of the situation, I encouraged her to take steps for her and the children to come to the States. It was not easy to do and she had to work very hard to overcome a number of obstacles. She found out that her biggest hurdle was convincing the U.S. government that while in the United States, the family would have enough financial support. I could not be of much help. I had come to the United States on a student visa, otherwise known as an I-20, which prohibited me from seeking gainful employment to supplement the income I got from my graduate assistantship, which was just enough for tuition, books and living expenses. Furthermore, in order to extend my stay as a student, I would have had to get admitted into another degree program after receiving my Masters degree.

I was fortunate to get guidance and help from the university's International Student Office. They advised me to seek admission into a doctoral program and, once admitted, ask for a renewal of my graduate teaching assistantship at the School of Speech. I was also advised to change my immigration status to that of an exchange visitor, otherwise known as J-1. That new status would allow Ruby to be employed by the university once she got there. There was a potentially unpleasant catch to that new status. I could not apply to stay permanently in the United States because under the rules of the U.S. Exchange Visitor Program, I would have had to return to the Philippines first and from there apply for permanent immigration status, otherwise known by its nickname of "green card." Many who went through that process took years to get their green card, if ever. But I wasn't about to worry about that as the more urgent task was to get my family to get out of the country as quickly as possible. So I followed the International Student Office's advice. Luckily, I was admitted into the Ph.D. program at the Newhouse School of Public Communications and the School of Speech generously extended my graduate teaching assistantship. Thus, I was able to extend my stay as an Exchange Visitor.

Ruby had to go to the U.S. consulate located in Cebu City to apply for the family's immigration visas. Unfortunately, none of the moves I made were enough to convince the American consul. What he wanted was documented proof that my family would not become a financial responsibility of the U.S. government. After two unsuccessful trips to Cebu, Ruby was about to give up when she remembered that there was something else she could try to do. It went against her own moral beliefs but because of the urgency of the situation, she relented. She contacted her godfather, Congressman Constancio Maglana, asking for his help.

As in many other countries, majority of people in the Philippines believe that if one wanted to get things done or to attain something, "It's WHO you know." Someone high up in the Philippine government COULD open doors.

Congressman Maglana was actually Ruby's second godfather by baptism. She was first baptized as a baby during the Second World War, in a Roman Catholic Church which was the only church near where she and her parents lived. After the war, the family moved to Davao City. Ruby's parents wanted her to be re-baptized in the Protestant religion, in the local UCCP Church where they had become members.

At nine years old, Ruby already had a highly developed artist's eye. She had admired the beauty of a young lady named Ludivina Lagunsad since the first time she saw her in church. She was Ruby's only choice for a godmother. Luding, as she was nicknamed, had just married a young lawyer named Constancio Maglana. In the Philippines, when a married person stands as a sponsor at a church ceremony, the spouse also becomes a sponsor. Thus, Atty. Maglana became Ruby's godfather as well. When we married in 1961, we also asked the couple to be among our wedding sponsors.

In 1965, the large province of Davao was divided into three provinces. Davao del Norte, one of the three new provinces was to be represented in the Philippine Congress and elections for the congressional position were held. Atty. Maglana, who had built a fortune in that area in the lumber business, ran for the congressional position and won. He was serving the end of his second congressional term when in 1972, Ruby wrote to him asking for a letter of support to present to the American consulate. He wrote the letter using the letterhead of his congressional office and sent it to Ruby. In the letter, he pledged to provide financial support for his godchild Ruby Agnir and her family should it be necessary to do so. Armed with those credentials, Ruby took her third trip to Cebu and presented the letter to the consul. Upon reading the letter, the consul said to Ruby, "I guess I cannot hold you back anymore." He was not about to doubt the word of one of the country's lawmakers.

Ruby and our three children arrived in San Francisco on the first week of July, 1972. They spent several days in California visiting with her brother Sadiri and his wife Aurora in Berkeley and with her uncle Andy and his wife auntie Fanny in Roseville. Afterwards, they flew to New York where they were met by my sister Ruth and her husband Diony. After a few days, the couple brought them in their car to Syracuse.

Ruby and the children could not have left the Philippines any sooner. On September 22, two months after they arrived, President Marcos declared martial law. Many activists and intellectuals were arrested including quite a few among my friends at Silliman who were involved in the nationalist movement with me. Some ran to the hills while others were imprisoned. There were reports of people being tortured, one of whom was a former Divinity School classmate of mine.

In the weeks and months that followed, I received updates from friends and relatives in the Philippines, especially from my oldest brother Willie. He was safe because he was in Marcos' camp as a reserve officer of the Philippine Army. He urged me to stay put and not entertain any thoughts of returning to the Philippines because he was sure that even with all his connections to the military, he would not be able to protect me. The country became a virtual police state and it took more than 14 years for that dark period in Philippine history to come to an end with Marcos' removal from power.

The arrival of Ruby and the children brought for me a new period of adjustment. For a whole year before that, I was a virtual bachelor, which was a mixed blessing because while I had a lot of freedom, I was homesick all the time. Now, I had a family to take care of. We moved to a larger apartment just a block away in the same Vincent Apartment complex where I had been. Our two daughters were of grade school age and we needed to find a school for them. Fortunately, there was a public elementary school a few blocks away and within walking distance so that was not a problem. Our youngest, Freddie, was only five and since there was no pre-school place nearby, he had to stay at home so Ruby and I had to juggle our hours so that there was always someone at home with him. Not having the money to pay for baby-sitting, we found this phase in our family life difficult, especially during that first year.

We needed to buy a car so we could get around. Several weeks before my family arrived, I got ready by obtaining a driver's license. I prepared myself by asking my Filipino friends how they got their licenses. They told me that they   each had to pass both a written exam and a driving test. I went to the Motor Vehicles Office in downtown Syracuse to apply for my driver's license. It was then that I got a lucky break. The clerk who attended to me said that since New York had "reciprocal relations with all U.S. states and territories," to use his own words, my Philippine license automatically qualified me for a New York license so all I had to do was show my Philippine license and my social security card. I dutifully handed him both. Within an hour, I walked out of there with a brand new U.S. driver's license.

Our first stateside car was a brand new orange-colored Volkswagen Hatchback. Buying it was our introduction to the so-called American dream, which for most people consisted in acquiring worldly possessions by credit. We bought the car at just the right time when we could fully enjoy it. It was the month of August and school opening was still a few weeks away so we drove around. Our earliest trips were to New York and West Virginia for family get-togethers with my sister Ruth and my brother Orly respectively. One memorable trip during that period was a visit to the "Enchanted Forest" in the Adirondacks where Ruby and I and our children had a wonderful time.

The next step was for Ruby to find a job to help with family finances. Fortunately, a secretary's position opened up at the Newhouse School of Public Communications which she applied for and was hired. Her new job was a Godsend for us because she was going to be working at the same school where I was a graduate student so we could be near each other. Her new boss was Dr. Wesley Clark who was the outgoing dean of the school. Dr. Clark was spending his final semester before his retirement following a glorious career during which the School of Journalism grew under his stewardship to become a premier school for training in mass media under the new name of Newhouse School of Public Communications. When Ruby joined Dr. Clark's staff, their office was housed in a temporary one-story prefab building a block away from the school's new campus where new buildings were under construction.

The new campus was named after Samuel Newhouse, a magnate of the newspaper industry who had donated the funds for the construction of the new buildings. It consisted of two large three-story buildings. One was designated for training in print media while the other was for broadcast media. It was in the latter building where I was going to be taking a lot of my courses at Newhouse. After one semester, construction in the new campus was completed and the buildings were inaugurated in ceremonies that were widely publicized. Samuel Newhouse himself came to grace the occasion.

With Dr. Clark retiring, Ruby had for herself a new boss and a new office located in one of the new buildings. Her new boss was Dr. Maxwell McCombs, a professor of Communications Research who had just arrived from his former post at the University of North Carolina at Chapel Hill. Dr. McCombs was going to divide his time between teaching and research. At North Carolina, he did pioneering research and publication in the field of "the agenda-setting function of the media" and was going to continue work in that field at Syracuse. I took a couple of courses with him and learned a lot from him on research methodology, which would later benefit me when it came time to do my doctor's dissertation.

Just as she did with Dr. Clark, Ruby enjoyed working with Dr. McCombs. He was a pleasant and engaging person with no hint of rank or status aloofness. For him and Ruby, working together was also a new cross-cultural experience which was mutually educational and amusing. Born and grown up in the South, Dr. Maxwell spoke with a heavy accent which Ruby found unfamiliar. Early on, there were times when while taking dictation, she would ask what he meant or ask him to spell a word.

As graduate teaching assistant at the School of Speech, I had a new job description. I was going to coach the varsity debating team. It was going to be a new experience because in many ways it was going to be very different from coaching debate in the Philippines. Unlike its Philippine counterpart, Amercan debating was extremely structured and rigorous.

College debating in the United States was conducted around a year-long activity called the National Debate Tournament, NDT for short. Started in 1947 by the United States Military Academy at West Point, New York, colleges from all over the United States were invited to send debate teams that would participate in a three-day tournament. A succession of seeding and elimination rounds led to a final round between the two best teams, whereby the winner took home the coveted award which usually consisted of a trophy.

112

In 1967, the NDT was taken over by the American Forensic Association, the national organization of forensics educators in the United States and introduced a lot of changes. One of the changes was the designation of a different host college for each tournament. Another significant change was the choosing of the tournament topic at the beginning of the school year. This gave participating schools a chance to prepare for the tournament which occurred near the end of the school year. Such preparation involved participating in a number of invitational tournaments during the school year.

The invitational tournaments were of two types. The first type was a qualifying tournament in which teams competed to garner points that would earn for them an automatic berth in the national tournament. Although any school was free to seek to be part of the tournament, the schools that were invited to these qualifying tournaments were usually those who had a remarkable record in the NDT. The other type was an educational tournament whereby participating schools were not seeking to qualify for the big tournament but rather looked at the event as an opportunity for their students to gain experience in academic debating. Syracuse elected for this second type. One reason for Syracuse's choice was that unlike the high-powered schools that had the resources to send teams all over the country and frequently, Syracuse participated in no more than a dozen tournaments for the year. To save on travel, we also usually chose tournaments that were within driving distance. Fortunately, Syracuse is located in the Northeast United States where some of the best colleges and universities in the United States were located including a number of Ivy League schools. Thus, we were able to attend tournaments hosted or attended by some of those prestigious schools.

Whichever type of tournament we participated in, we followed the same rules of debate. A typical tournament consisted of four or five rounds spread over two days held on a weekend. Occasionally, a tournament took three days, which was the case with most qualifying tournaments. Each team, consisting of two debaters, had to be ready to debate either side of the topic. A committee designated by the host school managed the seeding of teams and assignment of debate sides.

We were all required to debate the national topic which was chosen early in the school year through a process under the direction of the American Forensic Association. In the school year 1972-1973, my first year as coach, the national topic was "Resolved, that a system of medical care be established for all US citizens." The next year, the topic was "Resolved, that the federal government should control the supply and utilization of energy." Both topics represented a trend that started in the 1970's. Unlike previous decades in which the topic was a specific and clear proposal or hypothesis to be argued by the affirmative and negative sides, topics in this period consisted of broad proposals on domestic policy. The bone of contention between the two sides was not whether to follow the proposed policy. Rather, each debate was a contest on which side presented the best way to pursue the policy.

The broad nature of the topic opened the door to a multiplicity of cases and counter-cases. Each debater had to prepare for every eventuality, which meant hours spent gathering evidence and putting them on cards for ready retrieval. Most debaters would enter the debate stage carrying one suitcase and sometimes two, each full of evidence cards. Often, a debate had the appearance of a contest to show which side had more and better evidence cards. The system had its advantages and disadvantages. On one hand, the extensive research that debaters needed to conduct made them virtual experts on the subject, possessing enough material fit for a doctor's dissertation. On the other hand, the almost exclusive attention to content and the urgency in presenting evidence made for very little polish in speech delivery. Moreover, the cross-examination or interpellation phase which potentially can bring light repartee to otherwise overly serious moments was eliminated.

As the school year went on, we started to grow weary of debating the same topic over and over and longed for a break. A lucky break came toward the end of the school year in the form of a different type of debate tournament. It was held at McGill University in Montreal, Canada. Canadian debating is patterned after the British style of debating which, like debates held in the English parliament, emphasizes wit and allows heckling. Not only did the tournament give us a reprieve from the American national topic. It also helped us to develop a different skill, which is the art of the impromptu rhetorical comeback. Everything in the tournament set-up was designed to develop a delightful atmosphere including the choice of a tongue-in-cheek tournament topic. For example, the topic on our first year of participation was "Resolved that Canada should declare independence from the United States."

The two years I spent as coach of the Syracuse University varsity debate team was an experience I will never forget. I learned so much from the debate topics. As I write, I am half amused and half grateful as I listen to and read about the current attention the government and media are giving to America's dilemma over what to do with the management and delivery of medical care and renewable energy. It's like listening to an old record. A lot of what some regard as new and novel I consider old hat.

Meeting some of the most interesting people such as students and their coaches was another bonus. Above all, the exposure to American and Canadian debating added to my years as debate coach in the Philippines gave me an international perspective on the art of debate that prepared me well professionally and academically.

Until now, I had not said a word about church life which is unusual because, after all, I came to the United States as an ordained minister with a Divinity degree. Moreover, I don't remember any time when I was in the Philippines that I missed going to church on Sunday. That completely changed when I got to Syracuse. On my first year, I never went to church. One reason was that there was no church in the immediate vicinity. All the churches were in downtime Syracuse. I did not have a car and public transportation was not a practical option. In truth, being away from any religious activity was for me a welcome break. I did not miss church at all and had enough other activity to keep me busy.

Once we had a car and could travel around, we could take our pick of which church to attend. We wanted to be with a UCC Church nearby, preferably one that came from a Congregational tradition, just like the church in Davao City where Ruby grew up and where we became members and started a family. One church that exactly met our need was Fairmount Congregational Church UCC. Located in Camillus, a small village in the outskirts of Syracuse, it was about 10 miles and a 15 minute drive from our house. We started worshipping at that church, felt at home in it and joined the choir. Before long, the church found out about Ruby's rich background in church music so when shortly thereafter the position of church organist got vacated, they asked Ruby if she would be interested in the position. She did not need much convincing. She accepted the job right away.

We gained more than just an additional source of income. We acquired a new circle of friends with whom we engaged in a variety of activities, not just through music but through social and recreational gatherings as well. One interesting person was Dawn Mackay, the choir director. Dawn dreamed of becoming a medical doctor and was at that time a student at the Syracuse University College of Medicine. She and her boyfriend Jim Schwartz became our closest friends. They married soon after and we became very good friends and kept contact with one another even after we left Syracuse. They even helped us move to our next home in Western Massachusetts, loading our things on their truck and going the five-hour trip.

A year after Ruby started working at Fairmount, I got a call from a person who identified himself as Rev. Richard Cheffey. Dick, as he was called by family and friends, was the supply pastor of two yoked Presbyterian churches about 30 miles north of Syracuse. He explained that he was planning to resign from both churches and wanted to know if I would be interested in the position. He had learned about me from some of my friends at Fairmount who knew that I was an ordained minister. The two churches were located in the towns of Parish and Hastings, respectively, and were three miles apart. Both churches were small and had hardly any activity beyond Sunday morning worship so Dick suggested that the work would be light enough so that I could serve them without taking much time away from my responsibilities at Syracuse.

I found the idea of taking on a church assignment appealing. For one thing, it would take a load off Ruby's shoulders who had been the main family bread earner since they arrived the year before. However, there were some pros and cons to carefully weigh. Ruby would have had to give up her organist job at Fairmount because we certainly did not want nor had the wherewithal to be in two different places on Sunday morning. In so doing, we would have had to leave our close friends at Fairmount with whom we had spent so many pleasant times for the past year. There was also the disadvantage of our having to travel 30 miles as opposed to the 10 miles it took to get to Fairmount. The route to Parish and Hastings was fraught with danger especially in the winter time because we would have had to pass through a section that was traversed by the Northeast Jet Stream, which resulted in frequent snowfall there even in times when the rest of the surrounding area was completely clear.

One big incentive to take the church job was its potential as a stepping stone to full-time employment. After having spent the better part of the previous ten years as a graduate student dating back to my days at Silliman University Divinity School, I felt that I owed it to my family to start earning an income that could let me give them the kind of life that they deserved. I had acquired excellent credentials to qualify me for a college professorship. I was advised by very knowledgeable people that this was the best time for me to seek such a position. I had two graduate degrees, the more recent of which was the Master of Arts degree in Communication that I earned in 1972. Furthermore, by the end of the school year 1973-74, I would have accumulated enough classroom credits in my doctoral program, needing just the dissertation to complete the degree. People whimsically called the situation I was in as A.B.D., an acronym for "All But Dissertation." This was a time

116

when "over-qualification" was every jobseeker's downfall. Horror stories circulated about new Ph.D.s sending out hundreds of resumes, not getting any responses, and having to settle for jobs that were unrelated to or way below the level of their training. On the other hand, those who were most successful in obtaining professorial jobs were A.B.D.s like me. Thus, it made perfect sense to interrupt one's doctoral program, secure a professorial job and plan to resume the doctoral program later.

For me, however, there was an initial major hurdle. I needed to first change my immigration status from Exchange Visitor to Permanent Resident. Technically, this was next to impossible because of the U.S. government's requirement that an Exchange Visitor seeking a change to Permanent Resident status must first return to one's home country and apply for permanent residency from there. There was a rare exception to the rule, which was that if an employer could prove that an Exchange Visitor was needed and that no citizen or immigrant was available for the job, the rule can be relaxed. However, with so much competition from citizens and permanent residents for college professorial jobs at that time, my chances of getting one based on the exemption were next to nothing.

My chances were better with the pastoral position that Dick was offering. There was hardly any competition for that job because the income from the two small churches was too low to attract well-qualified ministers. Also, the government was inclined to be lenient toward churches in everything. I decided it was worth taking a chance on qualifying for the exemption so I accepted the offer to be the pastor of the two churches. With mixed feelings, Ruby resigned her position from Fairmount, citing health and family responsibilities. We bade goodbye to our friends at that church and prepared ourselves for a new adventure.

My Sunday morning routine consisted of getting to Parish in time for the service which began at 9:00 o'clock. I had to conclude the service by 10:00 o'clock so I could have enough time to travel to Hastings in time for the service there which started at 10:30 a.m. Both congregations were small with an average attendance of about 35 on an ordinary Sunday. Neither church kept an office so the place was closed for the other six days of the week and the only person who visited either place regularly was the sexton, who was an unpaid volunteer. Music was provided by a volunteer organist who accompanied the hymns. Neither church had a choir.

The similarities ended there. The Parish church was located in the center of town and was one of three churches in the vicinity, the other two being a Methodist church and a Roman Catholic church. The homes in the neighborhood were close to one another. Among the worshippers, no one was less than 50 years old. As such, there was no church program of any kind for children, teenagers or young adults. From the way they were dressed and the cars they owned, the church members belonged to the middle class. On the other hand, the Hastings church was located in a rural area and was the only church for miles around. It was surrounded by farm lands that were spread out. Unlike the Parish church, complete families of young and old worshipped at Hastings so there were opportunities for services and programs beyond a Sunday worship service. Virtually all of the worshippers were lower class folks.

One day during the week, Dick Cheffey came to visit me at home. I had just preached at the two churches for two Sundays so I assumed that he was eager to know how I felt about my new job. Instead, he came with some unsettling news. It seemed that one of the parishioners at the Parish church was unhappy and was causing some trouble. The troublemaker was an important person both in the church and the community. He was the primary owner and chief executive of a family business which delivered gasoline to service stations in the area. Being one of the town's wealthiest men, he was the main contributor to the budget of the Parish church, thus wielding a lot of influence.

It appeared that the man was not part of the committee from the church that had recruited me nor had knowledge of what was going on. He was away on vacation when I preached for the first time. Upon returning from vacation, he came to church on my second Sunday and was shocked to find out that his new pastor was not a full-blooded Caucasian like everybody else. The next day, he started making the rounds among parishioners of both churches asking them to rescind my pastoral call.

Dick apologized to me profusely for leading me to what appeared to be a trap. Apparently, he was taken completely by surprise. Although he knew that most of his parishioners were socially and politically conservative, he had no idea that he was harboring any racists in his congregation.

I knew about racism in America from all that I had read on American history and current events so I had no illusions. Still, it was unnerving to experience it first hand and so blatantly. I needed to decide whether to give up the job or hang on in hopes of being able to tolerate the situation until an alternative came up. I opted for the second and braced myself for further developments. I showed up the next Sunday expecting the worst. To my surprise and relief, nothing happened. The man either failed in his campaign to have me unseated or had a change of heart. From reading the congregation's body language, I concluded that it may have been both. One very telling sign was how the members of his family behaved. On that Sunday, the man's father, a retired elderly gentleman who was the founder of the family business, came up to me and warmly shook my hand. I could not believe that he was completely unaware of what his son had been up to. So the friendly way he greeted me was encouraging. To me, it meant that he did not support his son and may even have felt embarrassed and was making up for his son's poor judgment and behavior.

To his credit, the congregation's resident racist did not leave in disgust. He regularly attended church for the entire time that I was his pastor and although he rarely shook my hand after the service, he behaved himself. The rest of the congregation had a neutral attitude toward me. Apparently not wanting to make waves one way or the other, they kept me at arm's length. While it is customary for parishioners to invite their new pastor to their home, I never received such an invitation. And although I made it clear that I was available anytime, none ever called for me to care for them in times of need. I learned to accept all of that in the spirit of compassion and forgiveness.

So for all intents and purposes, I treated the Parish church as little more than a preaching station. I always felt relieved to be done with the earlier service so I could be on my way to the other church where I felt at home and warmly treated. In turn, I gave the Hastings congregation more than what my job description called for. I frequently called on parishioners, sometimes making the 30-mile trip during the week to do so. Even Ruby helped out and provided the music at the service when the organist was not available and we gave musical performances during special occasions.

The one activity that I enjoyed most at Hastings was playing softball with the young people. Once spring arrived and the snow and ice had melted, I formed a church team with the assistance of some of the kids' parents. We invited other kids in the area against whom we played every Sunday afternoon. I was completely in my element in the game which I enjoyed playing when was young. I was delighted that I still had some of the skills that I had developed as an infielder in my high school softball team. I impressed the kids with my switch-hitting ability which I had acquired by imitating my hero Mickey Mantle, the switch-hitting New York Yankee great who made his mark in Major League baseball as a player in the 1950's.

Meanwhile, I proceeded with my plan to eventually land a full-time job by upgrading my immigration status to permanent residency, otherwise known by its nickname of green card. I sent my application to the office of the U.S. Immigration and Natural Services at Buffalo, New York. I also sent a similar application to Canada. The latter move was no mere contingency in the event that I failed to obtain a U.S. immigrant visa. Ruby and I had learned a lot about the quality of life in Canada by visiting her cousins who lived in Ontario. Much of what we saw impressed us and we considered moving to Canada a serious option. Moreover, we got a lot of encouragement from Ruby's cousins who eagerly wished for us to join them.

Sometime the following December, I received a couple of surprise Christmas gifts. Within a couple of days of each other came two letters, one each from the U.S. Immigration and Naturalization Service and its Canadian counterpart. Both letters invited me to appear for an interview in response to my applications. I was faced with the enviable position of choosing between two equally attractive options. After discussing the matter with Ruby, I decided to respond to the American invitation. We figured that it would be more realistic to start in America and, if desired, move later to Canada instead of the other way around. Besides, I still had a doctoral program to finish at Syracuse. So I went for my interview in Buffalo which went without a hitch. A couple of months later, I received my much-coveted green card. It took all of six months to get it from the time I turned in my application, a record of sorts. Ruby and the children were carried along and they obtained their own green cards.

I reasoned that the ideal job for me was as professor in my academic field at a college nearby. That way, I could work full-time while continuing my studies at Syracuse. It was a long shot but I thought it was worth pursuing so I started looking for job openings that fit my specifications. Prospective jobs turned up in two places, namely Berkshire Community College and Greenfield Community College. Located in Western Massachusetts, both were close enough to Syracuse so that I could shuttle back and forth while working on my dissertation. Of the two, I preferred Berkshire because it was only three driving hours away while Greenfield was farther away by another hour. Also, the Berkshire area was well-known for its many attractions that drew visitors from all over. The place was a four-season vacation spot with its scenic mountain views and golden leaves in the autumn, first class skiing resorts in the winter and music and theater offerings in the spring and summer.

At the time, I knew nothing about community colleges. I just assumed that they were post-secondary schools that offered two-year associate degrees for those who were not bright or ambitious enough for a bachelor's degree. Only later would I find out how wrong I was. The community college was the best-kept secret in U.S. higher education, offering quality education that oftentimes was superior to that of some of its four-year counterparts. But because of my earlier ignorance, I was planning to use a community college job as a temporary way station until I got my doctorate and then would move up to a more prestigious job at a four-year college or university.

For several months, I did not hear from any of the two colleges in regard to my applications. So I assumed that I did not make it and both jobs were filled. I was about to give up when I decided to try something. I wondered if contacting the two colleges in Massachusetts would amount to anything. At least I thought that by doing so, I was showing my interest in them in case they would open up a position again in the future. It was already the last week in May so classes would have been over at both schools. First, I called Berkshire and I was referred to the acting head of the Division of Humanities who informed me that the position that was advertised was tabled because the head of the Division got sick. I then called Greenfield and talked to Dr. Douglas Webster, Humanities Division head. He informed me that the position had been tabled but there was recent talk of its being revived. He asked me if I was still interested in the position and if so, he would forward my papers, which were sitting in his office, to the office of the Dean of Faculty. I told him that I was interested.

Imagine my surprise when a week later I got a call from Greenfield Community College. The person at the other end was Dr. Jacob Padgug, Dean of Faculty. He told me that the college was interested in me and asked if I would be willing to go there for an interview. I did not hesitate and we scheduled the interview. A few days later, I traveled to Greenfield and met with Dr. Padgug and the two members of the faculty, namely Saul Greenblatt, who taught Speech and George Johnson, who taught Theater and handled theater productions. A week later, I got the wonderful news from Dr. Padgug himself who called me up to say that I was hired.

CHAPTER IX: GREENFIELD PHASE ONE

During my interview, I was told that there was a well-known Filipino doctor living in Greenfield. His name was Jose Peczon, an ophthalmologist. I was eager to meet this new compatriot of mine, figuring that he could help me to familiarize myself with my new home environment. So I obtained his home phone number and as soon as I got back to Syracuse, I called him up and introduced myself. He greeted me warmly and asked me to contact him as soon as I arrived in Greenfield.

A couple of weeks later, I drove to Greenfield and the first thing I did was to contact Dr. Peczon, who invited me to his home for dinner with his family. I met his wife, the former Donna Villaflor and their two young children Walter and Lisa. On that visit, Joe and Donna took me around to visit a few important places in the area.

I found out that Ruby and I had quite a few things in common with the Peczons. Jose, who goes by the nickname of Joe, was a fellow alumnus, a graduate of the College of Medicine of the University of the Philippines. Likewise, Donna was a graduate of the U.P. College of Nursing. She received her pre-Nursing degree from Silliman University before moving to Manila to continue her studies at the Philippine General Hospital. Later, we discovered another bond between our two families. It turned out that while Donna was in Silliman, she and Ruby became dorm mates for a brief time at Oriental Hall. We hit it off together and it was the beginning of a friendship that would last forever.

As I learned more from what I saw and read, I began to fall in love with the place and to reconsider my original plan of making Greenfield just a temporary station on my way to a more prestigious place. The town offered more attractions than I had anticipated. Located in the scenic mountainous Pioneer Valley of Western Massachusetts, it sat at the intersection of Interstate 91 and State Route 2 and was a favorite stopping place for tourists who came to enjoy the area's four-season attractions. Its population of about 18,000 classified it as a small but important town, being the seat of government and commercial center for Franklin County.

Educational opportunities abounded with so many prestigious schools nearby. Just a few miles up north was Northfield Mount Hermon School, a school established by the evangelist Dwight Moody. Down the road to the south was the famous Deerfield Academy. Greenfield Community College, situated in Greenfield, was the only post-secondary institution in Franklin County with a student population above 3,000. GCC enjoyed prestige as a feeder institution for students transferring to any of the nearby colleges in the so-called Five-College Area which included Smith College, Amherst College, Hampshire College, Mt. Holyoke College and the University of Massachusetts. Bright GCC students were known to automatically qualify for transfer admission to schools as far away as Harvard, Yale, Massachusetts Institute of Technology, and Williams College. As for cultural attractions, the town had at least a couple of outstanding ones. Greenfield was the home of the Pioneer Valley Symphony Orchestra, one of the oldest community orchestras in the United States. Numbering about 200 volunteer musicians who came from all over New England, it offered a variety of symphonic and choral music and drew audiences from all over Pioneer Valley and beyond. Arena Civic Theater, founded four years earlier, presented a variety of shows including Broadway musicals.

Sometime in the middle of July, 1974, our family moved to Greenfield. Assisting us in our move were our friends Jim and Dawn Mackay-Schwartz who loaded our belongings in their truck for the five hour trip. Our first home was a rental apartment in the complex called Greenfield Gardens. We had chosen the place for two reasons. One, renting bought us enough time to save enough money to buy a house. Two, it was located just half a mile from the college and I could even walk or ride my bicycle on a good day. That way, Ruby could have free use of our one car to get to work.

Ruby got a temporary job at the library of the University of Massachusetts in Amherst. Not ever having driven a car in her life, she needed to learn quickly. Fortunately, there was time for her to do that. School opening was still a month and a half away so I had the time to bring her to a place where she could pick up a bus to take her to the university. On weekends, I gave her driving lessons. She was able to pass the driving test on her second try so she started driving the 18 miles to work. In the meantime, we kept looking for another job that was closer to home. Early in 1975, a job opened up for her at the Channing L. Bete Publishing, a company located in the center of town, which reduced her travel distance to get to work to less than a mile from the house. Ruby enjoyed that job, which she kept for the next five years.

Part of the attraction of the town was a respectable public school system, a far cry from the often-maligned public schools located in some metropolitan areas. Our eldest, Mirla, was 12 years old and went to the junior high school located on Federal St, one of two main thoroughfares of Greenfield. Our two younger ones – Rowena and Frederick - were ten and seven and went to the nearby elementary school as fourth and second graders, respectively. Transportation was not a problem. While they could ride the school bus, they preferred to walk or ride their bikes to school.

Looking for a nearby UCC congregation as our home church was not a problem. There were three of them, which was highly unusual for a small town like Greenfield. Our problem was choosing the one to worship at. Each had its unique demographic and sociological characteristic. The largest of the three was Second Congregational Church. Located in the center of town at the intersection of Federal and Main streets, it was known as the worshipping place of the town's well-heeled society. Then there was First Congregational Church, which was not only the oldest among the three but was actually the oldest church in town. As is usually the case with most New England towns, the First Congregational Church was established in the same year the town was founded. Originally a congregation consisting of farmers, it eventually became a medium-sized congregation with a diverse membership. Among the three UCC churches, it also had the most modern facilities. Its campus was built in 1964, only 10 years old when we arrived. The third and youngest UCC church was located in the southwestern edge of town. It was the home church for most of the families who lived in the vicinity of a lumber company. In fact, it started out as a congregation of that lumber company's workers in the old days when it was a large furniture factory. For reasons that will be obvious later, we shall call this third church Westwood Church, which is not its actual name. Of the three, we chose First Congregational Church, joined the choir and became members before long.

As time passed, I became more and more convinced that I was going to spend the rest of my professional life, if not my entire life, in Greenfield. Ruby and I and our children felt comfortable having each found our niches in school, at work and in the community. I put to bed my original objective of finishing my doctorate at Syracuse University and focused on settling permanently. One big milestone was acquiring our own property. In 1976, two years after we arrived, we bought an old Victorian style house located on 33 Riddell St. which we got for $25,000. It was the very first house that Ruby and I ever owned, coming fully 15 years after we got married.

I owed my teaching job primarily to Dean Padgug. As Dean of Faculty, he had strongly advocated the addition of a full-time Speech faculty position. He was impelled in part by his own academic

124

background as a former Speech teacher and in part by the requirement of a Speech course in the General Education curriculum as well as some of the terminal vocational degrees at GCC. Before I arrived, Speech courses were taught by one full-time Speech teacher, Saul Greenblatt, and a number of part-timers. My joining the faculty solidified the academic area loosely called Speech and Theater, with Saul and I teaching Speech and George Johnston teaching Theater and directing the school's stage productions. The three of us had adjoining offices in the second floor of the south wing of the GCC building where all the other disciplines in the Division of Humanities were located.

Saul and I taught the two main Speech courses, namely Speech 101 (Oral Communication) and Speech 121 (Small Group Communication). Most students could choose either course to fulfill the Speech requirement of their degree program. The exceptions were those who were preparing to transfer into a four year program where Speech 101 was the preferred course. Every now and then, I would offer a higher Speech course, most frequently Argumentation and Debate. Teaching that last course was a welcome respite and an opportunity to use what I had learned teaching and coaching debate in the Philippines and in Syracuse.

My work at GCC went beyond the confines of the classroom. I got involved in a number of co-curricular activities as an advisor to several student organizations. One activity that I enjoyed was being advisor to the Forensics Club, a job similar to what I had in Syracuse. I formed forensic teams and took them to compete at weekend forensic tournaments hosted by other community colleges. Our favorite place to visit was Dutchess Community College in Poughkeepsie, New York. Part of its attraction was the beautiful scenic view afforded by the Catskills mountain range where the school was located. The place was also a historical area with Hyde Park, New York, the birthplace of Franklin Delano Roosevelt, just down the road.

Another enjoyable co-curricular activity of mine was as advisor to the GCC chapter of Phi Theta Kappa, the international honor society for two-year college students. We loved to attend regional and national Phi Theta Kappa conventions especially because it was through those conventions that we learned how well-known and respected GCC was in community college circles. Oftentimes, when we introduced ourselves to others as representing Greenfield Community College, they would respond by saying, "You mean THE Greenfield Community College?"

In my mind, Greenfield gave me the chance to finally "get the monkey off my back." I already had a full-time job as a college professor and could forget about being a minister, which I never wanted to be in the first place. Besides, the trauma of the Parish Presbyterian Church experience was still fresh in my mind. I was just happy being a layman and keeping a low profile. In fact, I did not join any local or regional group of ministers and did not seek recognition and inclusion as a minister with the Massachusetts Conference of the United Church of Christ.

All that changed in 1976 when a friend of Ruby's named Helen McBride came to visit. Helen was a member of the First Congregational Church of Shelburne Center, located about seven miles to the west along Route 2. They had just lost their minister of several years and they needed someone to serve as interim minister while they searched for a new permanent minister. Helen's husband Don was the head of the Search Committee and having heard about my being a minister, he asked Helen to find out if I would be interested in the job.

I had to think hard on how to respond to the invitation. I did not want to get into another trap like the one in Parish, New York. Also, I wondered whether I could tackle even a part-time ministry on top of my full-time job as GCC professor. There were a lot of positives, though. Unlike the case with the Parish church, I was not being invited by strangers but rather by people who had seen me for quite a while and presumably did some inquiring about my background before seeking me out. Also, after two years at my teaching job and having mastered the whole routine, I felt ready for something new. It was good to know that interim ministry is a short-term commitment that usually takes no more than a year. And then, somehow I had that nagging feeling that I was again being led by some force outside myself as in times past. I decided to give interim ministry a shot and accepted the invitation to serve the Congregational Church of Shelburne Center.

I was there between September 1976 and May, 1977, a period of just eight months. I felt it was too short and wished I could stay a bit longer. That was because at Shelburne Center I met and worked with some very wonderful people. Without exception, they were friendly, well-educated and cultured. Never for a moment did I feel burdened. I developed among them friendships that have lasted a long time. I thought that if interim ministry was going to be like that, I was ready for another one.

Rev. Lorain McLeod, a young graduate of Andover Newton Theological School, was hired as permanent minister. At that time, female ministers were not yet very common and, in fact, this was Shelburne Center's first time to have one. I felt that in a way I paved the way for her. Having had a non-traditional minister type in the

126

person of an Asian male made Shelburne Center ready to receive a female minister.

My next offer came the following year. On March, 1978, Westwood Church asked me to be their interim minister. I had no illusions about what serving that church meant. They had lost their minister under highly unusual circumstances. He had been convicted of rape and subsequently incarcerated. The congregation I was being asked to serve was a community that was badly hurting.

Their minister was hired in 1967 by the church and for ten years, he served them faithfully. Then on September 23, 1977, he was indicted for Rape and Abuse of a Child, the alleged victim being a member of the church's youth group. The technical term for the accusation was "statutory rape," which, by Massachusetts law, is defined as engaging in sex relations with a minor. The trial lasted five months and during that period, both the minister and Westwood Church were in the public eye as details of the trial were widely publicized in the local media. I was being asked to take over a congregation that was demoralized and divided. One group felt angry and betrayed while the other group felt an obligation to support their former pastor.

I decided to accept the offer to be their interim minister mainly out of compassion. As a result of the trial and the ensuing publicity, attendance and financial support had dropped off sharply and the church's survival was seriously in doubt. Some people, including clergy colleagues, doubted my wisdom in accepting the job. In the words of one person, it was a situation that "no one would touch with a ten-foot pole." On the other hand, what the church needed was a pastor for whom money was no object, who had a full-time job and had enough extra time. While there were not many, if any, in the area who matched the above description, I did.

The normal procedure in the United Church of Christ is that once an interim pastor is secured, the church initiates the search process for a permanent minister. The first step in that process is putting together a Pastoral Search Committee. It was obvious to me, however, that the church was not eager to start the process for understandable reasons. So I was not at all surprised when a few weeks into my interim ministry, the Diaconate, which was the body in charge of spiritual matters, asked me to stay on as permanent minister.

I told them that I could not grant their request because of a rule that whoever serves as an interim minister is automatically disqualified from the permanent position. However, I also told them that if they could convince the authorities to make an exception, I would agree to be their permanent minister. Accordingly, the Diaconate submitted my name to the Franklin Association Church and Ministry Committee as their choice for permanent minister. In view of the exceptional circumstances, the Church and Ministry Committee agreed to relax the rule and gave the church their blessings.

For the congregation, the change in my status from interim to permanent was a breakthrough of sorts. It provided them a psychological lift and helped to put the past behind, enabling them to look forward. We were now able to attend to the task of enhancing our worship, fellowship and pastoral care. The congregation started to grow again when some who had been turned away by the bad publicity over the trial returned and new members started to join.

A major reason for my success in the church's recovery was the involvement of the members of my family. After three years as Director of Music of the First Methodist Church of Greenfield, Ruby resigned that job to become volunteer Director of Music at Westwood. With her as choir conductor and Toni Miller as paid organist, the church enjoyed a rare combination of music services that few small churches had. Our three children – Mirla, Rowena, and Freddie – became the core of a revitalized Youth Group. They engaged in a variety of activities both at Westwood and the wider church. The most innovative aspect of the youth program was sending young people to summer church camp with the help of scholarships raised by church members. Conducted through the UCC Massachusetts Conference, the camps exposed the youth to a mix of recreational, religious and artistic activity. New young church leaders emerged from that program and at least one of them was inspired to enter the seminary and become a minister.

In 1980, we became a three-generation family. Papa Roman and Mama Tereza, who had retired, arrived from the Philippines to live with us. Very quickly and seamlessly, both became part of Westwood. After retiring from his job with the provincial government of Davao Province, Papa embarked on a second career as an ordained minister of the United Church of Christ in the Philippines. His biggest achievement during his brief career as minister was establishing a new congregation located in the outskirts of Davao City. Long after he left, that congregation continued to serve the community where it is. At Westwood, Papa helped me out with my pastoral work by conducting devotionals at the local hospital. As for Mama Tereza, she sang in the choir and joined the women's auxiliary group called the Ladies Aid which met weekly.

I had been pastor of Westwood for two and a half years and although I was permanent minister, I still regarded my tenure as an extended interim and was just biding my time before I would consider my work done of getting the church back on its feet. However, everything changed dramatically when the former minister reemerged to once again cause a problem for the church. For purposes of this narrative, we shall call him Ronald Lester, which is not his real name.

After his incarceration in February, 1978, Lester disappeared from the radar screen. However, he was very active all throughout while fighting to overturn his conviction. With the aid of his two lawyers, he filed motion after motion before the Superior Court of Franklin County, which had jurisdiction over his case. Between 1978 and 1980, he filed eight motions altogether, each of which was denied. Finally, he suffered a setback when both of his lawyers withdrew their services.

Lester decided to shift his attention to Westwood Church. Claiming that the church owed him three months' severance pay, he confided his intention to sue the church to some clergymen who had been regularly visiting him in jail. Although the latter tried to dissuade him from going ahead with his suit, he was adamant. On February 14, 1981, he filed suit against the Westwood Church demanding payment of three months' salary and benefits.

Needless to say, the suit did not sit well with the congregation. All it did was to reopen old wounds. Not willing to give Lester any quarter, they decided to fight the suit and engaged Atty. C., a local lawyer, to represent them. That put additional pressure on the church because while they now had to pay for a lawyer's services, Lester, who studied law by reading law books while in jail, was acting as his own lawyer and was in a position to carry on his suit indefinitely without spending a lot of money.

During the ensuing exchange of claims and counterclaims between Lester and our lawyer, I kept my distance. All my attention was focused on helping the congregation cope with the psychological and emotional effects of their new crisis. Inevitably, though, my role expanded and I got drawn into becoming part of the legal defense team.

It happened when Atty. C. sought my help. A key initial step in a legal complaint is a series of interrogatories that the plaintiff and the defendant direct at each other. One of Lester's interrogatories involved the matter of ministerial standing. He asked Westwood to affirm that when he became the church's pastor, the Franklin Association of the UCC, through its Ministerial Standing Committee, backed him up by granting him full ministerial standing. Atty. C. asked me for my help in answering Lester's question. This involved examining the records of the Ministerial Standing Committee, which had since changed its name to the Church and Ministry Committee. Accordingly, I contacted that committee's Scribe who gave me access to the Ministerial Standing Committee's records at the time when Lester became pastor of Westwood.

I found out that the Ministerial Standing Committee did grant to Lester full ministerial standing, which gave Westwood the go-ahead to have him installed as its pastor. However, in the discussions that had taken place at the committee, questions were raised over his ministerial credentials. My curiosity aroused, I decided to look deeper by conferring with the minister who was chairman of the Ministerial Standing Committee when Lester became pastor at Westwood. He told me that he was the one who had raised questions regarding Lester's ministerial credentials. He advised me to do further research by looking at Lester's background.

It appeared that Lester started his career in the late 1950's with the Maine Conference of the Methodist Church. The Franklin Association's decision to grant him full ministerial standing was based on his claim that the Methodist Church ordained him in 1958 while he was serving a church in Maine. I therefore needed to find out whether he really was ordained by the Methodist Church as he claimed and whether such ordination was sufficient to earn his ministerial standing with the United Church of Christ. I contacted the office of the Maine Conference of the Methodist Church and got full cooperation from Bishop George B. and Communications Officer Ellen C.

Through my telephone conversations and exchanges of letters with Bishop B. and Ms. C. and by reading the Book of Discipline of the Methodist Church, I found out that they have two kinds of ordination, namely Local Elder and Conference Elder. Local Elder ordination is granted to a layman who serves a Methodist congregation. It is a temporary ordination in that upon leaving that church, the Local Elder loses the ordination and is reverted to layman status. Conference Elder ordination is permanent; one who receives it is accorded the title of Reverend and can go from church to church, retaining full ordination status. For this reason, Conference Elders are referred to as traveling preachers. It is also the kind of credentials that enables them to be accepted as ministers by other denominations. To attain Conference Elder status, one must undergo a trial period which requires formal study for the ministry and maintenance of a high level of ethical behavior while undergoing trial.

The records of the Maine Conference of the Methodist church showed that Lester was placed on trial in 1960 but failed to attain Conference Elder status. In 1963, he asked for discontinuance of his ordination process and it was granted. Subsequently, his name was dropped from the Conference annual reports listing individuals on trial. I inquired from different authorities of the Methodist Church on what this meant and I was told in no uncertain terms that Lester had no ministerial standing when he left the Methodist Conference. Therefore, he had no right to claim that he was an ordained minister upon transferring to the United Church of Christ.

Did Lester willfully deceive the Ministerial Standing Committee by presenting his 1958 Local Elder ordination as his credentials for seeking ministerial standing in the Franklin Association? It was hard not to believe that he was fully aware that his Local Elder ordination was rendered invalid when his ordination process with the Methodist Conference was discontinued at his request. The clearest statement on this subject came from Bishop B. In a letter to me dated June 24, 1981, he stated that "... at the time of his acceptance into the United Church of Christ denomination, Lester had no standing in terms of orders." Further, in a letter Bishop B. sent on the same day to the Franklin Association Church and Ministry Committee chairman, he indirectly chided the UCC, stating that it was "... difficult (for him) to understand how (Lester's) orders were recognized in another denomination."

The stage was now set for the escalation of the conflict between Westwood Church and Ronald Lester. The revelations on the spuriousness of Lester's credentials strengthened our hand. After discussing the matter with our lawyer and the Diaconate, we devised a two-point strategy. The first was a counterclaim directed at Ronald Lester alleging that he misrepresented himself by claiming that he was an ordained minister in order to gain ministerial standing with the UCC. The second was a petition to the Franklin Association to terminate his ministerial standing immediately, based on new information. Atty. C. was going to prepare the counterclaim while the Diaconate was going to make the petition. I was going to be the resource person for both parties.

From being a passive observer at the start, I was now neck-deep in the fight against Lester. In fact, I was now leading the effort, motivated by a genuine commitment to truth. I spent hours preparing legal briefs and position papers to be used by the lawyer, the Diaconate, and the Church and Ministry Committee. Admittedly, however, I was spurred by intense resentment. Having spent the better part of three years revitalizing the congregation, it seemed that my efforts were about to be wasted.

In the meantime, I had some personal matters to face. I was observing the 10th anniversary of my own ordination into the ministry. It was ironic that just as I reached that landmark period in my career as a minister, I was also facing its biggest challenge ever. Moments like these in the past always brought about a welter of feelings that ranged widely from joy to doubt and depression. This time was no exception. In the spirit of Robert Frost's "The Road Not Taken," I would often wonder what could have been had my mother not encountered difficulty at pregnancy and childbirth, prompting her to bargain with God to let me live if she promised that I would be dedicated to the ministry.

It was my custom to indulge in nostalgia whenever the third week of June came around. I liked to gather the artifacts that would remind me of what transpired at my ordination. Among them were photos, newspaper clippings and my certificate of ordination. One artifact that I treasured most was the Bible that was presented to me. Over the years, I had used it so much that by this time, its cover needed replacing. But inside, it was intact. I loved to look at the dedication page which reads as follows: "Presented to Federico I. Agnir by the Southern Mindanao District Conference." It was dated June 21, 1971 and was signed by Jerry Aniñon, moderator; Perfecto Yasay, Sr., assistant moderator; Daniel Nebres, Calixto Sodoy and Crispin Faune. They were the same ministers who laid their hands on me at the ordination ceremony.

As I leisurely leafed through the Bible's pages, my fingers stopped at the first chapter of the book of Jeremiah. My attention was directed to the 4th and 5th verses of that chapter which read as follows: "Then the word of the Lord came unto me saying, Before I formed thee in the belly I knew thee; and before thou camest forth out of the womb I sanctified thee, and I ordained thee a prophet to the nations."

The passage hit me like a ton of bricks. I distinctly remember that its impact was so powerful that I began to shake uncontrollably. Like Jeremiah, I felt that God was speaking to me through that passage. The first part of that passage had a powerful enough impact. I wondered whether all those years I was running in the wrong direction. In my effort to escape from my mother's grip over my life, it never occurred to me that perhaps it was not my mother after all who chose me to become a minister. But if that first part of the passage legitimized my entering the ministry, the second part made it even more compelling. "A prophet unto the nations!" A minister to <u>all</u> people! I realized there and then that in all those previous years, the god I had been worshipping was a small god - a god that graced the family hearth, a god that I called upon for convenience, a god that I called upon to do my bidding. It was time to leave that small god and follow the God of all - the God of Abraham, Isaac and Jacob and Jesus and Paul and Filipinos and Americans. After ten years of searching and waiting, I finally found the real reason why I was a minister. That dramatic episode was my own religious conversion.

The day after my conversion, I wrote a letter of reconciliation to my mother. For a long time, we had not been talking to each other. Much of the reason for our lack of communication was my continuing resentment over her act of dedicating me into the ministry without my consent. My letter to her read In part: "I absolve you of all guilt. You did not choose me; you were merely the instrument for my call. From now on, I will stop fighting and just let God take over my life."

Just as it did for me, my conversion liberated my mother. In response to my letter of reconciliation, she wrote back to say how deeply touched she was by my words. It was just what she needed because she was having serious health problems. The year before, she had surgery that led to complications which nearly took her life. She never completely recovered and in 1983, she died. I was so grateful that she and I obtained closure before she was summoned to meet her Maker.

One other milestone in our family life occurred at that time. The size of our household started to shrink. In May, 1981, our oldest child graduated from Greenfield High School. She had spent the better part of her senior year doing research on colleges, eventually narrowing her choices down to several that were located in the Midwest. She finally decided on Oberlin College, a small private liberal arts college located in Oberlin, Ohio, a suburb of Cleveland. The college has several claims to historical significance, including first college to admit African-American students, and oldest continuously coeducational institution of higher learning. From the very beginning when it was founded by a couple of Presbyterian missionaries in 1833, Oberlin became associated with progressive causes. The town was known as a hotbed of the abolitionist movement and was a key stop along the Underground Railroad that provided a safe passage for slaves fleeing from the South. In addition to the above, Mirla was attracted to the school's reputable undergraduate degree program in Dance and Theater.

Not until Mirla got to Oberlin did we fully realize the impact on us of the so-called empty nest syndrome. In August, 1981, Ruby and I drove with her to the college for the usual registration and orientation. We helped her move into her new quarters at the dormitory. As we said goodbye to our daughter, I noticed that Ruby was unusually quiet, apparently having mixed feelings about what was going on. We started to drive back home and just as we turned the corner, Ruby completely went to pieces. I had to stop the car so she could give herself a good cry and waited till she could compose herself before we could go on our way.

As for my ministry at Westwood, a new phase opened. Although I was still technically a part-time minister, I wanted to make myself more accessible to my parishioners. I thought that the best way to do so would be to move into the parsonage. Following his conviction and incarceration, Lester and his family had vacated the parsonage and when I took over the church, the parsonage was rented out to a married couple who paid their rent by providing services to the church, he as custodian and she as my secretary.

We sold our house on Riddell Street and moved into the parsonage. Although the parsonage was smaller than the house we left behind, we had ample living room. Our second daughter Rowena, who was a few months short of 18 years old and soon to graduate from high school herself, decided that it was time for her to be on her own. It so happened that the family that bought our house had a daughter who was Rowena's friend so she asked if she could rent a room at their home. Our new household at the Westwood parsonage consisted of Ruby and me, Papa and Mama Ordinario and our youngest child Freddie who was a high school freshman.

By moving to the parsonage, we displaced the couple that had been living there. This angered the man's parents who were longtime members of the church and subsequently they left the church. But it was a small price to pay considering the benefits to my ministry. As a resident in the church premises, I was now practically a full-time minister. The place's physical layout was ideal. The parsonage and the church were only about 30 yards apart and were connected by a sheltered breezeway. Thus, I could leave my house at any hour of the day in any kind of weather and be in my office after a few seconds.

On my first week there, I caused a stir in the neighborhood. I had developed a habit of starting my day waking up very early and getting to my office sometimes as early as four o'clock in the morning. At that hour, I could be very productive because my mind was fresh and I was not being interrupted by phone calls and other distractions. However, I neglected to tell my neighbors about my work habits. So one early morning on that first week, a policeman came knocking on the door of my office. Neighbors who saw that the lights were on were afraid that the church was being burglarized and they called the police.

Our move to the parsonage was also good for Ruby. Channing L. Bete had moved to its new location in South Deerfield, a town eight miles from Greenfield. Not wanting to make the 16-mile round trip every day to get to work, she left Channing L. Bete and got a job at the Phoenix Mutual Insurance Company whose offices were down the street a short walk from the church.

I had become a new minister and a new man in one other way. As a result of my conversion experience, my spiritual life deepened. I spent more time in prayer and devotion. I needed divine guidance as I searched for new directions in my ministry. For one thing, I began to question whether I was doing the right thing in being a party to the escalation of the conflict between the church and Lester. The answer I had been looking for came to me during one of my daily prayers. I thought I heard a voice from God reminding me that my task as a minister was not to take sides in a conflict but rather to be an agent of reconciliation.

Lester and I were never close and I had not seen nor spoken to him since he was incarcerated. But I wanted to reach out to him so I went to the prison where he was held and asked to see him. Luckily, he welcomed me and we sat down together for a heart-to-heart talk. I leveled with him by revealing what I found out about his ministerial standing with the Methodist Church. He immediately got defensive and questioned my motive in visiting him. I assured him that I had good intentions. I promised not to make an issue of his ministerial standing if he would drop his suit against the church. And to sweeten the pot, I suggested that we could celebrate with a Service of Reconciliation.

I was improvising and did not even have an idea what shape or form a Service of Reconciliation would take. But I had a feeling that the concept of reconciliation would strike a responsive chord with Lester. I knew that he brought suit on the church not just for the money but to exact revenge on the church. But I also knew that he had a deeper longing to clear his name and to feel respected and loved like he was before.

He asked for time to think my proposal over and promised to get back to me. A couple of weeks later, he called me and asked to get together. He agreed to drop his suit against the church. In return, he asked that the church accept the resignation that he had submitted way back which the church failed to act on and to apologize for not responding to his follow-up letters. He also agreed to my proposal to have the Service of Reconciliation and asked to have a part in putting the service together. At his request, I agreed to a reception after the service provided he did not expect a lot of people to attend.

135

With the assistance of the lawyer, we drew up a document with the details of the agreement and presented it to Lester who approved it. The next step was to sell the whole package to the congregation. A meeting of the congregation was held on August 13, 1981,for the purpose of acting on the proposed agreement. The meeting was well-attended by church members. Also present as observers were local pastors Rev. Ron Evans and Rev. Henry Bartlett and Massachusetts UCC Western Area Minister Rev. Donald Overlock. As I expected, the part that met the most intense discussion and opposition was the proposal for a Service of Reconciliation. Quite a few had not forgiven Lester for what had happened and could not stand facing him again. The most vocal opponent was a man whose father was one of the founders and the first minister of the church. He stood up and in an angry voice said, "How dare that man step inside the church!" When I stood up to speak in behalf of the agreement, I felt the weight of the church's future and that of my ministerial career resting on my shoulders. After arguing for the need and advantage of letting bygones be bygones, I concluded by saying, "Ronald Lester was your minister for eleven years. The time has come for you to be a minister to him." The silence that followed my remarks was deafening. After what seemed like an eternity, someone stood up and said, "All right, we will have your Service of Reconciliation. But let it be clear that we are doing it for you and not for him. And don't expect us to show up for that reception." The congregation then voted to approve the proposed agreement.

The day after the meeting, both parties moved to fulfill their part in the agreement. The church through its various officers sent a couple of letters to Lester. One informed him of the church's belated acceptance of his letter of resignation while another acknowledged its error in and apologized for not responding to his various follow-up letters. In turn, a motion to dismiss Lester's suit was filed in the Hampshire Superior Court. It was signed by Lester as plaintiff and Atty. C. representing the church as defendant.

Although it had been agreed that the Service of Reconciliation would take place shortly after the two parties had approved the terms of the agreement, it took more than a year before the service could be held. Lester had asked several times to delay the service. The reason for his foot-dragging was that he wanted to come to the service as a free man. So he filed a petition for early parole and waited and waited for a response. Meanwhile, the members of the congregation had mixed feelings about the delay. On one hand, they felt that they had already done their part and were even half-wishing that Lester would just forget the whole thing. On the other hand, they did not like being kept hanging. They decided to take the bull by the horns by giving Lester an ultimatum. Pointing out that the meaning of the phrase "shortly after" had already been stretched to the breaking point, the church set October 3, 1982, as the final date for the service and told Lester that it would be held with or without him. He had no other choice but to comply even though he failed to obtain the early parole that he asked for.

Through a series of meetings, Lester and I agreed on the format of the worship service, who was going to participate and whom to invite. In order to preserve the spiritual nature of the service and to keep it from being perceived as a mere public relations ploy, we agreed not to publicize it and to invite only the members of the congregation, Lester's family, and a handful of clergymen, two of whom were going to participate in the service. The most important feature of the service was going to be a "Litany of Reconciliation and Consecration of Separation" in which Lester and the church moderator would exchange words of confession, forgiveness and blessing. For that part of the service, I wrote a script in which the two would say essentially the same words.

On the afternoon of October 3, 1982, Lester arrived at Westwood Church accompanied by a couple of guards from the Hampshire County jail. With him was his wife whose presence was a pleasant surprise because earlier she had made it clear to friends that she was not going to be attending. We had no way of knowing how many from the congregation were going to show up. Days before, a rumor went around that a mere handful of people from the congregation were going to come to do their legal obligation and that as soon as the service was over, they were going to step out quietly and not go to the reception. To our surprise, 85 people filled the church, 75 from the congregation.

The service went on without a hitch. Among its features were an anthem by the choir, a vocal solo by Ruby and a sermon by Rev. Henry Bartlett. I gave the communion meditation and officiated at the Sacrament of the Lord's Supper together with Rev. Don Fonda, a Baptist minister who had been providing pastoral care for Lester in jail. As expected, the Litany of Reconciliation and Consecration of Separation was as touching and heart-tugging as could be especially for Lester who was visibly shaken as he spoke his part.

I had discreetly planned for the worship leaders to exit by the side door so that those who did not want to shake Lester's hand did not have to. After sitting through the service, everyone who had entertained any doubts completely turned around. I expected a dozen people at the reception but everyone came down to the Fellowship Hall where it was held. There was so much hugging and crying that momentarily I wondered if I was really in a New England church. The miracle that we had fervently prayed for happened. As I reported to Rev. Overlock a few days later, in one hour we all grew up theologically by ten years.

Four years and seven months had passed since Westwood called me to be their minister. For me and the congregation, it was a long and rough ride with a happy ending. I had stated to them that no matter what happened, I was going to stay as minister for only seven years. So with just more than two years to go, I started to prepare for that moment.

One consideration in our planning was that our family was growing again. In October, 1983, our daughter Rowena got married to Steven Curtiss, her high school sweetheart. The wedding ceremony was held in the lawn of the Westwood parsonage with family and friends in attendance and Rev. Arthur Sweeney, our former pastor at First Congregational Church, officiating. On May 5, 1984, Rowena gave birth to a son whom they named Steven Frederick. Ruby and I became a couple of young happy grandparents; I was 45 and Ruby was 44.

We bought a house located on 55 Cleveland St. It was a large two-story Victorian architecture home with an addition at the back where the former owner had run a beauty salon. Ruby fell in love with the addition, which she decided to use as a music studio. After we moved into the house in the Fall of 1984, Ruby quit her job at Phoenix and started taking in students in piano and voice. Our move to a larger house was a Godsend for another reason. Rowena's marriage lasted less than two years. She and Steve separated and Rowena and little Stevie moved in with us. We were now a four-generation household. One chapter in our family life was ending and a new one was beginning.

CHAPTER X: GREENFIELD PHASE TWO

Friends and colleagues often asked me how I managed to work at two full-time jobs as college professor and pastor. They assumed that both my jobs were equally demanding even though I was technically a part-time pastor. Some even suspected that I was taking time off my work at the college so I could devote enough time to my pastoral duties. I had a number of possible answers to the question. One was that it helped that I lived just a mile from the college so I could easily shuttle between the two places. Another was that my teaching schedule was ideal. I took the classes that met early in the morning, sometimes as early as 7:00 o'clock, which nobody else wanted. So by noontime, I was all done teaching, meeting my student advisees and performing other co-curricular tasks. However, my best and favorite answer to people who popped the question was: "I have a slave at home."

My "slave at home" was an inanimate object called a microcomputer. In the first chapter of this book, I narrated how I discovered the meaning of the saying "Knowledge is Power" when I learned how to type at the age of ten and got ahead of all my classmates. I resolved then that whenever a new productivity tool comes around, I would be at the head of the line in learning how to use it. Thus when the microcomputer came along, I instantly fell in love with it.

I started learning to use the personal computer by spending many hours in the GCC computer laboratory. Stocked with about 20 Apple II's, the lab was intended for use by students majoring in Computer Science. Members of the faculty and staff were encouraged to use the facility but very few of them took up the challenge. It took quite a while for them to appreciate the personal computer's value. Doubtless, fear of the new and unknown was a big factor behind their hesitation.

Before long, I became quite good with the personal computer. I started writing some simple programs in the Basic Language and using the Apple's office applications, chiefly Word processing and database management. Using the computer at both my jobs enabled me to save a lot of time without loss of productivity.

I decided to share my new-found knowledge with my colleagues. In 1982, I ran a one-day computer workshop for church workers at the lab. I advertised the workshop to churches of all denominations and got a strong response from fellow pastors and priests in the area who filled the lab. They were thrilled to learn how they could save a lot of time by using the computer in preparing their sermons, church bulletins and newsletters, and in keeping track of their parishioners. For me, it was the beginning of a new career as a computer consultant.

The next step was to acquire my own home computer. At that time, the price for a complete system consisting of a computer, peripherals and standard programs ranged from $3,000 to $4,000. I was hesitant to spend all that money on a new system. Given the pace by which the technology was changing, I was afraid that it would not take long for my system to get outdated. I wanted a less expensive option that would still give me enough computing power for my purpose. I was even willing to get a used computer for a start.

That's when I got a marvelous break that opened new doors that I never expected. I was visiting a friend who was the computer person for a local finishing school. A year before, he had bought for the school a personal computer called Compucolor II. Apparently, he ran into all kinds of problems with it and repeated calls to the manufacturer got him nowhere. Finally the computer stopped functioning and would not even turn on. At the time I visited him, the computer was sitting in the school's storage room. I asked if he would sell me the system. I figured that if the price was right, I could take a chance on having it fixed. After consulting the school headmaster, he let me take the computer and all the disks that came with it for $100.

GCC had a talented handyman named Perry Cole who seemed capable of fixing anything. He had helped me before when I had problems with various types of equipment. I brought the computer to him the next day asking him to find out what was wrong with it, making sure to tell him that if it was fixable, he should first let me know how much it would cost before doing anything. A few days later, I visited Perry to see what he found out. To my surprise, he had gone ahead and fixed it figuring that I would not object since all it needed was a small part costing only 50 cents.

I found out that the Compucolor was made by Intelligent Systems Corporation in Norcross, Georgia. The company had earned its reputation by developing software for the military. The Compucolor was its attempt at getting into the fast-growing microcomputer industry. Intended to compete against the leading personal computer brands at the time, such as the Apple II, the TRS-80 and the Commodore PET, it offered such attractive features as color graphics, a compact package that housed an 8080 microprocessor and an internal disk drive, its own operating system, and a built-in Basic programming language.

Unfortunately, the Compucolor, with all its fine features, was never well promoted and failed to capture a significant share of the personal computer market. As sales lagged, technical support became spotty and unreliable. Soon, the company stopped producing it. Only about 2000 units had been made, most of them sold abroad to Australia, Italy and Canada. The Compucolor was the epitome of a great unfulfilled promise. Years later, when the IBM Personal Computer and its various clones had assumed their place at the top of the personal computer field, a top-ranking IBM executive was asked what he considered the best personal computer before the IBM Personal Computer. His straight answer was: the Compucolor.

What kept the Compucolor alive was a group of hobbyists who wrote applications and shared their creations among themselves. I was fortunate to have been able to contact two hobbyist user groups, one in Toronto, Canada and another in Huntsville, Alabama. From them I obtained free application programs that they had written, the two most useful of which were a word processor and a database management program, both of which I used extensively in both church and school.

About that time, Intelligent Systems Corporation was trying to unload its inventory of unsold Compucolors and was offering them at bargain prices. Word came to administrators at GCC and the School of Education at the University of Massachusetts about 40 Compucolors that were being offered at $400 apiece, one-fifth of the regular price. The two institutions decided to take advantage of the offer, with the School of Education taking 15 units and GCC taking the other 25.

The computer had a flaw that Intelligent Systems Corporation neglected to tell its buyers. The batch that GCC and UMass got was a model with a temperamental external disk drive. GCC installed its 25 Compucolors in the Business Division for use by their students. Not long after, the computers stopped working and the school decided to discard them all. They all wound up in the school's junk room waiting for the recycling truck.

It appeared that the problem was an erratic disk drive speed regulator. I wrote to my hobbyist friends and was told that they had encountered the same problem but had come up with a solution. They created a program that could monitor the disk drive's speed with a display on the computer screen. So whenever the screen showed the speed going out of range, it could be restored to its proper setting by turning the screw that controls the speed with a screwdriver. I asked my hobbyist friends for a copy of their program and they gladly gave it without charging me a cent. Perry and I tried it out on one of GCC's

Compucolors and, much to our delight, it worked. He also came up with an easy and efficient way to do the procedure. Instead of exposing the drive's innards when removing the disk drive's case for access to the adjusting screw, he simply cut out a hole on the case directly above the screw and put a cap on it.

Suddenly, all of GCC's 25 Compucolors became operational and were free for the taking by anyone interested. Faculty and staff from the various academic departments competed to get hold of a unit. Perry and I became their resource team. While he installed and maintained their computers, I provided copies of application programs that I obtained from my friends and taught everyone how to use them.

Understandably, most of those who rushed to acquire the computers came from my own Humanities Division. A free computer installed on one's desk plus free instruction on its use from a colleague close by was just impossible to resist. One area which benefitted most from the sudden computer windfall was the office of the Humanities Division. The division secretary's use of a super productivity tool became the envy of the other academic divisions.

In the meantime, an opportunity to develop a new course came up. I proposed setting up a special section of Basic English Composition for computer-literate students which I would teach. The school administration approved my proposal and equipped one classroom with Apple II computers. Students lined up to sign up so that filling up the class was never a problem.

As a result of my pioneering efforts, the school honored me with a special citation. Awarded by the GCC Board of Trustees, the citation read as follows: "Presented to Federico I. Agnir in sincere appreciation of your valued contribution in promoting interest in computers in the Humanities Division."

More doors of opportunity opened for me. The UMass School of Education started an innovative postgraduate program designed for community college faculty. To make the program more attractive, some courses would be taught at the students' campus if there were enough enrollees to fill a class. More than a dozen of us from GCC enrolled in the program so a lot of the beginning courses were taught by School of Education faculty who traveled to GCC for the classes which were usually held in the afternoon.

The program was an open-ended course of study which allowed participants to decide how far to go with it. Most were in it just for the exposure. Some planned to go all the way to a doctorate while others were looking to possibly obtain a Certificate of Advanced Graduate Studies (C.A.G.S) or a second Masters degree. After a year of

142

basic courses on community college education, the group that met for classes at GCC dispersed and those of us pursuing an advanced degree continued our studies at the university's Amherst campus. Each of us chose a department according to one's area of specialization. From the outset, I had decided that my dissertation was going to touch on the impact of computers on community college teaching. I enrolled in the Doctor of Education program under the aegis of the Department of Instructional Leadership of the School of Education. I chose that department mainly because it offered a number of courses in Future Studies, which tied in well with my intended dissertation subject.

Fortunately, I was able to shorten the time it took to complete my course work. It helped that I was able to transfer some of the graduate credits that I earned at Syracuse University, the most important of which were those on statistics and research methodology. I was going to need what I learned from those courses when it came time to work on my dissertation.

With the aid of my dissertation advisor, Dr. Howard Peelle, I chose as my subject the attitudes toward the computer among community college teachers. Toward that end I planned to conduct a survey among the faculty members of three community colleges in Massachusetts, namely Greenfield Community College, Mt. Wachusett Community College and Berkshire Community College. I chose those three because they were all rural, close together and shared a lot of common characteristics.

For the survey, I devised a 21-item questionnaire that measured attitudes on seven issues related to computers. The issues were: computers' impact on the quality of life, computers' impact on one's employment, computer errors vs. human errors, computers and depersonalization, human control over computers, computers and the improvement of education, and computers' invasion of privacy.

In deciding on how to administer the survey, I avoided the mailed questionnaire method because of its notoriously low average response rate. I thought of administering the questionnaire at faculty meetings but, for a variety of reasons, the administrators of the three colleges advised against it. I settled for person-to-person administration whereby an interviewer would sit down with each faculty member and obtain from the latter answers to each of the 21 questions. This method guaranteed a 100% response rate. I hired at every school student interviewers whom I paid $3.00 per interview. Fortunately, GCC funded my project, hoping that my findings would be of value to the school's faculty development program.

143

I received 159 valid responses which I proceeded to code and input into the university's mainframe computer. Luckily, I had remote access to the computer from home so I was able to do the data analysis at all hours of the day without having to travel to the Amherst campus. It also helped that I knew how to use the SPSS (Statistical Package for the Social Sciences) language which I learned at Syracuse. And I had a spreadsheet program called Lotus 123 which could create graphs as visual illustrations of my data. Thus I was able to accomplish in a few days what otherwise would have taken me several weeks.

I was still far from finishing. A lot of researching and writing was still needed before I could present the product to my dissertation committee. I decided to put the project aside for the time being to attend to other business.

It was the spring of 1985. I was retiring from Westwood Church after seven years at the helm. Although some of the leaders expressed regret at my leaving, they understood my reasons. The demoralized and divided church that I had taken over was now healthy and it was time for me to go so that they could be led by somebody else, hopefully by a full-time minister. We set ourselves to the task of preparing for my departure.

My last Sunday at Westwood was memorable. A touching moment was when the church moderator read aloud my resignation letter as part of the worship service. As he read it, he was visibly moved and was actually sniffling between sentences. I understood how he felt because his whole family of three generations and I had become very close. His three children were all active in the Youth Group. In fact, when I told his mother that I was leaving, she wept. Another unforgettable episode was a surprise practical joke that the congregation played on me. Some weeks before, I had related to the congregation my story about a past parishioner who had explained to me why he always brought to church dark glasses which he kept in his pocket. He told me that whenever the sermon got boring, he would put on the dark glasses so that the pastor could not tell that he was sleeping. Apparently the Westwood congregation clearly remembered that story. As I started my sermon, somebody coughed. It turned out to be a prearranged signal and the next instant everybody including members of my family were wearing dark glasses.

I became active with the Massachusetts Conference of the United Church of Christ. The word had reached them about my work with computers and I was asked to run a couple of activities at the conference headquarters in Framingham. One was a week-long computer camp for young people. The other was a one-day workshop for church secretaries and treasurers. Both were to take place one after the other in the summer of 1985. For both events, Digital Equipment Corporation generously donated the use of 20 minicomputers.

Neither type of activity was new to me. Two years before, several UMass School of Education classmates and I conducted a month-long computer workshop for children in San Antonio, Texas. And in 1982, as I related earlier in this chapter, I ran a workshop for local pastors and priests at GCC.

The computer camp was part of the conference's annual summer church camp program and was widely advertised, drawing 20 young people from the various UCC churches in Massachusetts. As with the other summer church camps, the week's activities were a mixture of teaching, recreation, fellowship and worship. I enjoyed working with the young campers who were all bright, energetic and eager learners.

The workshop for church secretaries and treasurers was something else. Virtually all the attendees were from small churches. A lot of them were older women and some had never handled a computer in their life. From the outset, I could tell from their body language that quite a few were anxious. My eyes caught the attention of one septuagenarian church secretary who seemed to be more anxious than everybody else. Suddenly, she stood straight up and screamed, "I can't stand this anymore." Whereupon she bolted out of the room, ran straight to her car and drove away.

I learned something from that experience. When teaching a class in something as new as computers, you need to consider the age of your students as well as the disparity in their background knowledge. The larger the class size, the more chances of a wide disparity. From that day on, I stopped teaching computers to groups larger than a handful.

To put a popular saying in a politically correct way, all work and no play makes for a dull life. From the outset, Ruby and I sought a good balance between our professional and social lives. Greenfield's rich and varied cultural environment gave us a lot of options for community activities that we could engage in together. Music is the one area which we have always enjoyed doing. So we grabbed every opportunity to perform as soloists or as part of a choral group.

One of the most popular musical events in town was an annual fundraiser called "The Follies," a project of the local hospital's Women's Junior Auxiliary Board. The event was appropriately named because it was an opportunity for young and old, particularly the latter, to let it all hang out in an evening of musical fun. A professional who specialized in that kind of activity was engaged to put the program together. He was a traveling impresario who was hired by other towns all over to do the same thing. He ran the same show wherever he went so he was able to put together in a couple of weeks what would otherwise have taken months for a local group starting from scratch. Ruby, Mirla, Rowena and I auditioned for the show and were taken. Two of them sang a duet while I did a song made popular by Maurice Chevalier entitled "Beautiful Girls" together with half a dozen women who surrounded me and swayed in rhythm while I sang. For us, the best part of the evening was making new friends and being introduced to the town's musical community.

A more serious musical activity was singing with the Pioneer Valley Symphony. Founded in 1939, PVS is one of the oldest community orchestras in the United States. Numbering about 200 volunteer musicians who come from all over New England, it offers a variety of symphonic and choral music and draws audiences from all over Pioneer Valley and beyond. Ruby and I sang in several of their choral presentations featuring works by classical masters like Mozart, Hayden and Bach. Held in the spacious auditorium of Greenfield High School, every performance was packed by admiring audiences that came from everywhere.

Community Theater was another activity that Ruby and I loved to do. Arena Civic Theater, founded in 1970, presented a variety of shows including Broadway musicals. At the time we arrived, ACT productions were staged in the cramped quarters of the Franklin County Fairgrounds Roundhouse, making for a study in creative genius in the use of space. In the years that followed, ACT attracted theatrical talent from all over and inspired the emergence of other community theater companies in the area, making Franklin County a community theater capital of sorts.

I got on stage for the first time in Greenfield when Saul Greenblatt asked me to take over his part in an ACT play entitled "The Pleasure of His Company." Written for Broadway in 1958 and made into a 1961 film starring Fred Astaire, Lilli Palmer and Debbie Reynolds, the play revolved around a man named Pogo who shows up to attend his daughter Jessica's wedding and winds up trying to charm and seduce everybody including his own daughter and his former wife, to everybody's consternation. My role was that of the family's Chinese houseboy named Toy.

One scene in the play involved a conversation between Toy, Pogo and Jessica, with all of them speaking Chinese. The play's script did not carry any Chinese words and just assumed that the actors were

146

going to provide their own. None of us three knew any Chinese so Director Ann Christern, who also happened to be the ACT founder, told us to go and obtain our own Chinese words. I went to a Chinese restaurant, copied the names of some of the dishes, strung them all together, threw in a few Chinese names, and I had for myself Toy's lines. We never revealed where we each got our lines, but in our rehearsals we sounded quite authentic.

The play opens with Toy all alone on stage, muttering to himself in broken English as he putters around the room. So on Opening Night, the curtains opened and there I was in front of the audience of about 100 that packed the Roundhouse. Because of the cramped space, the audience was only a few feet away from me and I could make out everybody's face even though the lights were slightly dimmed. To my utter horror, I saw seated in the front row a couple of Chinese-looking young men. As our trio went into our Chinese conversation, I glanced at the two when my turn came to speak. The shock registered on their faces was indescribable. After the play, I hurriedly sneaked out instead of staying for the usual chat backstage between the players and the audience.

Ruby's Greenfield stage debut was as a lounge pianist in a play entitled "The House of Blue Leaves." This was followed by ACT's presentation in 1982 of Rodgers and Hammerstein's musical "Oklahoma" in which she had a singing part in a dance sequence as one of the Dream Girls. Her big splash into local theater was as Bloody Mary in ACT's 1984 presentation of Rodgers and Hammerstein's "South Pacific." Her performance was lauded in reviews at local papers, one of which called her "an authentic Bloody Mary." Inspired by the enthusiastic way she was received and a chance to practice a skill that she had studied and trained for, she went on nine years later to establish a company theater company called Green Room Players. The 25 plays that she directed with that company over a period of ten years earned for her a reviewer's plaudits who called her "the quintessential musical theater maven."

We also got involved in Masonic activities. It was Ruby who took the lead, which was ironic because in the Philippines I was the one who was active with Masonry where I became Master Councilor of the Jose Abad Santos Chapter of the Order of DeMolay. Many DeMolays usually wind up joining a lodge of Master Masons once they become senior DeMolays. However, I did not immediately join a Masonic lodge when we got to the United States. I either lost interest or was too busy or both.

One day our next door neighbor who was a member of Arcana #50, the local chapter of the Order of the Eastern Star, invited Ruby to a meeting. Ruby was impressed by everything she saw, especially the friendliness of the chapter's members. Before long she had joined the chapter. Soon after, more members of our family got involved. Papa Roman and Mama Tereza, who were longtime members of the OES in the Philippines, arrived to live with us and were thrilled to know that their daughter had become their OES sister. In turn, our two daughters became members of the Order of the Rainbow for Girls. Ruby quickly rose to Arcana's highest leadership position as Worthy Matron. It is customary for a Worthy Matron to pick as her male counterpart a family member who is also a Mason. Usually, it's the husband but since I was not yet a Mason, she picked Papa to be the chapter's Worthy Patron.

I was the last member of the family to join. In September, 1986, I was initiated into Greenfield's Republican Lodge of Free and Accepted Masons. That qualified me to join the Order of Eastern Star, which I did the following month. At that time, Ruby was serving as Associate Matron, the second highest position in the chapter. Three months later, she was installed as Worthy Matron and, naturally, she had picked me as her Worthy Patron. My rise from Masonic lodge membership to the highest male leadership position in an OES chapter took four months, a record of sorts. Something even more unusual happened later. Ruby was asked to be Installing Officer for the next set of chapter officers and I to be Installing Patron. For a new kid on the block, it was an honor usually reserved for a longtime chapter member or a visiting dignitary.

As the heads of our chapter, we were encouraged to visit other chapters all over Massachusetts, something we enjoyed doing as we gained many new friends from all over. There were quite a number of state-wide gatherings, the most exciting of which was the three-day annual Grand Chapter which featured a lot of colorful pageantry and important state-wide business culminating in the election and installation of new state officers. Ruby was honored with a number of state appointments including Deputy Grand Matron and Grand Representative. Two later appointments that she treasured most were in recognition of her musical talent and training. They were as Artist (Soloist) for the 2000 Grand Chapter and as Grand Organist twice, in 1994 and 2001.

One other activity that made us feel good about ourselves was membership in Mensa, the high-IQ society. Mensa is an international organization in which the sole qualification for membership is an IQ in the top 2% of the population. One day we came across a feature article about the organization in a Reader's Digest magazine. In it was a sample test for readers to check their IQ. We took the test and did very well so we decided to take the official test at the nearest test site, which was in Springfield, Massachusetts. Fortunately, we both passed and were taken in. Parenthetically, we sometimes wonder what would have happened if one of us passed and the other did not. The thought never occurred to us when we decided to take the test. Our daughter Mirla later qualified and joined the organization, making us, to the best of our knowledge, the foremost Filipino Mensa family in America.

Ruby and I belonged to the Connecticut &Western Massachusetts Chapter of Mensa. It was a very busy chapter with two or three activities happening during each week. But to join the activities, we would have had to travel at least 30 miles each way. We were the only Mensans in Greenfield and the closest other one to us lived in Deerfield, a town six miles away. That was when we fully realized one of the disadvantages of settling in a small town located far from the big city.

My ministry continued to prosper as I continued to be recruited by other churches. In 1985 I was asked to serve as interim minister of East Springfield Congregational Church. Their pastor had just retired after serving them for more than 20 years. Although I had to travel 30 miles to the church, I liked the experience of preaching at an urban church for the first time in my life. Springfield is the second largest city in Massachusetts and is considered the hub of Western Massachusetts. The church was a medium-sized congregation with an average of about 200 attending their one service on Sunday morning. Most of the members were working class folks, many of whom had retired from a nearby chemical company.

I was there for seven months, a period that went very quickly with hardly any bump in the road. The only issue that came up was that the church had become heavily dependent on a weekly Bingo game for their finances and some members grumbled over the church's use of gambling to support itself. Instead of getting involved, I decided to leave that issue to the incoming permanent minister. On the other hand, there were some high points during my time there. The church office was being managed by a couple of lady volunteers. They were the church secretary and the church newsletter editor. Seeing that they were still using a typewriter to do their work, I convinced the church to purchase a computer system for the office and I trained both of them in its use. Another bright spot was their worship music, thanks to their talented organist/choir director and a number of good solo voices. Their

Christmas cantata was a special one entitled "A Night of Miracles" by John Peterson, a well-known cantata composer. Ruby and I joined them, with me singing in the tenor section and Ruby as substitute organist so the regular organist could conduct.

April, 1986 came along, a date Ruby and I had looked forward to since it was going to be our 25th wedding anniversary. We decided to celebrate the event by going out to dinner with our children. The three of them insisted that the dinner was going to be their treat so we left it up to them to make all the arrangements. They told us that they had chosen as our dinner venue an upscale restaurant in Northfield which sat high on a hill and had a very beautiful view of the valley. So one early Saturday evening in late April, we proceeded toward Northfield. Mirla and Rowena went ahead to make sure about our reservations while we rode in Freddie's car. On the way there, Freddie told us that he had to make one stop somewhere to collect some money from a friend. It looked like he and his "friend" were going to meet at the Thomas Memorial Golf Club in Turners Falls because that's where we were headed. As he stopped and parked near the clubhouse, he asked us to go inside with him for a bit, making an excuse like there was something there that he wanted us to see. We followed him and as we entered, we came upon two dozen of our family and friends who greeted us with a loud "Surprise!!"

They showered us with a lot gifts, among which was a generous amount of money which, we were told, we could use to go someplace for our "second honeymoon." As it turned out, we had to wait a few weeks before leaving because I had one more church commitment. First Congregational Church of Greenfield had been searching for a permanent minister following the retirement of Rev. Art Sweeney. At the time, they had an interim minister taking care of them. They had found the permanent minister they were looking for but before they could formalize arrangements, the interim minister was called to another assignment. First Congregational asked me to take over until the new minister could arrive. I felt both obligated and honored to be asked. It was the very first church that we joined upon arriving in Greenfield a dozen years before and we still had many friends in that church. Besides, I was going to be there for only a few weeks.

It was July by the time we were ready to embark on our "second honeymoon." We chose to go to Las Vegas. It may have been a mistake to go there at that time of the year. It was the middle of summer and temperatures soared into the high 90's and low 100's. Going outdoors was risky so we stayed indoors most of the time. I also did not reckon with how tired I was. On the morning of our second day there, I started to experience chest pain. Not wanting to take any chances, we called an ambulance and I was taken to the hospital where I stayed for a week and underwent a battery of tests to rule out a heart attack. Fortunately, the tests came out negative. But the whole experience was very stressful for me as well as for Ruby who was left behind in the hotel room while I was in the hospital. The episode left psychological scars from which I took a long time to recover.

Soon after coming back home, I started a new pastorate at Leverett Congregational Church. The Leverett congregation was in many respects different from any other that I had served. The town was situated a few miles from the UMass campus and served as a bedroom community for people who worked there. It reminded me of my first church assignment right out of seminary when I was assistant pastor at the Church of the Risen Lord at the campus of the University of the Philippines. Everybody in the congregation treated me well but it did not take long before I got restless. For one thing, I longed to be readily available to my congregation in the same manner that I had been at Westwood. That would have meant moving to the parsonage. There was a parsonage which they called the Dixon House named after a former pastor. But it was much too small and was being used for Sunday school classes.

I had been at Leverett for two years when an opening came up at South Deerfield Congregational Church. I was attracted to it because there was some kind of turmoil within the congregation. After what I had gone through at Westwood, I felt drawn to churches that were having problems, especially if it involved the minister. Their minister was a lady who, in the eyes of the congregation, had an abrasive personality. That led to a number of fights during congregational meetings, some of which turned into shouting and finger-pointing matches. This turned off some parishioners and made them stop coming to church. Once again, I was called to be an agent of reconciliation so I accepted the offer to be the church's minister.

Ruby and I moved into the parsonage. We no longer needed the space that our Greenfield home provided when we were a four-generation family. Ruby had closed her music studio after running it for a couple of years. Papa and Mama left for California to live with the family of Ruby's younger brother Sadiri. Rowena had gone to a Boston school for a year to train to be an electrologist, leaving Stevie with us. Upon finishing her training, she and Stevie left to practice her new profession, first in Brattleboro, Vermont and later in Palm Bay, Florida. Freddie had graduated from Greenfield High School. He qualified for admission to Rensselaer Polytechnic Institute in Troy, New York, and was offered a scholarship by the U.S. Navy. However, he enrolled at GCC and, upon finishing his Associates degree, transferred to the University of Massachusetts as a Mechanical Engineering student and roomed outside the campus with his friends.

We rented out our Greenfield home to a couple that took very good care of it. The man was very handy and would repair anything in return for a small reduction on their rent. They felt so proud of their home that they frequently showed it off to their friends. Ever year, they held an open house and invited us, much to our amusement and delight. Considering all the horror stories that we heard about renting out one's property, we had to be the luckiest of landlords ever.

It did not take me long to settle into the woodwork at South Deerfield. More than at any time, I felt that my two jobs complemented each other so well. As a professor of Speech Communication, I could claim that, unlike others, I was always practicing what I was teaching. I would half-jokingly invite my Public Speaking students to come and listen to me preach so that they could critique me in the same way I did them in class. On the other hand, I regarded my meetings with the church leadership as laboratories for my course in Small Group Communication.

I owed much of my success at South Deerfield to a former Westwood parishioner who joined the South Deerfield church soon after I became its minister. It was an easy and logical move for him because his home was actually in South Deerfield. He was a prominent citizen of the town and had a lot of friends in the church. He became an officer of the church and was my main support, often throwing blocks for me whenever a potential conflict would come up. A brother Mason, he also sponsored me into both the 32nd Masonic degree and the International Brotherhood of Shriners.

My career at GCC also flourished. I was promoted to full professor and granted tenure, which meant I was permanently employed and could not be removed except for just cause. I was also made Coordinator of the Speech Communication and Theater department. It was little more than a prestige job because it did not result in reduction of my course load. My main job was to set up the semester's course schedule and to represent the department at meetings. I loved the appointment because it showed that the school recognized that I was very much a presence at the school despite having another job. Furthermore, I got the appointment despite not being the most senior member in the department.

I also did my share in bringing honors to the school. In 1988, IBM and the League for Innovation in the Community College teamed up for the purpose of integrating computers into the community college curriculum and training community college teachers in the use of the new technology. One of their initiatives was to run a Competition for Excellence in which community college teachers were invited to submit proposals on the use of computers. The names of winners were going to be published nationwide and each given an award consisting of a complete IBM Personal Computer System. As my entry to the competition, I wrote an interactive computer program called Speech Topic Selection Tutor. The program helped the user, usually a Public Speaking student, decide on a speech topic by narrowing one's choices based on a number of criteria. My program was picked as one of 100 winners. There were 74 community colleges with winners and out of that number, 16 had multiple winners including GCC which had two. The other GCC winner was Ira Rubenzahl, a Mathematics teacher who created computer exercises for calculus. Another GCC honor was that it was one of only two community colleges in Massachusetts with a winner and the only one west of Boston.

Having done all the research and the gathering and analysis of data for my dissertation, all I had to do was to write it. For three years I kept putting it off using one excuse after another. Unable to write even the first sentence, I realized that I was suffering from a common affliction called writer's block. I was ready to give up when I thought of going to a psychologist.

The psychologist was a lady who could relate to my dilemma. She herself was a Ph.D. holder and knew what I was going through. She told me that my problem was that I was trying to write the master work of my life and wanted it to be perfect. She said that no one outside of my dissertation committee was going to read my dissertation. Her words had a miraculous liberating effect on me. I started writing and finished the dissertation in two months. In September, 1989, my Dissertation Committee composed of Dr. Howard Peelle, chairman; and Dr. Charlotte Rahaim and Dr. Donald Fisher, members approved my dissertation. I submitted it to the School of Education and received my Doctor of Education diploma all in the same month.

A copy of my dissertation was sent to University Microfilms International in Ann Arbor, Michigan for archiving. The company is a facility for filming dissertations as an alternative to printing for publication. It also circulates updated lists of dissertations to libraries nationwide for the benefit of researchers. A few weeks after I submitted my dissertation to UMI, I received requests from two complete strangers for copies of my dissertation. Either the psychologist who got me going by telling me that no one outside of my dissertation committee was going to read my dissertation was lying or my topic was just too good. In any case, what she did for me solved my writer's block problem and I was grateful to her for that.

The graduation ceremonies were scheduled for May, 1990. At age 51, I felt too old to be marching at graduation ceremonies. It had been 31 years since I last marched at graduation and that was in Silliman for my Bachelor of Divinity degree. I had missed one graduation ceremony in 1972 for my Master of Arts degree at Syracuse University and I was thinking of missing another one, satisfied that I already had my diploma. But Ruby urged me to attend. Little did I know that she had set up an elaborate surprise.

On the morning of Graduation Day, there was a knock on the door at the parsonage. I opened the door and was greeted by three of my siblings who had traveled from their respective homes in the United States together with their spouses. There were my older sister Esther from Atlanta, Georgia; my older brother Orly and his wife Betty from Martinsburg, West Virginia; and my younger sister Ruth and her husband Diony from Hillcrest, New York. They all came to celebrate my graduation with me.

More surprises were on the way. After the graduation ceremonies, I was led to the church where a party had been prepared in my honor by the congregation. It felt so good that my graduation became an occasion for a family reunion as well as a demonstration of affection from the members of my church.

A number of other family milestones and celebrations happened about that time. Our children advanced in their careers. Two got married and had children. After graduating from Oberlin in 1985, Mirla set out on a lengthy career on stage. She moved to New York in order to have more opportunities to get on quality shows. We followed her progress and tried to get to her shows especially the ones that traveled to places nearby. After acting in a number of regional and off-Broadway shows, she got her big break in 1991 when she joined the original Broadway cast of *Miss Saigon*. Ruby and I went to the show's Opening Night which turned out to be a mixed bag. On one hand, it was a delightful experience to hobnob with a lot of stage and film celebrities who attended the party that followed the performance. On the other hand, there was a demonstration against the play in front of the theater by a crowd protesting against the alleged stereotyping of Vietnamese women as call girls. Mila was a stand-in for Gigi and

Yvonne so each time she got either part, she would let us know and we would try to get there. She stayed with the show for almost five years after which she left for graduate school at the University of California in Irving, eventually obtaining a Master of Fine Arts degree.

Freddie and Sharon who had first met at Greenfield High School, started dating as students at GCC and later at UMass, started their own family. On November 15,1990, their first child Kayla was born. Three years later, on April 22, 1993, their second child Rachel arrived. After Freddie and Sharon received their degrees in Mechanical Engineering and Graphic Arts respectively, they moved to Tennessee where Freddie took a job with a company that manufactures automobile parts.

Rowena married Eric Rantanen in 1992. Both of them graduated from UMass; hers was a Bachelor of Arts degree in Music and his in Mechanical Engineering. They had two marriage ceremonies. In January of that year, they had a civil ceremony at the parsonage with members of both families in attendance. Later in August, they had a church wedding in South Deerfield Congregational Church attended by family and friends. I officiated at both weddings. Our tribe continued to grow with the arrival of three Rantanen grandchildren. Elysse was born on February 2, 1994 and Katie on July 6, 1995. Our sixth grandchild Laura would later bring up the rear on October 9, 1997.

In the spring of 1995, I served notice to South Deerfield Congregational Church that I was leaving. It did not come as a surprise to the congregation nor was there any issue behind my resignation. Seven years had gone by since I became their pastor and they were aware that just as with Westwood, it was a benchmark that I intended to keep. There was another reason why I had to leave. A new challenge came, which would turn out to be the biggest one in my entire ministerial career.

155

CHAPTER XI: GREENFIELD PHASE THREE

In 1986, a new permanent minister took over First Congregational Church of Greenfield. To protect her privacy, we will give her the fictitious name of Cheryl Bradley. Rev. Bradley and I became instant friends for a number of reasons. For one thing, I had paved the way for her arrival by briefly serving as the church's interim minister. For another, she knew a lot about the Philippines and its people. Before she joined the UCC, she had spent several years as a missionary to the Philippines for the Seventh Day Adventist Church. She and I had a number of interesting discussions especially on the subject of discrimination, a favorite topic of ours for obvious reasons.

Despite being First Congregational Church's first-ever permanent female minister, Rev. Bradley had little reason to doubt that she would be well received. She immediately impressed the congregation with her preaching skills and caring ways. The congregation grew rapidly as new members flocked to the church. I myself benefitted from her presence. Needing a pastor myself, I turned to her for support. For the two years that followed, I often sought her counsel whenever I had a problem. She became a steadying influence on me throughout that period.

I also admired her professionalism and sensitivity. Unlike some pastors who tend to be excessively protective of their turf, she often invited fellow ministers to conduct services at First Congregational when she felt it appropriate to do so. One such occasion was the memorial service for Rev. Arthur Shaw. A former minister of First Congregational Church, Arthur became a full-time professor at Greenfield Community College after leaving the church. He and I became fast friends when I joined GCC in 1974. In fact it was he who advised me and my family to choose First Congregational Church when we were church-hunting. One day in February, 1989, Arthur had a fatal heart attack while driving to work. At the family's request, the memorial service was held at First Congregational Church.

Cheryl knew about the special relationship between Arthur and me and correctly assumed that I would have loved to participate in Arthur's memorial service. I did not even have to ask. Instead, she asked me to plan and take over the whole service and avail of all the facilities of First Congregational Church. She discreetly stayed away from both the service and reception both of which were well-attended by Arthur's former parishioners and GCC friends and colleagues.

There was one practice that Cheryl introduced which endeared her to her parishioners. Following the Sunday worship service, everyone was invited to stay for a feedback session on the pastor's sermon. Those sessions were always lively and friendly and sometimes became catalysts for action on some problem or issue that required congregational attention.

It was one such session that set the stage for a major controversy that was to rock the church for years to come. On that fateful Sunday sometime in the winter of 1993, Rev. Bradley preached a sermon in which she decried the negative attitude that the community held toward gays and lesbians. She called upon everybody to be more open toward them. At the feedback session that followed the service, attendance was larger and the discussion livelier than usual. When she was asked what the church could do, Rev. Bradley informed them about Open and Affirming, ONA for short. The latter was a program of the United Church of Christ to encourage each church to welcome gays and lesbians and fully include them in all aspects of church life. It meant that the church had to decide whether or not to become an ONA church.

Rev. Bradley made sure to warn the group that Open and Affirming was not to be taken lightly and that it required serious study. Accordingly, the group decided to form a study group on the Open and Affirming question. Open to all who were interested, sessions were held monthly between April and October, 1993. Resource persons from outside were invited, some of whom were in favor of the ONA and others against. Some of the meetings were small and private while others were large and public. Discussions were very lively and often contentious.

It was very clear from the discussions that the church membership was clearly and equally divided. Occasionally, tempers flared up during the meetings. As positions on both sides hardened, the congregation prepared for a showdown by scheduling an election to decide whether or not First Congregational Church was to become an ONA church. A grinding political campaign ensued, with each side seeking every little advantage it could. Church members, including those who had not been worshipping for a long time, were urged to come and vote. As the showdown approached, some long-time church members expressed alarm and sought outside help to defuse the situation. Some of them even came to me. However, no one could do anything as things had reached a point of no return.

Members were summoned to a church meeting on November 15, 1993 for the purpose of deciding on a resolution to have First

Congregational Church of Greenfield become an Open and Affirming Church. At the meeting, the vote was taken and the resolution passed by a slim margin. Technically, the vote resolved the issue but the narrowness of the vote told the true story. The church was still divided, even more so than before the vote was taken.

At the instigation of the anti-ONA group, a congregational meeting was called for the purpose of voting on a proposal to pay off the mortgage on the roof by using the principal on a variety of legacies. Approval of the proposal was going to severely affect the church's finances by cutting off a source of revenue that was being used to balance the budget. The proposal was bitterly contested, the opposition coming mainly from the group that had voted in favor of the ONA who saw the new proposal as a move to paralyze the church. They also regarded it as a vicious punitive action against Rev. Bradley for instigating the ONA crisis. At the meeting held on January 18, 1994, the proposal to pay off the mortgage passed.

A few weeks later, a group of ONA dissenters dealt the church a second financial blow. They organized what they called the One Dollar Club, whose members agreed to each reduce their financial pledge to one dollar a week. Most of the club members were long-time church members and some of the church's biggest pledgers.

For Rev. Bradley, it was the last straw. In April, 1994, she tendered her resignation. In turn, half of those who voted for the ONA stopped coming to church or joined other churches. After being pastor of First Congregational Church for eight years. Rev. Bradley's leaving was a sad ending to a ministry that had started with such great promise.

On September, 1994, Rev. James Smith became the interim minister of First Congregational Church. Tensions over the ONA crisis and the forced departure of the previous minister continued to prevail and hampered his work as pastor. In an effort to resolve the impasse, he drafted a Statement of Reconciliation and asked congregation members to sign it. Very few signed the statement and had minimal impact on the way members treated one another.

A Pastoral Search Committee was formed to seek a permanent minister. When some members of the committee called on me asking that I be available to be pastor of the church, I was not surprised. I had already established a reputation as an agent of congregational reconciliation and healing. I knew many of the congregants, a lot of whom were there when I joined the church in 1974. I had served the church briefly as its interim before Rev. Bradley came. And I was available, having just finished my tenure at South Deerfield. I accepted the invitation and was hired. When the chairman of the Pastoral Search

Committee presented me before the congregation, he referred to me as one who loves and knows First Congregational Church of Greenfield and said that if one was going to help the church resolve its problems, I was as good as any. On October 1, 1995 I was installed as pastor.

It was good that when I moved to South Deerfield seven years before to live in that church's parsonage, I decided to rent out my Greenfield house instead of selling it. First Congregational had no parsonage so I moved back to my house, feeling a bit guilty as I had to displace the renters who had enjoyed living in my house and taken very good care of it all those years. My house was perfectly located, being just a few blocks away from the church.

My first priority upon taking over was to seek peace between the warring factions, which was no easy task. The anti-ONA group was very vocal in demanding that the ONA vote be immediately abrogated, arguing that the departure of many of the pro-ONA people following Rev. Bradley's resignation meant that ONA was no longer favored by the majority of church members. On the other hand, those who had voted for the ONA and remained had had enough and were not willing to go through the painful experience again. It was also clear, although they did not openly admit it, that had a second vote been taken, they would have decisively lost. Within that latter group was a few who took a militant stand, insisting that having voted to be ONA, the congregation should vigorously pursue its implementation. There was no common ground and it seemed that any attempt I would make to resolve the problem was bound to displease some members. I just hoped and prayed that whatever I decided to do was going to result in minimal damage.

I decided to take the bull by the horns. At the church's annual meeting the following Spring I asked that we let Open and Affirming stand but that we keep a low profile for the moment. I also promised that after two years, I would encourage the congregation to revisit ONA and decide what to do. The anti-ONA group accepted my offer. As for the pro-ONA group, three couples did not like my proposal and forthwith left the church. I found out through the grapevine that all three had children who were homosexual. I felt sad to lose them but relieved that there were not more of them.

I looked forward to that two-year period, grateful that I could use my time to focus my attention on things that had nothing to do with ONA. My enthusiasm was short-lived. I was curious to know which churches in the area were ONA so one day I logged on to the website of the United Church of Christ. To my dismay, not only was First Congregational Church of Greenfield listed as ONA but it was the only one so listed among the more than 25 churches in Franklin County. I did some investigating and found out that First Congregational Church never officially asked to be listed by the United Church of Christ as ONA. Nor did the church even officially report to the UCC what transpired at the November 15, 1994 when the congregation voted to be ONA. I called up the UCC headquarters and was told that the listing was instigated by a special ministry within the UCC called the Gay and Lesbian Coalition, GLC for short. UCC advised me to contact the GLC.

It was clear to me that the UCC had no legal basis for listing First Congregational Church as ONA without obtaining the congregation's permission. Besides, the UCC's unilateral action was inconsistent with UCC's policy of upholding the autonomy of every member church. Therefore, First Congregational Church had every right to demand its removal from the ONA listing. I even thought of making a legal case out of it by engaging the services of a lawyer but I desisted, not wanting to get the congregation entangled in a legal battle like the one at Westwood.

I kept everything to myself and hoped that no one in the congregation would find out about the listing. I also wondered what I would do should any homosexual come to our church because of the ONA listing. It took almost a year to get an answer. One day, a couple of men showed up at my office seeking to join First Congregational Church. They identified themselves as homosexuals and said that they found out about us from the UCC website. I sat down with them and told them that they were welcome to our church but in fairness to them I revealed what had transpired. Fortunately, another UCC church in Franklin County had just become ONA. It was a small church in a nearby town about 10 miles away. When I told them about that church, they thanked me and left. I later checked with the pastor of that church and he confirmed that the couple had indeed joined his church.

I had dodged a bullet but I was haunted by the thought of possible unpleasant future scenarios. What if a homosexual comes to Greenfield from far away to start a new life? What if the person accepted an offer to relocate knowing that there is an ONA church in town? How would that person react upon finding out that the ONA listing was a lie? Can we be sued for misrepresentation?

In the meantime, problems continued to come up, much of it still a result of the resentment over the ONA crisis. While we had agreed on a moratorium of two years before bringing up the ONA subject again, the years that followed were characterized by an uneasy truce. Most people were pleased that the wrangling that followed the 1994 vote had died down but it was difficult to set up a proactive course because the congregation, wittingly or unwittingly, preferred to focus its thoughts inward, almost exclusively preoccupied with issues of survival and day-to-day problem solving. I could not get a meaningful Mission program going. Worse, the *agents provocateurs* missed few chances to take pot shots at any external program that I tried to promote, especially if it involved the UCC. Partly due to their machinations and partly as an artifact of the congregation's long-standing isolationism, the Missions budget was very low and, in fact, in one year's budget the line item for the UCC program called Our Christian World Missions stood at zero.

I was quite relieved when the two-year moratorium ended, which gave us the opportunity to take up the ONA matter again and clear the air once and for all. As agreed, we had a congregational meeting for that purpose. To my dismay, the congregation wanted to bury the issue some more. In fact, some of them threatened to leave the church should ONA become the subject of public discussion again. The congregation's attitude was summed up as follows: "Bury the issue. Let sleeping dogs lie. The less we hear about ONA, the better." I publicly acknowledged the congregational consensus and promised that I would not bring up the ONA issue again unless they wanted me to. There was a universal sigh of relief.

I then concluded that consistent with the desire of the congregation to suppress any discussion of ONA, it would be appropriate to ask those publicizing us as an Open and Affirming Congregation to stop the practice. I had insulated the congregation from ONA material by diverting all incoming mail on the subject to my house. But despite the obvious incongruity, we continued to be advertised as an Open and Affirming congregation through brochures and the ONA web page which was linked to the UCC page along those of "other UCC ministries." And as I feared, a few computer-literate church members discovered the listing and started to raise a ruckus.

I decided to take up the church's case with the UCC Gay and Lesbian Coalition. Fortunately, a high-ranking Coalition officer, Rev. Abigail Davis (not her real name), lived in Massachusetts only an hour and a half hours drive away. I went to meet her and asked for her help in getting the advertising stopped. She sympathized with our plight but was pessimistic about the chances of my request being approved. However, she promised to bring the matter up before the ONA Advisory Committee which was scheduled to meet in Chicago in a couple of months.

As I feared, Rev. Davis later reported to me that the ONA Advisory Committee refused my request to stop the advertising. In her letter to me, she said that after considerable, thoughtful conversation, it was the unanimous decision of the Committee that First Congregational should remain on the ONA list until such time as the congregation (or a body of the church which has authority to act on its behalf) makes a decision to rescind its ONA status and communicates that to the ONA Program. She conveyed the committee's opinion that "to request that it not be listed but continue to be considered ONA is a contradiction in terms; an essential aspect of what it is to be Open and Affirming is the public announcement of this commitment."

For most church members, everything was business as usual but I felt like I was sitting on top of a proverbial iceberg where things were normal on the surface but hiding underneath was a deep problem. I personally bore the brunt of that problem as more gays and lesbians, their sympathizers and friends showed up at the church on the strength of the church being listed as ONA. Having to go through the same routine of explaining the dilemma to them every time while feeling the guilt of, in effect, turning them away was wearing me down.

I came upon a way to break the impasse without creating a big stir. I found an opening by reading Rev. Davis' letter in which she had stated that the ONA Program Committee would accept a rescinding of the 1994 ONA vote by a "body of the church which has the authority to act on its behalf." I decided that such a body would be the Executive Board. In studying the church's by-laws, I found a couple of items which stated that the Executive Board was responsible for defining the congregation's "annual program goals" and "program policies." Concluding that ONA came under the rubric of both "program goal" and "program policy," I then proceeded to convince the Executive Board that it would be in the church's best interest to abrogate the Open and Affirming policy. It took me a while to convince the Board to agree to my proposal and I had to reach deep into my entire bag of persuasive and argumentative skills. I wrote a lengthy paper in the style of a legal brief in which I pointed out that not only was it necessary and beneficial to do what I was suggesting but that it was the only practical way to solve our long-standing problem. One of the things that convinced them was my suggestion that rather than do a purely negative act of rescinding Open and Affirming, the congregation should adopt a substitute policy which I called "Open and Caring." They agreed that such a new policy accurately described the thinking of the congregation at that time. I also reminded them that by constitutional mandate, their action would have to be ratified by the congregation at its next annual meeting.

At the meeting of the Executive Board on December 18, 2001, I submitted my proposal package. It consisted of three motions as follows: 1) to change from an "Open and Affirming" Church to an "Open and Caring" Church; 2) to notify the Gay and Lesbian Coalition and the United Church of Christ of the above change and to indicate that in effect this rescinds the 1994 congregational action declaring ourselves as an Open and Affirming congregation; and 3) to direct the Gay and Lesbian Coalition and the United Church of Christ to remove us from any and all of their lists that indicate First Congregational Church of Greenfield as an Open and Affirming church. The result of the voting on all three motions was recorded in the Executive Board's minutes as "firmly in favor."

Two days after the Executive Board's vote, I wrote letters to Rev. Davis and the webmaster of the United Church of Christ informing them about the vote. Both responded before the end of the month, each acknowledging receipt of my letter. Noting my qualifying remark that in order to be final the vote would be submitted to the church's annual meeting, they both indicated that they need not wait for the congregation's approval and that they were going to immediately stop listing and advertising First Congregational Church of Greenfield as an Open and Affirming church.

At the annual meeting of the congregation the following Spring, the action of the Executive Committee was approved with hardly any discussion. It helped them to know that the UCC and the GLC had made good on their promise to stop advertising the church as ONA. It had been eight years since the church voted to be Open and Affirming and six and a half years since I became pastor of the church. At long last, the proverbial monkey was off the church's back.

Of all the churches that I had the privilege and honor of leading as pastor and teacher, First Congregational Church of Greenfield presented the biggest and most difficult problems. And yet, ironically I can say that I found the entire experience personally satisfying and beneficial in more ways than one. For one thing, I learned so much while dealing with the ONA crisis. One of my notable achievements was successfully convincing the church to stick with the United Church of Christ. During the crisis, the anti-ONA members made a lot of noise about wanting to leave the UCC but I was able to silence them. I did so by emphasizing the denomination's strengths and pointing out the advantages of belonging to a denomination over that of being alone. I made it clear that the Gay and Lesbian program and the UCC are not synonymous and that those churches that are not ONA are just as deserving of love and respect as those that are. I was blessed with allies among top UCC officers whom I invited to help me educate the congregation.

I became a virtual expert on the Open and Affirming Process, making me a valuable resource for churches considering the ONA. I genuinely believed in the need for the kind of safe havens that ONA would provide to gays and lesbians and thought it imperative for those churches which wanted to be ONA to do it right. As their resource, I could guide them through the various steps toward becoming a legitimate ONA church and, more importantly, help them avoid the kinds of traps like what First Congregational Church had to deal with.

My views about the need for some ONA churches were developed in part because of a personal agenda. I have a niece who is a homosexual. Like many of her kind, the personal conflicts that tore her apart drove her to a deep depression and caused her to drop out of college. I learned about her plight from her parents who took me into their confidence. At the time, I and I alone among both parents' siblings knew about their secret. For their own mental and psychological well being, I urged them to come out of the closet even just within our immediate families but they were reluctant to do so.

In the meantime, I resolved to love and accept as well as protect my niece. As though *déjà vu* was staring me in the face, I found that the church that her family had been attending went through an upheaval over their denomination's equivalent of the ONA, which led to the resignation of their female pastor. The congregation split, with many, including my niece and her parents, leaving the church.

In order to protect my niece, I searched for ONA churches where I thought she would be comfortable. It was no easy task because far too many churches that had voted to be ONA were doing nothing to act on it which to me indicated that they either regretted their decision or were being secretly dishonest. I eventually found a good ONA church a few miles near her and parents' home and I encouraged my niece to check it out. Today, as I write this book, her parents are now active members of that church. In the meantime, my niece and her partner eventually came out and got married at a nearby state which had passed a law legalizing same-sex marriage.

Among those who joined the church during my tenure, none was dearer and closer to me than Rev. Arthur Sweeney. He was the pastor when my family and I joined the church in 1974 and was the predecessor to Rev. Bradley. During the four years that I was a church member before I left to serve other churches, he treated me as an unofficial assistant pastor. After retiring in 1986, he joined other churches or served as interim minister of some small churches. Soon after I took over First Congregational, he and his wife Arlene joined the church. Our former roles got reversed as I started to treat him as my unofficial assistant pastor. Later, his position got formalized when, at my instigation, the church installed him as the church's *pastor emeritus*. He helped me not only by taking over on occasions when I had to be briefly away but by being a calming presence and voice to the anti-ONA group, most of whom were his former parishioners who still looked up to him. Little did I know at the time that his biggest role in my ministry was yet to come.

Having successfully resolved the church's ONA crisis, I then needed to decide how much longer to stay. As pastor, I was on my seventh year, which had been my benchmark with churches I had previously served. So if I were to follow my own script, it was time for me to say good-by. However, there were other considerations that made me think twice. I was 63 years old, just two years short of the normal retirement age of 65. There was a bigger reason. As with most towns in New England, Greenfield and First Congregational Church were established on the same year which, in this case, was the year 1753. The 250th anniversary was coming up and already plans were being made for a year-long joint celebration that would start in 2003. As pastor, I was asked to serve on the Celebration Committee. Some of the events being planned were going to take place at First Congregational Church. I wanted so bad to be involved in those celebrations, hence my decision to stay on longer.

I was looking forward to an enjoyable two-year glide path toward retirement when I got the shock of my life. One day in April, 2002, I received a phone call from my family doctor. She told me to report to my urologist immediately. What happened was that a routine blood test that I took a month before revealed that I had a high PSA. It was my first time to hear about that term which I found out stands for prostate specific antigen. A high PSA means anything including irritation and inflammation of the prostate gland but in a lot of cases it can indicate prostate cancer. A normal PSA is between 0 and 4 and my PSA was at 24, which was the reason for my family doctor's urgent phone call. My urologist treated me a number of times with antibiotics to try to lower my PSA but it stayed at 20 or higher. So he ordered a biopsy to test for prostate cancer which took place on May 15. A few days later, the urologist summoned me and gave me the bad news. The biopsy revealed that I had advanced prostate cancer. The tell-tale sign was a Gleason score of 8 which, based on a scale of 1 to 10, indicated that my cancer was the aggressive kind.

In the next two months, I spent virtually every waking hour searching for the best treatment for my illness. I went on the Internet, read a lot of literature on prostate cancer, talked to men who had undergone or were undergoing treatment for cancer, joined prostate cancer support groups and traveled to various doctor offices and hospitals in and out of Massachusetts. I found out that there was a vast and bewildering array of treatments, each of which had its own share of supporters as well as detractors. After weighing everything, I finally chose a little-known treatment protocol called proton beam radiation therapy. At that time, there were only two places in the whole world that offered it. One was the Massachusetts General Hospital in Boston and the other was Loma Linda University Medical Center in Southern California. I applied to both places but only Loma Linda accepted me. The Boston facility, which had been in operation for only a year did not want to take a chance on me given the advance stage of my cancer. On the other hand, Loma Linda, the pioneer of hospital-based proton beam treatment, had been operating for a while and had an excellent track record.

The whole Loma Linda program, including admission, laboratory tests, treatment planning and the treatment itself, was going to take about two and a half months. It meant that I had to be away that long from both my jobs at the church and GCC. Fortunately, the church did not have to search far for someone to take charge in my absence. Rev. Sweeney graciously stepped up and offered his services.

I chose proton beam therapy after a long process of elimination. I discovered that, with very few exceptions, prostate cancer doctors recommend not what they consider the best treatment but what they or their colleagues do. A patient seeking treatment needs to be a smart shopper, taking into consideration such factors as survival chances, cost and quality of life.

At the time, the standard treatment for prostate cancer was radical prostatectomy, which is removal of the prostate. The treatment was reserved only for early stage prostate cancer whereby the cancer is still confined to the prostate gland. I was not qualified for surgery because my statistics at diagnosis showed a high probability that the cancer had already escaped the gland. So the alternative for me was radiation treatment, of which there were two kinds. The more common of the two was photon beam, better known as X-ray. Photon was delivered to the prostate by three methods, namely external beam radiation treatment (EBRT), seed implant (SI) and high dose radiation (HDR). I had chosen HDR and was already scheduled to start treatment in December, 2002 at Lahey Clinic in Boston when I got the green light from Loma Linda. I immediately cancelled my Lahey clinic appointment.

As explained to me, the superiority of proton over photon is in its ability to target the cancerous organ more precisely. This allows for a larger and more effective dosage than that of photon. Moreover, because it has a relatively narrow path and stops at its target without exiting, it results in very little collateral damage to surrounding healthy tissue compared to photon which has a broad path and travels through the entire body. The proton beam is a by-product of the atomic age. In fact, before Loma Linda, the only places where one could get proton beam treatment were at various atomic energy research laboratories and only for rare conditions such as inoperable brain cancer. The Proton Beam Treatment Center at Loma Linda was the result of the efforts of Dr. James Slater, Sr. Trained both as a physicist and physician, Dr. Slater was completely aware of proton beam's huge potential for curing a lot of cancers so he dreamed of proton beam treatment in a hospital setting. The price tag for building such a facility was very high but he was able to get financial support from the Seventh Day Adventist Church and the California legislature. When I was diagnosed in May, 2002, the Loma Linda proton treatment center had been treating patients for 12 years. At first, the medical community was very skeptical but their attitude eventually began to change and plans for construction of other proton treatment centers emerged, including some at highly prestigious cancer treatment centers in the United States.

Ruby and I arrived at Loma Linda on the last week of October, 2002. I was assigned to Dr. Rodney Jabola, a nice and gentle young man who I found out was a second generation Filipino-American. I was very impressed with his thoroughness. Our first meeting lasted almost two hours during which he made sure that I completely understood the treatment that I was to undergo. After about a week of lab tests and other preparatory procedures, I started my therapy on the first week of November. Because of my high PSA and Gleason scores, Dr. Jabola prescribed a primary treatment of 16 proton doses followed by a secondary treatment of 28 photon doses. The proton dosage was for disabling the prostate gland while the photon treatment was needed to take care of possible nests of micro-organic cancer cells that may have escaped into surrounding tissue. Administered Monday through Friday, the total number of 44 treatments took nine weeks. I finished my treatment on the second week of January.

Ruby and I look back at our Loma Linda experience as one of the finest two months that we ever spent together. Following its maxim of "treating the whole man," Loma Linda offered a total healing experience that extended far beyond the medical. Whether it was help with housing, individual counseling, availability of recreational facilities or opportunities for social networking, everything that patients and their families needed was provided. One feature that we patients all looked forward to was the weekly Wednesday night meeting when we shared testimonies about our experiences, met new patients and occasionally heard from former patients who were visiting. Some of the most interesting people were the "graduates," which is what we called those who were concluding their treatment that week. All were excited to go home and to have a chance to tell their story to others.

Because the treatment had little or no side effects, we all were able to stay active while we were there. The luckiest ones were those who were scheduled early in the morning because after their treatment, which took no more than thirty minutes including undressing, treatment and dressing up, they had the rest of the day to play golf or engage in some other activity. I was one of those lucky ones who were scheduled for early treatment. That gave Ruby and me many chances to visit relatives and friends in the area or to go sightseeing.

We returned to Greenfield in the middle of January, 2003, and scarcely could pause because we had a full agenda ahead of us. Fortunately, thanks to Rev. Sweeney's stewardship during our absence, our reentry was smooth. It was shortly after that I came to find out what a tremendous sacrifice Rev. Sweeny had made in taking over. Being a very private person, he never let on that he was quite sick. Soon after, he wound up in the hospital. He quickly went downhill and died before the end of the year. I had lost a beloved friend and mentor.

Our attention focused on preparing for the celebration of the church's and the town's 250th anniversary which was starting in a few months. I was very fortunate to have Ruby, who used her performing arts skills and resources in designing special events for the celebration. She was able to draw support from a number of young men and women who followed her around as she went from place to place. Some of them sang for her in the various community and church choirs that she had directed. Others were actors of the Green Room Players, the community theater company that she founded. Some of them were often heard to say, "We will follow Ruby to the ends of the Earth," a testimony to their love and loyalty for her.

The Green Room Players started in South Deerfield Congregational Church in 1993 when I was the pastor there. A number of church members came up with the idea of a play as a fundraising project. Needing someone who could choose a play, put together a cast and direct the play, they did not have to look very far. With her degree in Speech and Theater and her extensive acting and directing experience, Ruby perfectly fit the part. The play she picked, entitled *One Toe in the Grave* was an artistic and financial success. A theater company was born and Ruby decided to call it "Green Room Players." The first play's success encouraged the church to make it an annual fundraising activity. Two more plays were produced at South Deerfield, one in 1994 entitled *The Second Time Around* and another in 1995 entitled *Let's Murder Marsha.*

When I left South Deerfield to become pastor of First Congregational Church of Greenfield in the Fall of 1995, the Green Room Players moved with us and made First Congregational Church its new home. By that time, the company had expanded its annual offerings to two plays, one of which was a comedy and the other a summer musical. The addition of a summer musical to the GRP repertoire coincided with the opening of Shea Theater in nearby Turners Falls, providing a professional venue for several theater companies in the area including Green Room Players. Shea Theater was formerly a theater for concerts and operas, but which was closed and abandoned for years until the decision to reopen it. GRP presented nine of its 12 musicals at the Shea. The full-length comedies were shown at the Fellowship Hall of First Congregational Church.

With the exception of one, I was the producer for all of GRP's summer musicals. Every now and then I played a bit part at Ruby's request. In 2003, we set out to plan for the year's summer musical. I was due to retire the following year after which we were going to move to Florida where we had already purchased our retirement home. So we figured that in all likelihood the musical was going to be GRP's last since nobody was expressing a desire to continue running the company without us. The play was also going to be special in another way. It was the 10th anniversary for GRP, having been founded in 1993.

I asked that for my last hurrah, I was going to pick the play and have a major role. I chose Rodgers and Hammerstein's *The King and I* with me taking the part of the King. It was a familiar role for me because several years before, I had played the same role at the Shea Theater for the Country Players of Northfield. I had a personal reason for wanting to be on stage. I wanted to show to the public, many of whom were aware of my illness and my lengthy absence for treatment, that I came back as healthy and vigorous as when I left. Befitting the occasion, it became GRP's largest and most prestigious production. In part to accommodate the anticipated large crowd and in part as an arrangement with the Greenfield High School which was the play's beneficiary, the play was held at the school's auditorium.

A number of GRP members had gone on to perform on Broadway and overseas theater. We were able to convince those who were Greenfield High School alumni to take time off to be part of the play. One of them was our daughter Mirla of *Miss Saigon* fame. She choreographed the play and danced the role of Simon Legree. Lindsey Dunn, a young and beautiful dancer, was the daughter of the choreographer of many GRP musicals. She was coached by Ruby for her successful Broadway audition. Taking time off from Broadway touring productions in Europe, Lindsey came back to dance the ballet role of Little Eva. Kevin Duda, who at the time was performing in the Broadway presentation of Rodgers and Hammerstein's *Cinderella* and was the understudy for the Prince, came to play the part of Luntha. Kevin was Ruby's voice student for years and had appeared in many GRP musicals before going to Broadway. Another Greenfield High School and GRP standout was Kristy Putala. A graduate of the American Musical and Dramatic Academy in New York, she had made a name by acting and singing on cruise ships and in off-Broadway plays. She came to play the role of the leading lady, Anna Leonowens.

The play ran for two weekends and was very well-received with rave reviews in local papers. In one of the reviews, a special section focused on the "Shall We Dance" scene and noted how energetic I was despite coming off a recent illness. There was a secret behind my accomplished dancing that the public did not know. Kristy, who was also a choreographer, taught me how to dance the polka and whirl around without getting dizzy.

GRP's presence at First Congregational Church benefitted the church in many ways. All of the net proceeds of the plays were donated to charitable causes, thus making GRP an indirect extension of the church's mission and outreach. Beneficiaries included the church itself, the Franklin Pastoral Counseling Center, the Salvation Army, the Greenfield public schools, and the Muscular Dystrophy Association. The latter was GRP's biggest charity, receiving almost $10,000 over a number of years. Ruby and I always enjoyed traveling to Springfield to present a check at the annual Jerry Lewis Muscular Dystrophy Association telethon.

Members of GRP also helped with the church's program by singing in the choir and participating in the church's special events. One special event was the presentation of a play called "The Talking Church." At the request of the church's 250th celebration committee, Ruby wrote the play, heavily basing it on a research paper written by Sylvia Gallagher, the church's historian. Most of the play's cast were members of Green Room Players.

The biggest event for the year 2003 at First Congregational was the joint 250th anniversary celebration of the town and the church. Held in the church on a Sunday afternoon in June, it drew a large contingent of participants consisting of prominent citizens of Greenfield and public officials of the Commonwealth of Massachusetts. The two-hour program featured a number of designated people taking turns narrating various aspects of the town's 250-year history. My part was to tell the history of the town's religious institutions. Music was provided by an ecumenical choir organized and conducted by Ruby and composed of singers from Greenfield churches of all denominations. One of their anthems, "Ode to Greenfield," was composed by Ruby for the occasion. The celebration concluded with a fellowship hour in the Fellowship Hall.

I retired and preached at my final worship service at First Congregational Church on Sunday, June 27, 2004. The service was very well-attended. Many of those attending, aside from First Congregational members, were parishioners from the two other Congregational churches in town. They had cancelled their services that day to encourage their congregants to attend my retirement service. The morning's activities were a joint effort of the three churches. Once again, singers of the three churches combined to form the celebration choir, which Ruby conducted. The liturgy was led by a leader from each of the three churches. The ladies of the three churches also organized the potluck lunch that followed the service. Even such a service as baby-sitting was a joint endeavor.

The theme of the worship service was my retirement. While I was dwelling on that theme, an episode took place that sent the audience into stitches. Part of the service was The Children's Time which I led, as usual. I started by telling the group of about a dozen children that I was retiring. One eight-year-old kid asked innocently, "Why are you retiring?" In the group was Danny, an 11-year-old, whose interruptions during my children's sermons I had gotten accustomed to. In a voice loud for everyone to hear, he exclaimed, "Because he is old!"

A special feature of the liturgy was an Order of Passage in which the church and I exchanged words of thanks and pledges of support. Adapted from a similar order from the UCC Book of Common Worship, it was presided over by the moderator of the Franklin Association of Churches. David James, religion columnist for Greenfield Recorder, the town's leading newspaper, was in attendance. He was so impressed by the liturgy that a week later, he wrote a column entitled "Ministers, churches, participate in ceremonial good-byes." All

171

but a couple of paragraphs in the article were about our Order of Passage.

Perhaps the most memorable feature of the celebration was the participation of the New England Ringers (NER), which was acclaimed as the Northeast's premier community handbell ensemble. About a year before, the ensemble's director, Edward Henderson, Jr., approached me asking if they could use our Fellowship Hall for their rehearsals. Many of their members were church musicians from different New England States, some traveling great distances to their weekly Sunday afternoon rehearsals. They thought that Greenfield, being centrally located, was an excellent place for their rehearsals. Since there was hardly any Sunday afternoon activity at the Fellowship Hall, I welcomed the idea and brought the matter up with the Church Council. While it was customary to charge outsiders for the use of our facilities, I convinced the Council to exempt the NER, arguing that their presence would enhance our church's reputation and be considered a part of our Mission and Outreach program. The arrangement worked very well and once in a while I would drop in and listen to their rehearsals.

Early in 2004, NER started planning their Summer Tour, which usually took place in July and August. This time, they decided to start the Tour a week ahead on the last Sunday of June and to have their performance in the Greenfield area. They were able to arrange for a performance at First United Methodist Church in Greenfield on the afternoon of June 27. The obvious reason for their secret maneuvers was that they found out that I was retiring and wanted to attend my retirement service, if not be a part of it. It meant that they each had to miss their own Sunday worship service at home with some having to arrive the day before and staying overnight.

It did not take me long to discover their secret. So one Sunday afternoon early in June, I approached the group and invited them to be a part of the service, which they were just quite thrilled to accept. I also asked for two favors. One was that they would make as a part of their musical offering a number performed together by the ensemble and the organist. They did have such a number entitled "Music of the Spheres" for which they asked that Ruby be the organist for that number and that it was going to be performed at the end of the service. The rest of their repertoire consisted of four selections played at the beginning of the service. At the end of the service, the congregation gave them a standing ovation. It was a tribute to the whole service and a special appreciation for the participation of the New England Bell Ringers.

My other request was for one of my compositions to be played by handbell. I had previously seen live and on TV some performances wherein one person played an entire piece. I was fascinated at the sight of the player picking up one handbell after another for each note, without missing a beat. They did have one who was such a player. I had a composition entitled "Go, Lovely Rose" and it seemed to me just the right song for such a performance. Because the composition was a secular song, we agreed that it would be played during the fellowship hour following the worship service.

The lunch that followed the service presented the kind of problem that any event sponsor would love to have. So many people turned out for it and could not all be accommodated in the Fellowship Hall. Graciously, the New England Ringers volunteered to have their lunch in a separate room.

With the exception of Mirla who was in graduate school, our whole family attended. Freddie and Sharon and their two children were there and so were Eric and Rowena and all four children. Other Agnir clan members present were my niece Carla Agnir Caguindagan and her two children who traveled from New Jersey for the occasion..

After the lunch, there was a program during which we were showered gifts of money and a special one from an artist and his wife consisting of a painting of the church that he had done. The performance of "Go Lovely Rose" was billed as a premiere because it was the first time ever that the song was played in public and in the manner it was performed.

Then it was our turn. After acknowledging everybody's presence and the generosity by which we were treated, we broke into song. Ruby had written her own lyrics for "Thanks for the Memories," the song popularized by Bob Hope. Her version covered the highlights of our nine-year stay at First Congregational Church in a half-serious and half-funny way. It was a fitting ending to 30 years of wonderful memories of the very place where it all began.

CHAPTER XII: BACK TO MY ROOTS

The longer I stayed in the United States, the more I felt a strong urge to go back to my roots. Although I was happy where I was, I longed for a balance in my social life whereby I was equally comfortable and adept at interacting with both Americans and Filipinos. Moreover, I felt guilty that I was not doing anything to give back to the institutions at home that had done so much to help me get to where I am. One such institution is Silliman University where I obtained my Master of Divinity degree. There was no Silliman alumni association within 200 miles, not even any in Boston. Once in a while, I would attend a meeting of the alumni association in Michigan where I had a number of friends and former classmates, as well as my sister-in-law Elsie who lives in Ann Arbor. On at least one occasion, I also attended a special function of the New York/New Jersey Alumni Association. I enjoyed those rare visits but wished I did not have to travel so far to meet fellow Sillimanians.

By 1999, I had been in the United States for 28 years, 25 of which were spent in Massachusetts. Silliman's 100th anniversary was just two years away and I worried about possibly missing any important Centennial celebrations here or abroad. About that time, I came across an article by Dr. Paul Lauby in a United Board newsletter entitled "Looking for Mr. Money Man." In that article, he talked about the steady decline of Silliman's financial health. One major factor behind such decline was the decrease in foreign missionary support which Silliman had depended on for many years. He proposed that the overseas alumni step up to fill the gap. He calculated that if every overseas Silliman alumnus would give even just $100 each to Silliman, it would have a dramatic impact on Silliman's financial health. What was needed, he wrote, was someone to motivate the overseas alumni to act, thus the article's title. I felt that I owed so much to Silliman, especially to my mentor Dr Lauby. Right there and then, I resolved to be the Mr. Money Man that he was looking for.

Accordingly, I got in touch with the United Board for Christian Higher Education in Asia (UBCHEA) and was referred to Nan Hawkins, the Director of Communications and Alumni Giving for the United Board. From her I learned about the Stony Point Conference. That conference was held in June, 1998 at the Presbyterian Conference Center in Stony Point, New York under the sponsorship of the United Board. It was a gathering of representatives from 14 Silliman alumni associations in the U.S. and Canada. Silliman

President Agustin Pulido had arranged for that gathering in order to have conversations on how overseas alumni could work together to help their Alma Mater. Out of that conference emerged a joint resolution by the attendees, whose key provision was a promise to form an umbrella organization. I asked Nan Hawkins how much progress there was toward the goal of that umbrella organization. She had not heard about any. I then concluded that if the umbrella organization was going to be formed in time for the Silliman Centennial in 2001, there was no time to waste.

I decided to get in touch with the Stony Point leadership, starting with Fred Baliad whom the Stony Point attendees had chosen to lead the project. He acknowledged what Nan Hawkins had told me about the lack of progress. After talking with a few other Stony Point attendees, I found out that the project stalled because of illness on the part of some key people and a communication infrastructure that was not working. I offered Fred my help, which he welcomed.

In November 1999, we started a series of planning meetings. The first one took place in Ann Arbor, Michigan with members of the Michigan-Ohio-Kentucky (MOK) Alumni Association attending. I chaired the meeting, prepared the agenda and took care of communications, thus setting up a pattern for subsequent planning meetings. The first order of business was to coordinate with Silliman. So in January, 2000, I traveled to Dumaguete for the purpose of getting Silliman's permission to establish the organization in the same year as the Silliman Centennial, and to ask for President Pulido's attendance at the new organization's inauguration.

Upon arriving in Dumaguete, I met with Dr. Pulido. He and I had known each other since 1967 when I served as assistant pastor at the Church of the Risen Lord at the Diliman campus of the University of the Philippines. At that time, he was a U.P professor serving as chairman of the Chemistry Department. A member of the church, he was chair of the Church Council when I arrived as a young pastor fresh out of seminary. After a couple of years, we parted ways when he was called by Central Philippine University to be president while I returned to Silliman to join the faculty. The last time we had seen each other was in 1971 in Silliman just as I was leaving for the States. He was still president of Central Philippine University and was visiting the campus to attend his class reunion.

This visit was my first to Silliman since then and was happy to see my old friend again. All along I had wished that he would someday become Silliman president and I was thrilled that my dream came true. He greeted me warmly and was delighted that finally something was being done on the 1998 Stony Point proposal. He promised to be present at the new organization's inauguration but requested that the gathering take place before June, 2001 so he could return to the campus in time for the start of the Silliman Centennial celebrations which were scheduled for the beginning of the academic year. I promised to convey his request to the planning group.

In April, 2000, we held our second planning meeting in Ann Arbor. Attending by teleconference was Nan Hawkins. A new participant was Lawrence "Nsoy" Lacuesta who had represented the Ontario Alumni Association at Stony Point. We decided to hold the gathering in May, 2001 in Chicago mainly because of that city's central location. The job of persuading Chicago to host the gathering was assigned to Joaquin Uy, Fred Baliad and Rene Querubin who traveled to Chicago to meet with the association's leadership. The three got a lucky break. At the time they got there, Pacita Flores, who was one of the association's founders and a continuing influential voice in their affairs, was in the Philippines. Had she been around, she would have surely prevailed on the association to decline our request for them to host the gathering. More than any, she knew how much work was involved. When she arrived, she was furious upon learning about Chicago's decision to host the gathering. However, faced with a *fait accompli*, she softened her position and in the end turned out to be one of the event's hardest workers. What helped to mollify her was the promise by the MOK and Ontario associations to co-sponsor the event.

We had two more planning meetings, both held in Chicago. The planning group grew larger as more representatives from the various other Silliman alumni associations joined. It was at that time that I got Jonathan Duazo and Renato "Bong" Sabolboro to help me with Internet communications. Jonathan, who was one of the Stony Point attendees, put together the organization's first website while Bong set up the Internet listserv called suanatipon@yahoogroups.com. The latter was the forerunner of Tipon-Silliman@yahoogroups.com which Bong and I set up together. It has since become the organization's workhorse Internet communication medium.

It was during one of the Chicago planning meetings when we decided what to call the gathering. In response to my invitation to suggest a catchy name, someone offered the word "tapok," which in Cebuano means "gathering." It just so happens that in my native language of Ilocano, "tapok" means "dust" and I mentioned that to the group, jokingly adding that we did not want our new organization to be "swept into the dustbin of history." For a more geographically and linguistically inclusive term, I suggested the word "tipon" which means about the same thing in several Filipino languages. I also pointed out the term's historical significance, being the root word for *Katipunan,* the name of the secret society that initiated the Philippine Revolution of 1896 that gained our country's independence from Spain. The group approved my suggestion, and so it was that the first gathering and all subsequent ones were called "Tipon Silliman."

I almost wound up biting off more than I could chew, trying to take on so much responsibility. Fortunately, Chicago had an active and articulate secretary in Ellen Paray Macasieb who became my right-hand person for communications. She and I put together most of the letters summoning alumni from all over North America to the gathering, and inviting various guests from both sides of the planet. Joining President Pulido were dignitaries from Silliman including Chairman of the Board of Trustees Leonor Magtolis Briones, as well as officers from the United Board led by Nan Hawkins. Dr. Paul Lauby, who had retired from the United Board, was also attending.

The new organization got off in grand fashion with a wide array of activities that the three sponsoring associations put together. Tipon Silliman 2001 was held from May 16 to May 20, 2001, with Chicago's Hyatt Regency O'Hare Hotel as the convention venue. The convention featured a golf tournament, a welcome party, a breakfast meeting with Dr. Pulido and workshops on diverse topics including fundraising, retirement planning, growing up Filipino in America, and investment opportunities in the Philippines. The internationally renowned Silliman Choristers, who were concluding their second tour of the United States, were in town and they concertized during one of the evenings. A Lake Michigan cruise and a trolley tour of Chicago were also scheduled.

On the evening of Saturday, May 19, the social highlight was held. A dinner/dance took place during which President Pulido addressed the convention. The Outstanding Sillimanian Awardees in attendance were honored and the newly-elected officers of the new organization were inducted. The convention's concluding event was a worship service held on Sunday, May 20, at the Chicago Filipino Presbyterian Church with Dr. Paul Lauby preaching. After the service, everyone gathered for a picnic dubbed "salu-salu sa paniudto," which is Cebuano for fellowship over lunch.

My job was to preside over the official creation of the new organization. I wrote its Constitution and By-Laws which laid out the organization's objectives and political structure. Following the letter and spirit of the Stony Point proclamation, it upheld every member association's autonomy, a principle that was reflected in the new organization's name, Silliman University Alumni Council of North America, SUACONA for short. The chief governing body, responsible for setting the organization's policies, was the Board of Directors. It was composed of the organization's elected officers and the president or designee of each member association, each of whom was entitled to one vote regardless of the member association's size.

SUACONA started with 17 alumni associations drawn from the existing ones at the time. Among those 17 was the organization's newest member, the Silliman Association of New England. That association was less than a month old, having been founded on the third weekend of April at a gathering of Sillimanians from the New England states that we held in Sturbridge, Massachusetts. Known by its acronym of SANE, it became the butt of friendly jokes when honorary member Nan Hawkins announced that she and other members were "inSANE.".

At a meeting on the morning of Saturday, May 19, the member association representatives ratified the Constitution that I wrote, elected the first set of officers, and approved the recommendation of the Planning Committee for the next Tipon to be hosted by the New York/New Jersey Alumni Association. The first set of elected officers were Sylvester Almiron, Jr.,chair; Renato Querubin, vice-chair; Coleta Campanale, secretary; Pacita Flores, treasurer; Lawrence Lacuesta, PIO; and Paul Imperial, auditor:

Before the meeting to elect officers, some members of the Planning Committee asked me to run for office. I declined, saying that my work was done. However, I consented to being an advisor, if asked. The leadership took me up on that offer. Thus it was that throughout SUACONA's entire existence, I was advisor to the organization in various capacities as needed, official or otherwise. My duties included setting up a new website; creating new Internet listservs for the Executive Board, the Board of Directors and other bodies; acting as quasi convention chaplain by leading devotionals and services and being available for counseling; setting up teleconferences, and keeping track of the growing database of Sillimanians abroad. From the start to the present, I was consultant to all of SUACONA's presidents. As of this writing, five presidents have served SUACONA, namely Sylvester Almiron, Jr. who served two consecutive two-year terms, Renato Querubin, Joel Pal, Zenaida Duran Bennett and Gideon Alegado. In 2005, a more formal role for me came up when an *ad hoc* position called Executive Director was created for me to fill. In that official capacity, I traveled for two years all over North America to meet the various chapters and attend their special functions as well as promote SUACONA projects.

It was then that I was asked to take charge of a SUACONA project that virtually became the fulfillment of my long-standing desire to become the Mr. Money Man that Dr. Lauby had dreamed of. In 2003, the Silliman Board of Trustees had come up with a proposal for tapping the financial resources of the overseas alumni. It was called the Portal East and West building project, a couple of commercial buildings to raise rental revenue for financing special academic and development programs. To help pay for their construction, the Trustees sought SUACONA's help which the latter gladly accepted. Work started on the Portal West building with seed money which the university hoped to replenish with outside donations. Seeking to make good on its promise to help raise the construction cost, SUACONA declared the funding of the building as the organization's flagship project. It then formed a committee which coordinated the fund drive by recognizing donations through two Trees of Life located at the building's lobby. Appropriately named the Tree of Life Committee, it started with six members.

In 2005, I took over the committee's chairmanship and recruited more members till it grew to its final size of 17. Meeting almost every month, we raised half of the original target amount of $700,000, oversaw the inauguration of the Tree of Life and its companion Interactive Screen and laid down, in cooperation with Silliman, policies and procedures to guarantee the building's continuation as a symbol of the generosity and loyalty of Silliman's alumni and friends. While most of those who bought the leaves, rocks and trunks that formed the Trees of Life were individuals and alumni chapters in North America, a few alumni and friends residing in the Philippines chipped in. In July 2009, partly to shift to new funding priorities and partly to encourage more local participation in the Portal West project, we turned over the management of the Tree of Life fund drive to Silliman. SUACONA then turned its attention to other fundraising projects including help with disaster victims, the conversion of Oriental Hall into the University Student Center and the purchase of a brand new Allen organ for the Silliman Church.

My busiest time as a SUACONA leader took place between the years 2005 and 2009 during which I traveled to Silliman every year and sometimes twice, mainly to check on the progress of the Tree of Life. I was very fortunate to have the assistance of Silliman's counterpart of the Tree of Life Committee. There were two of its members without whom I would never have been able to accomplish what I did. Abe Cadeliña was the architect of the Tree of Life, which consists of two huge tree drawings on the North and South walls of the lobby. Each tree has 350 leaves, six rocks and a trunk, all of which are offered to prospective donors for a corresponding amount. It was Abe who drew up the plans, supervised their construction, ordered the manufacture of the plates that represent every donated leaf, rock and trunk and personally installed each of them. Bob Macalolot, a professor in the school's Computer Science department, programmed the interactive Screen. I came up with the idea for the latter and donated the money for its purchase and installation. Located at the center of the lobby, it affords a close-up view of each leaf, rock and trunk, which is needed since some of the leaves are too high up on the wall for the naked eye to read. Since then, the Interactive Screen has become a virtual treasure trove of information. When the facsimile of a certain leaf, rock or trunk is touched, it brings up a page with details about the donor or whoever is being memorialized by the donation.

2005 was a banner year in my Silliman alumni affairs involvement. At the Founders Day festivities that year, I received the university's Outstanding Sillimanian Award (OSA) along with seven other recipients. As written in my award certificate, the honor was given in recognition of two of my accomplishments, namely my work in the United States as an agent of church reconciliation and healing, and for my role as the midwife to the creation of an umbrella organization for Sillimanians in North America.

In 2011, SUACONA held its sixth biennial convention in Fairbanks, Alaska. The organization was ten years old and, fittingly, the convention's theme was "Celebrating a Decade of Growth and Christian Stewardship." I took personal delight over the fact that the organization had not only grown but reached that milestone while still in one piece. That was in happy contrast to that of many Filipino organizations in America which either break up or die shortly after their founding because of internal politics. Much of SUACONA's longevity and success is a symbol of the Silliman spirit.

SUACONA'S 10th anniversary was celebrated with a candle-lighting ceremony. A committee headed by sitting SUACONA president Zeny Duran Bennett had solicited sponsorships of $300 each for ten symbolic large candles which were then arranged in a semicircle. I presided over the ritual of candle-lighting by reading a script that I had written for the occasion. The script narrated the story of SUACONA from its very beginnings, using ten sub-themes. As each part was read, someone who best represented that part of that story lit a candle. After all candles were lit, a huge birthday cake prepared by the host Alaska chapter was unveiled, cut up and shared by all.

Although Ruby missed the inaugural meeting of SUACONA, she soon caught up and became as hard a SUACONA worker as I. Her big contribution was in the area of music. She applied the skills that she developed in Massachusetts as a festival choir organizer. Beginning with Tipon Silliman 2005 in Anaheim, California, she would whip together a Tipon Chorale consisting of convention attendees and with just one or two rehearsals get them ready to perform at the various social functions and devotional services.

At the Alaska Tipon, the delegates decided that the next Tipon would be held in Silliman, the first time ever for the event to be held outside North America. Scheduled back-to-back with the annual Founders Day, it gives an incentive for many of our fellow émigrés to come home. Once again, Ruby and I will be working together, with me in charge of the religious services and she and the Tipon Chorale providing the music. In addition, we have something new that we prepared just for Tipon Silliman 2013. She and I composed a song entitled *Hymn to SUACONA* which will be premiered at the convention. She wrote the lyrics and I wrote the music.

My next alumni project was my high school graduating class. In early July, 2004, just a week after my retirement from First Congregational Church of Greenfield, I took stock. My senior class graduated from Ilocos Norte High School on April 1, 1955. Forty nine years and three months had gone by since then. It meant that only nine months remained before the 50th anniversary of our graduation. That was how much time we had to prepare for our Golden Jubilee.

It was a long shot with seemingly insurmountable odds. For one thing, compared to other classes, our class had no experience in class reunions. Although there were small local gatherings among our classmates in the previous 49 years, this reunion was going to be the first real gathering that would summon everyone from every corner of the planet. I blamed myself for our late start. I was too busy with other things and neglected my responsibilities as class president. I failed to maintain close contact with all my classmates, especially with those in the Philippines. As of July 1, 2004, I knew of the whereabouts of only seven of my 471 co-graduates and had seen or talked to only four of those seven.

One of those four was Edward Bueno. After our graduation, Edward went on to medical school and after passing the medical board in the Philippines, he migrated to the United States. I learned about his presence from the Peczons because Donna Peczon was somehow related to Ed's wife Mary Lou. The Buenos had spent some time in Pittsfield, Massachusetts before moving to Tennessee. In 1975, a year after I arrived in Greenfield, Ed came back from Tennessee and joined the medical staff of Franklin County Medical Center as an anesthesiologist. It was our first time to see each other since we graduated. The chances are infinitesimally small for two classmates who were only three seats apart for four years meeting each other after 20 years in a small New England town 10,000 miles from home.

Another one of those four classmates was Renato Ramos, who was my high school buddy. Like Edward, he went on to medical school and wound up practicing as a surgeon in Bloomfield, Michigan, a suburb of Detroit. Ed and I invited him to visit Greenfield and in 1976, he and his family came. The three of us had our own mini-reunion. A reporter of the Greenfield Recorder learned about the unique gathering and wrote about it in an article which appeared a few days later.

I discovered one big reason why we were so unprepared for our class reunion. In my absence, I had depended on my fellow officers, confident that some of them would pick up the slack. However, I found out that with the exception of one who could not be found and another who had died, all of my fellow officers had migrated to the United States. That was why there was no one left in the Philippines to get things started. On the other hand, the presence of my fellow officers in the United States turned out to be an advantage because we could do much of the planning in the States and get a head start before going to the Philippines to set things up there.

I found out that 118 of my 471 classmates had migrated to North America. The largest group, numbering 48, wound up in Hawaii. Strangely, very few of them were even aware that there were so many of their classmates living in that state. In some cases, some of them were neighbors or at least lived in the same town but were completely oblivious to one another's presence. That changed as soon as the word got out that we were planning to have a reunion. An intense search for everyone's whereabouts ensued.

Ironically, the one who jumpstarted the search was not one of our fellow graduates. That person was Catherine Pascual Lo. Catherine was our classmate until the month of January of our junior year when her family left for Hawaii. With her talents and energy, she combed the islands in search of Class 1955 graduates. Later, the trio of Lolita Menor Mabini, Hortencia Duldulao Aczon and Constancia Reyes Garma joined Catherine and together they came up day after day with new contacts. Between the foursome, they accounted for 40 who were living in North America. Exercising my executive privilege, I declared Catherine our honorary co-graduate. My decision was enthusiastically welcomed by all.

In September, 2004, I traveled to Laoag and met with the steering group there, which was headed by Conchita Agtarap. For quite some time, she and Bobby Samonte had been working on a list of contacts in the event that we might have a reunion. Sadly, when Bobby died, Conchita was left to carry the ball. She made a number of trips to many places including Manila to get those addresses.

While I was in Laoag, we had three planning meetings, which were joined by Wilfredo Fermin, Firmorico Francisco, Erlinda Fonacier Carbonell, Natividad Simon Caday, Lilian Frio, Presentacion Marcos and Norberto Manuel. After I left, they decided to meet every month. The group continued to grow with the addition of Venancia Bumanglag Sampayan, Ofelia Agbayani Agustin, Maria Santos, Gloria Villanueva Reyes, Melchora Ventura Caspe, Jerry de la Rosa and Venus Bautista Morales. Policarpio Miguel, my sometime political rival and sometime ally during our student days, had migrated to Palawan. He returned to Laoag to build his retirement home and joined the steering group.

Likewise, I had fun helping the Manila group get organized by attending their first two meetings. The first one was held at the home of Femy Fermin Buyco and was attended by Ruth Felipe Simeon, Lydia Navarrete Sankula and Rhodora Avila Panelo. Ruth, a retired pediatrician, graciously accepted the job of chairing the Metro Manila group and hosting their monthly meetings. Joining them in subsequent meetings were Diego Sagisi, Nemesia Madamba Inco, Rosalio Felipe, Naty Corpuz Bumanglag, Gloria Felix Paras, Freddie Patricio, Efren Nagtalon, Sixto Luz, Nelcy Padaca Jimenez, Rizalina Martin Gasmido, Loreto Domingo, Fe Almazan Bernardo, Criselda Marcos Juliano and Rosario Galang Doragos.

Upon returning to the United States, I had the wonderful experience of meeting with Jun Arcangel, Andy Lazo and Lydia Ocampo Sadler. In November, 2004, Ruby and I were moving to Florida with our first of two U-Haul trips and we stopped in Virginia for the meeting that was called and hosted by Lydia. Their respective spouses were with us. After the delicious meal prepared by Lydia, we met and planned. All three of them took on big responsibilities, with Jun helping me out in typical vice presidential fashion, following up with our classmates both here and abroad on their participation. Lydia and Andy both headed the financial campaign for North America. Aside from our expenses for the event, the money we were raising was to enable us to donate something important to our Alma Mater.

When I moved to Florida, I did not expect to see any classmates there. Yet I was delightfully surprised that Tony Caday, a retired physician, has a vacation home in St. Petersburg. He and his wife Ruby happened to be around during our first weekend at our new home. I had a wonderful time with them over breakfast at the airport as they were leaving back home to Virginia. The biggest Florida surprise was that Pacifico Cordon, Jr. was just 20 minutes from where I live. He is in Brandon where he and his wife have had their family medical practice for quite a few years. He was very excited when he received the invitational packet and was determined to come to Laoag, which he had not visited since 1967. Later I was to learn that another classmate, Anicetas Natividad Nanowsky, was in the Miami, Florida area and had set up a number of successful small businesses there.

I left for the Philippines on February 3, 2005, stopping in Southern California. Second to that of Hawaii in the number of U.S. immigrants from our class is the state of California with 35, many of them concentrated in the greater L.A. area. I spent a few days there to get together with everyone especially those who were not going to attend the Laoag reunion. I was a guest of Romelia Regidor Legaspi and her husband Alfonso at their home in Oxnard. The couple also hosted our mini-gathering on Saturday, February 5. What a wonderful time we had! While most came from the greater Los Angeles area, two others – Celestino "Bowie" Baraoidan and Rosita Lumabao Taylan - drove all the way from Stockton, about five hours up North. Fausta Buted Marcos, Teresa Bonilla Soriano, Lilia Hermosura Dizon, Jacinta Lucas Bareng, Constancia Corpuz Javier, Sergio Domingo and their respective spouses completed the happy circle.

From there, I went to Honolulu on February 6 and was given a royal welcome at the airport by a party headed by Lolita Menor Mabini, Hortencia Duldulao Aczon and Olivia "Lee" Corpuz Acoba. I counted nine leis that they put around my neck and with a mixture of embarrassment and elation I managed a smile as other passengers gawked at the sight, obviously wondering who this dignitary was and where he came from. It was Lee who answered their unspoken question. Turning to the crowd, she proudly exclaimed while gesturing toward me, "He is our president." From the expression on their faces, I guessed that their next unspoken question was, "Of what country?"

The next day, we were joined by Adelaida Manuel Caneda, who turned out to be a townmate of ours in Davao in the early 60's. The group gave me the grand tour of the island of Oahu and Lolita and her husband Ben feted us at their beautiful home close to the ocean at the island's famous Northern shore. The Waikiki hotel that they put me in not only allowed me to take in the Hawaiian beach ambience but also gave me a needed respite before making the final hop to the Philippines.

I arrived in Manila on February 10 and what followed was a whirlwind of activity as I shuttled back and forth between Manila and Laoag. I enjoyed the fellowship with each respective group as we met and planned some more or simply had a good time together. One of the new experiences was a change of venue in Manila when we were hosted on February 26 by Julio Navarrete, who, aside from being a successful lawyer, had become a budding culinary expert who took delight in his creations. Another change took place in Ilocos Norte when we were hosted by Monica Tadena Cabang at her home in Solsona. She was happily married to Maximino Cabang, who joked that Monica may have been a fast runner, in reference to Monica's past as a track and field star, but he must have been faster because he caught her.

Our most thrilling pre-reunion event happened on February 18 when about 30 of us were on hand for the installation of our donation to the school. Class 1968 had just donated a one-room Journalism building and very fortuitously, our class donated the building's first major piece of equipment in the form of a risograph machine and color copier. With that gift, the school obtained the premier state of the art printing system that enabled them to produce high quality printed material for a fraction of what they used to pay to outside contractors. It also opened new opportunities for the Journalism department, such as earning money from outsiders for special printing jobs.

On the first week of April, Ruby, who had stayed behind while I went ahead to set things up, arrived. With her was our grandson Stevie. When we moved to Florida, Stevie came along and stayed with us at our new home. He wanted to see the country where his mother was born and spent the first eight years of her life. He was very lucky because my niece Yoly Viernes Asuncion took him around sightseeing the whole time we were in Laoag.

The reunion took place on April 8-10, 2005. On the first day, we made courtesy calls on Ilocos Norte Governor Ferdinand Marcos, Jr. and Laoag Mayor Michael Fariñas. Later that evening, we were hosted by the Laoag and Ilocos Norte group for a Fellowship Dinner and Welcome Party held at the Palazzo Hotel.

We started the next day's festivities with a parade around town, with most of our classmates riding a *caleza*, the Ilocano version of a horse and buggy. Leading the parade was the float that carried our class beauty queen Gloria Felix Paras who was crowned Miss Ilocos Norte in 1955. After the parade, we gathered at the school campus for a Memorial Mass and a Homecoming Program. Among the program features were the reading of a poem written for the occasion by Catherine Pascual Lo, speeches by me and Jun Arcangel, the formal presentation of the publishing system that we had installed two months earlier, and a response by Mr. Fausto Duque, one of a handful of our surviving teachers. Lunch was held at the quadrangle and was hosted by the Metro Manila group. In the evening, we had a dinner and dance hosted by our U.S.- based classmates. The music was provided by the INNHS orchestra. An interesting sidelight was that of the principal of the school, Dr. Dany Daquioag, singing several solo numbers. As for me, there was something that I had waited more than 50 years to do, which was to express my thanks to a special group of young ladies. Back in July, 1954, I won by a squeaker in my bid for the senior class presidency on the strength of a landslide vote by one all-girl class. I got their vote by serenading them the day before the election. There were a few reunion attendees from that class. I asked them to step forward as I took my guitar. I then serenaded them again with the same song that I had sung almost 51 years before.

The final day was spent traveling. We visited the picnic area at Delomot, Pasuquin, Ilocos Norte. We wound up having lunch at the Ilocos Norte Conservation project in Pasuquin. Our host was the Ilocos Norte Water District whose chairman was Emeric Asuncion, who also happened to be my nephew-in-law. After lunch, we went to a nearby beach for swimming, games and just lazily enjoying one another's company. Late afternoon came and it was time to say farewell with a mixture of joy and sadness.

Our Golden Jubilee set a number of records. At the time, it was the largest graduating class in school history. Not only was our 50th anniversary the occasion for our very first reunion but we had the shortest time to get it together, which was only nine months. Ours was the first reunion class ever to show off its beauty queen with her riding a float in a parade around town. And we were the first Golden Jubilee class to have a website.

After Ruby and I retired in 2004, we set our sights on the University of the Philippines. The place was special to us because it was there where we met as students, dated, got married and returned to work for a couple of years. So whenever we traveled to the Philippines, we made it a point to visit U.P. to meet some of our friends from the 1950's who were still there. We always managed to spend a Sunday there during which the pastor of the Church of the Risen Lord would ask me to preach and Ruby to sing at the worship service.

In the summer of 2007, Ruby and I were in the Philippines and visited the U.P. campus. We had a mission, which was to convey the request from our fellow UPCYM alumni abroad and distant places in the Philippines for an UPCYM reunion to coincide with the celebration of the centennial of the University of the Philippines, which was coming up the following year. In the minds of all our friends abroad, it was a simple and less expensive way to sort of kill two birds with one stone. They hoped to combine two sentimental journeys into one by taking part in the celebration of the 100th birthday of their Alma Mater while visiting that section of the campus where they could relive with old friends some of the happiest years of their youth.

On August 19, a few of us UPCYM alumni met at the home of Ben and Leddy Cariño (nee Vidallon) in Quezon City to plan the proposed reunion. Attending the meeting aside from Ruby and me and the Cariños were Froilan Bacungan, Pio and Gloria Caccam (nee Quitco) Reuben Ganaden, Chit Domingo Tapales and Renato Paraan. Our first act was to create the organization that was going to plan and manage the reunion. We called ourselves the UPCYM Alumni Committee To Support the U.P. Centennial and adapted the acronym UPCYM ACTS. Then, realizing that 2007 was also UPCYM's 60th anniversary, we decided that UPCYM ACTS should hold two separate reunions.

The UPCYM 60th anniversary celebration was scheduled for November, 2007 while the UPCYM Centennial reunion was set for either July or August, 2008. We agreed that the two celebrations would have the following objectives: 1) To support the mission of the Church of the Risen Lord (which grew out of the UPCYM) as the Protestant and Ecumenical Ministry in the foremost university of the country, underscoring the importance of the UPCYM and CRL's presence in the University; 2) To bring together the different generations of UPCYMians in fellowship and action in support of this mission; 3) To revive and strengthen the UPCYM programs through which it served the church, university, and country; 4) To generate new support for the UPCYM and CRL so that they can start new programs to further strengthen the link between the university and the CRL.

We parted ways promising that we each would promote the forthcoming reunions. My part was to spread the word among overseas alumni and encourage them to attend. Accordingly, as soon as I got home, I created a listserv called upcymalumni@yahoogroups.com and engaged Rey Paraan to be my co-moderator. Together, we built the list of email addresses until it reached more than 200 members. I uploaded photos from my albums and from fellow UPCYM alumni. As I received updates from the Philippines on the progress of the preparations, I put them in the listserv. As the listserv grew in size, so did the volume of messages from fellow alumni who were excited at hearing from friends and schoolmates whom they had not seen in years.

The 60th anniversary celebration took place on Sunday, November 25, 2007. Its features were a worship service at CRL, a luncheon at the Gumersindo Garcia Hall, a memorial service in the afternoon and a concert in the evening by the UPCYM choir alumni. The guest preacher was Dr. Daniel Arichea who traveled from Durham, North Carolina where he was a Methodist Bishop in Residence at Duke Divinity School. Himself an UPCYM alumnus, Bishop Arichea was a pre-law student at U.P. from 1950 to 1952. With the exception of Cris Mina who was visiting from her home in Las Vegas, all the reunion attendees were Philippine residents, with some coming from Visayas and Mindanao. Ruby and I decided to save our travel dollars for the big reunion, which was scheduled for August 14-17

The week of August 10-17, 2008 was a special time to link up with friends from college days who came for the UPCYM reunion. The reunion's main feature was a two-day international conference with "Faith and the University" as the theme. On the first day, a galaxy of UPCYM alumni stars was there to present papers on the reunion theme. It included Chief Justice of the Supreme Court Reynato Puno, Justice Hugo Gutierrez, Justice Raoul Victorino, Silliman University president Ben Malayang, Prof. Leonor Briones, Dr. Mahar Mangahas and Dr. Jurgenne Honculada Primavera. The next day, the theme was "Faith Journeys – From Faith Communities to Changed Lives." I joined several other speakers, including some from non-Protestant faith communities, in presenting papers on how our lives were influenced by our campus religious experience. On Sunday, I preached at the concluding morning service. Ruby was organist at two worship services and conducted a portion of the alumni choir concert that evening.

After spending half of my life abroad, I turned full circle and went back to my roots. Without exception, every visit to my homeland was a delightful and meaningful experience. A favorite pastime often took place the moment I stepped out of the plane. Inside the taxicab on the way to the city, I would engage the cab driver in a conversation about what was happening at home. Pretending that I was just away on a short business trip, I would ask him questions such as who won last night's basketball game. I was able to get away with my charade because, thanks to the Internet, I was fully conversant with local current events. Moreover, despite years of absence, I still spoke fluently the three Filipino languages I had acquired with no trace of a foreign accent. On those occasions, I felt like I never left home.

PHOTO GALLERY

The Agnir ancestral home in Claveria, Cagayan

Agnir family portrait taken in 1956

1955: PMT Corps Commander Agnir and his officers

Ordinario family in 1951

Miss RMC 1954

**1959: Singing "Blest Be The Tie That Binds"
with friends Elmer Banci and Aida Alapan**

On our Wedding Day, April 28, 1961

**With family and friends at
Divinity housing, 1966**

**The newly ordained and
his family, 1971**

**The new Ed. D. graduate (1989) flanked by Ruby, siblings
Esther, Orly and Ruth and their spouses**

**"Shall we dance" scene in
The King & I**

**Inaugurating the Tree of
Life in Silliman, 2008**

Receiving the Outstanding Sillimanian Award, 2005

ABOUT THE AUTHOR

Rev. Dr. Federico Agnir spent most of his adult life combining simultaneous careers in education and the ministry. He served as assistant pastor at the Church of the Risen Lord at the campus of the University of the Philippines and as a professor at Silliman University before migrating to the United States with his wife and three children. There he continued his bi-vocational career in New York and Massachusetts, most of it in the latter state where he lived for 30 years. He taught for 28 years at Greenfield Community College, retiring as head of the Department of Speech Communication. As pastor, he earned a reputation as a "church doctor" by taking over a number of congregations, all of them Caucasian, which were traumatized by recent conflict, reconciling them and nursing them back to health.

He earned degrees from the University of the Philippines (Bachelor of Arts, 1959); Silliman University (Master of Divinity, 1968); Syracuse University (Master of Arts, 1972) and University of Massachusetts (Doctor of Education, 1989)

He and his wife, the former Ruby Ordinario, engaged in community activities together, mostly in music and theater where they ran a community theater company in Massachusetts for ten years. They are members of several Masonic organizations including the Order of the Eastern Star and the Shriners. In 1978, they joined the American Mensa Society and in 1984, their eldest child Mirla also joined, making the Agnirs the foremost Filipino Mensa family in America.

In 2001, he played the key role in the founding of SUACONA, the umbrella organization of Silliman alumni in North America. Since retirement in 2004, he has busied himself as an alumni reunion organizer and fundraiser, successfully directing the Golden Jubilee celebration of his high school graduating class and raising funds for Silliman University's Portal West building. In recognition of his achievements as a community leader, role model and agent of reconciliation, Silliman chose him to receive the Outstanding Sillimanian Award in 2005.

The Agnirs live in Wesley Chapel, Florida where they continue their community activities. In April, 2011, they celebrated their 50th wedding anniversary.

CPSIA information can be obtained at www.ICGtesting.com
Printed in the USA
LVOW05s1642211213

366196LV00001B/3/P